# World Encyclopedia of Tropical Fish

# World Encyclopedia of
## *Tropical Fish*

edited and with photographs by

## Keith Sagar

OCTOPUS

# Contents

First published 1978 by
Octopus Books Limited
59 Grosvenor Street
London W1

© 1978 Octopus Books Limited

ISBN 0 7064 0705 9

Produced by Mandarin Publishers Limited
22a Westlands Road
Quarry Bay, Hong Kong

Printed in Hong Kong

# Introduction

Nearly all the permanent waters of the world, still or moving, salt or fresh, are stocked with fishes, over 20,000 species of them. The greatest proliferation of species and the most exotic of them are found in the lakes and ponds, swamps, streams, rivers, estuaries and coral seas of the tropics. Most of the species of freshwater tropicals commonly kept by aquarists come from South America, Africa and South East Asia; most of the marine species from the Pacific and Indian Oceans and the Caribbean.

The majority of nature's beautiful creatures are seen at their best at liberty in their natural surroundings. If we look at mammals or birds in cages, we know that this is a poor substitute. However healthy and well-cared for they may be, captivity takes the bloom from their beauty, constricts their vitality and compromises their dignity. This is true also, to a degree, with fishes – nothing is more pathetic than a blank-eyed goldfish swimming round and round an otherwise empty bowl: there is no excuse for that. But fishes, being water creatures, not of our element, are very difficult to see in their natural surroundings, and often, in any case, show little of their colour there. And

End papers: Harlequins *Rasbora heteromorpha*
Title page: Copperband Butterfly *Chelmon rostratus*
Contents page: Common Clowns *Amphiprion ocellaris* with their anemone
Below: Neon Tetras *Paracheirodon innesi*
Left: *Anthias pleurotaenia*

they are small enough for it to be practicable for us to recreate their homes within our own, to make a miniature underwater world, a complete ecological system, with animals, plants and minerals in a balanced relationship. With no other creatures can this be so easily achieved. There is no smell, no mess, no prohibitive expense, and infinite possibilities for imagination and creativity, for breeding and exhibiting and photography.

Fishes were kept as pets in China a thousand years ago. The first book on fish-keeping, Chang Chi-en-te's *The Book of the Vermilion Fish* appeared in the sixteenth century. Chang described the beauty of his pet, how he fed it, and mentioned its reaction to temperature changes. In 1665 Pepys mentioned in his diary:

'My wife and I were shown a fine rarity: of fishes kept in a glass of water, that will live so for ever; and finely marked they are, being foreign.'

It is impossible to guess what they might have been, and whether or not they were tropical. A century later the keeping of goldfishes in ponds or bowls had become a common practice in England. The concept of a 'balanced' aquarium was first put forward by A.W.T. Brande in 1819. In his book *A Manual of Chemistry* he described the way in which living plants reoxygenate water, so that an aquarium could be set up which would not need water changes. Philip Gosse founded the world's first public aquarium at London Zoo in 1853, and the following year

wrote a book on fish-keeping in the home. A decade later came the first certain importation of a live tropical fish to Europe – the Paradise Fish (*Macropodus opercularis*), a very attractive and hardy fish which is still kept by European aquarists.

The next major advance was the principle of circulating water with pumps, a method invented by English

Left: Rainbow Butterflies *Chaetodon trifasciatus*
Above: Regal Angel *Pygoplites diacanthus*
Right: Anglerfish *Antennarius* sp.

9

aquarists but first put into operation at the Paris aquarium opened in 1860. The Hamburg and Berlin aquariums also opened in the 1860s.

All three had seawater tanks, and the Berlin aquarium was the first to use artificial seawater. The Germans rapidly took the lead in all branches of the subject. Their scientists were the first to organize expeditions to find and classify new species. Their traders were the first to open up collecting stations and ship tropical fishes in large quantities to Europe and America. Their amateur hobbyists were the first to discover how to breed many species in captivity.

But it is only in the last fifty years that tropical fish-keeping has developed into the popular hobby it is today. Since the Second World War, air transportation and large-scale commercial breeding have brought prices down and led to a boom in the hobby. Singapore is probably the fish centre of the world, with its ideal climate. Fish farms there produce millions of fishes each month for distribution to all parts of the world. There are thousands of small fish farmers all over the Malay Peninsula who dig shallow fish pools wherever they can afford the space, introduce a few pairs of fishes and some commercially popular plants and leave nature to do the rest. Or they utilize the rice paddies in the same way. There are very large, highly commercialized fish farms in Florida. In Japan, a large industry has grown up breeding the cold-water species, such as goldfishes and carp of fantastic shapes and colours. In Hong Kong, breeders have mastered some of the most difficult species, such as Neon Tetras, and are now breeding them on a commercial scale.

Hundreds of species are now kept in home aquariums and many are bred there. Moreover, aquarists have 'created' countless new varieties and transformed many only moderately attractive species into quite beautiful creatures. The humble Guppy (*Poecilia reticulata*) is the most remarkable example. Nature provided the diminutive male Guppy with splashes of several colours, but he was more like a palette than a painting, until selective breeding produced the many gorgeous varieties of fancy Guppies we know today.

Some species have been seriously depleted by over-fishing to supply the hobby; but others threatened by pollution or the destruction of habitats are safe from extinction because of the large breeding stocks held in captivity. This applies only to freshwater species. Marine tropicals cannot yet be bred in captivity. Much attention is being devoted to the problem, and a breakthrough may not be far away. But we are running out of time. In the interests of conservation the present uncontrolled pillaging of the reefs (for corals and shells as well as for living specimens) cannot be allowed to continue.

Right: Moorish Idol *Zanclus canascens*
Below: Green Swordtails *Xiphophorus helleri*

# Freshwater Tropical Fish
## in the Home Aquarium

There is no limit to the ingenuity of aquarists and almost anything that will hold water has been at one time or another converted into an aquarium. Old television sets and beer barrels have been adapted with great skill, but they, together with the more conventional metal-framed aquariums are now somewhat old hat – we have arrived at the plastic age. The beginner with limited capital is well provided for with a first-class range of relatively inexpensive one-piece plastic aquariums supplied complete with condensation tray and canopy. Whilst these are more easily scratched than glass, they have the virtue of being almost unbreakable in normal conditions and they do not leak. Those who can do so, however, are recommended to consider the installation of an all glass aquarium with a capacity of at least twenty gallons. The frameless, all-glass tank is made possible by the development of silicone-based rubber sealants of great strength and dependability. Rusting frames and leaking tanks (with consequent electrical hazards) need be tolerated no longer.

There is now greater flexibility in design than ever before, since all-glass tanks can be made in almost any conceivable shape. They are neat enough to be attractive with only a canopy and stand, or they can be housed in custom-built cabinets to match the furnishing of the rooms for which they are intended. A well constructed, arranged and maintained aquarium can be the centre-piece in the decor of a room. In a room without a fireplace, an aquarium makes an excellent alternative focal point. On the other hand, an aquarium which has been badly set up or allowed to run down can be an eyesore.

Depth adds greatly to the aesthetic effect of an aquarium, but remember that if your tank is more than two feet deep you will not be able to reach the bottom and that will be a great inconvenience.

The siting of the aquarium is important, for both aesthetic and operational reasons. It would, for example, be a mistake to position the aquarium where direct sunlight falls on it for any length of time. The fishes would have no objections, but the tank would soon be choked with unsightly algae. On the other hand, if the tank is placed in a dark spot it will enhance the surroundings and the artificial lighting can be operated in such a way as to

Rosy Tetras *Hyphessobrycon rosaceus* and Neon Tetras *Paracheirodon innesi* in a well-planted aquarium

13

control any unwanted and unnecessary plant and algae growth.

The condition of the water is of fundamental importance. Temperature, clarity, pH value (loosely referred to as acidity or alkalinity), hardness, colour and oxygen content are perhaps the most important properties. The greatest problem is that created by the aquarist himself when, in his enthusiasm, he seeks to keep a wide variety of fishes in the same tank. Many of these may have originated from very different environments and it is all too often difficult for them to thrive in the same conditions. In community tanks a whole series of compromise conditions must be created if reasonable success is to be achieved. Water temperature should be 75°F. (23.5°C.) though Mountain Minnows are happy at much lower temperatures and Discus at much higher.

The term pH denotes the degree of acidity and alkalinity of the water. The pH is expressed in a scale of numerical values on either side of 7 which is neutral.

Solutions are increasingly acid as the value falls below 7 and alkaline as the value rises above it. There are many simple and reliable kits on the market which enable accurate pH control to be maintained. They consist of a colormetric scale together with buffering solution. Unless the aquarist intends to specialize in particular species, the best compromise is 6.9 (slightly acid) for a community tank. There are, of course, exceptions. Black Mollies, for example, can live and breed quite happily in a pH of 8.3 whereas the Neon Tetra and the Killifishes are quite at home in pH values of around 6.0 or even lower. Frequently (though not invariably) there is a relationship between pH value and hardness of water.

The hardness or softness of water is related to the amount of calcium dissolved in it. The more calcium, the harder the water. Here again the optimum hardness or softness varies with the species of fish being kept, but speaking in general terms most fishes do best in a relatively soft water and are affected adversely by a high calcium content. The exceptions are the Mollies and most brackish-water fishes, such as Scats and Malayan Angels which require hard water with a high specific gravity.

Water colour (not to be confused with clarity) often depends on whether or not carbon is included in the filter bed and may often be affected by the intensity of the aquarium lighting. Tinting of water occurs primarily when conditions in the aquarium become unbalanced. A green tinge is developed when excessive light is present which is responsible for the uncontrolled growth of algae. There are several conditions which generate a brown tinge but perhaps the most common is lack of light coupled with plant decay. The presence of wooden decor components or peat substances may also be a cause. Clarity can be restored quite easily by filtering the water through activated carbon.

Filtration is, without doubt, fundamental to successful fish-keeping. Any consideration of the topic of filters is complicated by the fact that there are almost as many types as there are days in the year. Probably the simplest and cheapest are best. The undergravel filter plate provides a perforated floor on which the gravel lies. Water from the aquarium passes through the gravel, through the perforations of the plate and is then hoisted back into the aquarium with the aid of an air lift tube. This constant filtration process is relatively simple mechanically but in terms of chemical changes it is complex and fascinating. The question in the mind of most enquirers is, 'Whatever happens to the dirt?' And the answer is a fairly simple one – it is 'digested' in the gravel. As the water passes through the gravel bed it brings a constant supply of oxygen with it and this fosters the growth of aerobic bacteria on the gravel surfaces. Waste matter or 'dirt' carried with the water coming into contact with the aerobic bacteria is broken down into its simpler components and thus converted into gas(es), water, soluble mineral salts and a small amount of residue called mulm. Very little maintenance is necessary. All that is required is that the gravel should be thoroughly agitated or stirred every few months in order to release the accumulated mulm and this can be removed by the simple process of syphoning off.

The filter plate should cover most of the base of the aquarium. The throughput rate should be adjusted so that the total volume of water passes through the system every two hours. Real advantages of this simple filtration system are that so little of it need be visible, and that it needs little or no maintenance.

The commonest alternative internal filter is the box type. All box filters operate on the same principle, that of passing the water through a disposable medium of one kind or another. Examples of the mediums used are filter wool, carbon, gravel, etc. In the case of filter wool it must be appreciated that we are not referring to ordinary cotton wool which would, if used, result in heavy organic pollution, but to a special non-organic material made from synthetic fibre. Glass wool should be avoided, it is dangerous material to play around with. The latest form of wool filter is in the form of a mat, which has been woven into a flat sheet and can be cut to any size, washed when necessary and re-used. Activated carbon (made from bone or shell) is the best type, and will produce crystal-clear water; but it does tend to neutralize the pH and is therefore not suitable if acid water is required. Carbon should be renewed about every three months.

'Hook on' external box filters are available in both power and air lift forms. The aquarium water is drawn by a syphon technique into the chamber, the motor or

airlift pumping the filtered water back into the aquarium. The power filter is operated by an electrically driven water impeller and consists basically of the filter box and motor unit connected to the aquarium by means of flexible hose. Earlier models created problems related to failure of hose connections and flooding created by faulty water-flow control; the units now in production are of high quality and dependability – accidents are rarely encountered. The filter medium is of the same kind as used in internal filters but the turnover rate is of course very much greater and the electric motors used are so quiet that they are practically inaudible. All in all they really do enhance the quality of aquariums and convert the ordinary to the luxurious not only in function but in appearance also.

Temperature control of the aquarium is of course an essential aspect of successful operation; reliable equipment is desirable and it is most unwise to purchase cheap or shoddy equipment when the health or even the lives of your fishes depend to a great extent on it. For many years past aquarists have been using combined heater/thermostats. These have the distinct advantage of having only a

Left: Jewel Cichlid *Hemichromis bimaculatus*
Above: Piranha *Serrasalmo nattereri*

single electric lead from the aquarium and the user cannot therefore accidentally overload the thermostat. Many an accidental 'boiling' has occurred because of wiring several relatively high-powered heating elements to a single small thermostat which was unable to cope with the load it was asked to carry. The power or strength of heaters used in aquariums should be just adequate to maintain the required temperature in the coolest conditions envisaged. The idea of having plenty of power to spare is not a good one. A further precaution well worth taking is to place the heating element just immediately above the gravel; this ensures that the entire volume of water in the tank is heated even if the filtration and aeration processes fail. It is worth mentioning too that the heater should never be switched on unsubmerged; it is likely to overheat and crack the tube. Thermostats, too, are many and varied but there is only one type other than the internal which is in common use – the external 'clip on' type, usually incorporating a warning light and adjustment control. There is a heavy duty model too, specially designed to take several heaters with safety. It is possible to use one such thermostat to control several tanks providing of course that the power of the heaters is proportionate to the capacity of the tanks. It is highly desirable for all aquariums to have cover glasses or condensation shields in order to prevent moisture coming into contact with light fittings or even with the canopy itself. One quite popular type of aluminium canopy is designed to function without a cover glass but this is dangerous both electrically and chemically – aluminium oxides can contaminate the water, and in the case of a marine tank this can be fatal for both fishes and invertebrates.

Lighting deserves careful attention not only for the added aesthetic pleasure it may give but because fishes need it and it is essential to plant growth. A basic guide to the inexperienced would be that a forty watt bulb or tube eighteen inches above the gravel will be adequate for an area of two square feet, if in operation approximately ten hours a day. Space-age technology must be thanked for giving us fluorescent tubes specially designed to promote plant growth. These also enhance the colours of the fishes, especially blue and red. The higher initial cost of these tubes is more than compensated for by the longer life and lower running cost.

What you do with the back of the aquarium can make or mar the whole effect. If you paint it you cannot change your mind. Colour reproductions of thickly planted tanks can be placed behind the back glass. Sheets of blue or green plastic can be bought which have the advantage that they can be placed inside the tank to hide all air-lifts and heater wires. Or an illusion of great depth can be created by placing a pale-blue background some distance behind the tank or placing the tank with its back to a window, and sticking to the outside of the back glass a sheet of translucent blue or green protective film such as is sold for covering books and documents. If there is space behind the tank, corals and sea-fans can be placed there to add to the optical illusion of extreme depth.

Gravel is normally used as compost and is preferable to the artificial and often garishly coloured composts on sale. Let the fishes and plants provide your bright colours. The gravel should be thoroughly washed several times, then spread over the filter plates to a depth of two inches at the front and three to four inches at the back. The filter plates should be placed away from the back and sides of the aquarium to allow for the planting of deep-rooted plants there, which would otherwise have all the sustenance drawn away from their roots by the filter.

Next, position the rocks. These should not be so large as to take up most of the swimming space, nor so jagged that fishes might injure themselves against them. Water-smoothed rocks taken from a river bed are best.

To introduce corals and sea shells into a freshwater tank for decoration would be courting disaster because the calcium content of the shells or coral would slowly affect the degree of hardness and pH of the water. The same rule should be applied to any form of marble, or such rocks as limestone or tufa which are both high in calcium. Suitable rocks include sandstone, granite, quartz and slate. All stones should be of the same type. Small rocks or chippings placed at the foot of the larger pieces

look well. If stratified rock is used a much more natural effect is obtained by making sure that the strata all run at the same angle, preferably horizontal or just slightly tilted. The base of the rocks should be buried in the gravel to give the impression that only the tips of great slabs are visible. In addition to rocks, gnarled roots or pieces of thoroughly saturated bogwood can be used as decor. These can often be found or bought in grotesque shapes.

When the gravel and rocks are in position, half fill the tank, pouring the water gently on to a sheet of paper or plastic or floating board to avoid disturbing the gravel. Install your heaters at this stage and test them (making sure they are fully submerged). You are now ready to begin planting.

The idea of a 'balanced' aquarium, the plants taking in the carbon dioxide produced by the fish during respiration, and giving off oxygen, is a myth, because though the plants do this by day, they actually reverse the procedure at night. The main value of plants is aesthetic. There is no more

Ram *Apistogramma ramirezi*

attractive way of decorating a tank than with natural plants and rocks.

Most aquariums are too thinly planted. If you cannot see the back of the tank for plants, so much the better. You have got too many plants only when you cannot see the fishes. The tallest and thickest plants should be placed along the back and sides of the tank, particularly in the back corners where they can be used to hide air-lifts and heaters. *Vallisneria* is suitable for this purpose or such fine-leaved vigorous plants as *Cabomba* or the fern-leaved plants such as *Ceratopteris* (Indian Fern) or Wisteria. In front of these, given plenty of room, can be the broad-leaved feature plants such as *Aponogeton, Echindoras, Hygrophila, Ludwigia,* and the larger *Cryptocoryne* species. In the foreground can be planted the smaller species of *Cryptocoryne,* Hairgrass and also the various pigmy plants such as *Nymphaea* × *daubenyana*-a tiny waterlily. If your aquascape requires the planting of some plants over the filter-plates, small plantpots can be used, which must,

of course, either be buried or hidden by rocks.

When you are satisfied with your aquascape, fill the tank to the desired height, and leave it with all the systems running for a few days before adding fishes.

There is, of course, no need to have the aquarium entirely filled with water. Surface area is more importance than gallonage, and a partially filled tank offers great opportunities to the imaginative aquarist for creating a sense of the continuity between the life of a stream or river or lake and that of its banks. Many exotic plants grow at the water's edge and many aquatic plants bloom above the surface.

The purist would argue that, since his aim is to bring a little section of aquatic nature into his home, he must restrict himself to fishes which actually are found living together, perhaps even to a shoal of a single species,

Above: Harlequins *Rasbora heteromorpha*
Below: Silver Hatchets *Gasteropelecus levis*
Right: Platy *Xiphophorus maculatus*

together with plants which would form their natural habitat. Though most aquarists would not wish to go as far as that, there is no denying that shoals do look much more attractive than mixed collections, and that large clusters of a few species of plants look better than individual specimens or small clumps of many.

Let us assume for the moment that the aquarist who has just set up his first tank cannot resist the temptation to keep a wide range of species in it. He should not be too impatient to buy, but should read several books and talk to several experienced aquarists and dealers.

Do not overcrowd your tank. One inch of fish to each gallon is enough. Obviously fishes which are large enough to eat or aggressive enough to damage other fishes must be avoided. You cannot, for example, keep large cichlids if you intend also to keep any small fishes at all. Tiger Barbs will frequently nip the fins of other fishes, though they are less likely to do this if you have a shoal of them than if you have only one or two. Some fishes, Tinfoil Barbs for example, will quickly strip all your plants. Water which is soft and acid enough to suit tetras, dwarf cichlids and gouramis, is unlikely to suit mollies, scats or Malayan Angels.

The habits of fishes should be taken into account. Catfishes and loaches stay on the bottom and are useful

scavengers. Hatchets and Half-beaks stay on the surface. The shape of your fishes is also important where the overall aesthetic effect is concerned. Most of your fishes will be torpedo-shaped. It is effective to have a few fishes of other shapes to contrast with these – angels, hatchets and fighters, for example. A few slow-moving fishes, fighters or cichlids, will contrast with the quicksilver danios or rasboras. A few black fishes, mollies or Black Veiltail Angels will again make a dramatic contrast with their brightly coloured tank mates.

Single specimens never look as good as pairs, nor pairs as good as shoals, where a shoaling species is concerned. Why not buy a small shoal, ten or twelve specimens of your favourite shoaling fish, then just add a few other species to contrast with them in appearance and behaviour. Some fishes such as White Cloud Mountain Minnows or Harlequins or any of the barbs or danios, which may not be particularly spectacular or interesting as individuals, acquire a new magic when a small shoal of them gracefully swim as one across a spacious tank against a background of luxurious vegetation.

Each aquarist will soon discover his own favourites (and must learn to be tactful when shown someone else's favourites, which leave him cold). I can only say what, for me, would constitute an ideal community for a

fifty-gallon tank: ten or twelve Cardinals, ten or twelve Harlequins, two Black Veiltail Angels, two Leopard Catfishes, two Marbled Hatchets, a pair of fancy guppies, a pair of Hi-fin Swordtails, one male Pearl Gourami, one male Siamese Fighter, one male *Apistogramma ramirezi*.

The majority of beginners tend to over- rather than under-feed. Uneaten food settles on the bed of the aquarium and is quickly covered in fungus. Any sign of cottonwool-like growth on the gravel is a strong indication of gross overfeeding. The fishes should consume all the dry food added to the tank within five minutes, otherwise they will lose interest. Four basic types of food are available: dried, freeze dried, fresh and live. The most popular of the dried foods is in flake form; it contains all the basic necessities and has vegetable matter, proteins, carbohydrates, minerals and fats in its composition. Many brands are available and the dependability and standard of most is very high. There are still many advocates of the types of food which were common some years ago, foods such as ant eggs, mosquito larvae, dried daphnia and the like, but it is doubtful whether the fishes receiving the food share the enthusiasm of their keepers. The accelerated freeze-drying process in its essential elements consists of deep freezing at very low temperatures and applying a vacuum; temperature is then raised slightly which causes

Above: Giant Gourami *Colisa fasciata*
Right: Silver Hatchet *Gasteropelecus levis* with Marbled
Hatchet *Carnegiella strigata*

the phenomenon of water 'boiling off' well below freezing level. When the food is put in water it is reconstituted in virtually the same form as before freeze-drying.

Former dehydrating methods left dried-up shells and little else. F.D. (freeze dried) daphnia or tubifex worm reconstitutes into a perfect food almost as good as 'live' would be. Artemia or Brine Shrimp is now freely available in F.D. form and is suitable for fishes of all types. By fresh food is meant scraped raw meat (especially liver) and fish.

Nothing we have said should prevent the keen aquarist from providing live food when it is clean and available. All fishes naturally prefer it. Most dealers sell live daphnia, tubifex, glassworm and bloodworm, or the aquarist can catch his own daphnia in a local pond. Daphnia or water-

fleas are actually fresh-water crustaceans about the size and shape of fleas but not, of course, related to them. They will almost always be found together with their smaller relative, cyclops, which is just as good for food. Tubifex worms are harvested from mud-banks in rivers. They will stay alive for weeks under a dripping tap. Dealers also sell starter-cultures of whiteworms (Enchytrae). These are kept in small boxes of damp earth with a piece of glass resting on the surface of the soil. They are fed on pieces of brown bread soaked in milk. They will breed if not too hot or cold (the cupboard under the sink is a good place). They gather in knots around the bread and on the cover-glass and can easily be removed with tweezers for feeding. When a small earthworm is thrown into an aquarium of fishes which may never before have seen one, interest is created even in the most reluctant feeder. The messy business of chopping the worm up into suitable small pieces is of course a necessary preliminary. A recent development is vitamin supplements in tablet or powder

form. Although they are not strictly foods they are well worth using occasionally.

In the case of accidental overfeeding we are confronted with the problem of efficiently 'cleaning' the aquarium. An ordinary syphoning technique with flexible tube and bucket may be used, but beware of drawing fish into the tube. Many types of small under-water vacuum cleaners are available operated by electric motor or air pump. These will draw the mulm or floating debris into a collecting bag thus allowing the filtered water to pass back into the aquarium. It will also be necessary to change up to 25% of the water. This should be done, in any case, about once a fortnight. Tap water is rarely if ever similar in character to 'aged' aquarium water and if a change can be foreseen it is worthwhile to collect rain water, which must of course be clean. It is quite a simple matter to tie a plastic bag to a downspout (after letting the initial flow wash dust or dirt) and water collected can be stored in any suitable plastic container until required.

Should algae build up on the internal glass surfaces suitable scrapers made from plastic or hard rubber as well as sponges and razor-blade holders are available, but never use the razor-blade scraper on a plastic aquarium. Or there are magnetic cleaners which enable one to clean the glass on both sides without so much as removing the canopy or rolling up one's sleeves. The novelty value of this device is such that volunteers for glass cleaning are never scarce.

Careful observation of the behaviour patterns of the fishes – their feeding habits, breathing rate, swimming movements and attitudes to other fishes will tell you of impending trouble. Any deviation from normal will be conspicuous. They can be watched carefully for symptoms of disease and treated in good time. Changes are not always due to illness or water conditions. Fishes coming into breeding condition can often be very aggressive. When you switch on a light in a dark room, many fish will have lost all their colour and be sitting on the bottom of the tank. Within a few minutes they regain their colour and start to swim about again.

Illness will often show when a fish swims with closed fins, becomes listless, breathes heavily and loses colour during the day. Sometimes there are external symptoms in the form of white spots or fungus growth and this of course must be treated. When making diagnosis of illness always have regard to three basic possibilities (i) it can be a disease, (ii) it can be a difficulty related to water conditions, or (iii) it can be a difficulty related to community tank compatibility.

So far as water condition is concerned, a check should be made in respect of temperature, aeration, filtration, pH value and possible sources of contamination such as paint fumes, insect or deodorant sprays, or tobacco smoke. The risk of pumping contaminated air into the tank can be avoided by placing the pump in some infrequently-used room where the air is fresh and clean, or even under the floorboards or in the garage. Even small pumps will blow air along many yards of airline if kinks are avoided.

Having eliminated water conditions or incompatibility as the cause of abnormal fish behaviour the hobbyist is left with the possibility of disease or illness, and the more obvious ailments should be looked for first. 'White Spot' is the commonest of fish diseases and is not always obvious or easy to see. The small white parasite spots usually appear first on the transparent areas of the fins and subsequently on the body. This is a contagious disease and early diagnosis and treatment is most advantageous. Several excellent cures are available of Malachite Green, which does not require the inconvenience of changing temperatures or altering the lighting routine of the aquarium. It will seldom do any harm to treat for White Spot when fishes are ill from something which cannot be diagnosed. There are many variations of this disease such as Velvet or Dust which respond to the same treatment.

Fin-rot and fungus are fairly easy to identify. Most of the common fungus infections can be cured by the addition of common salt to the water, but in stubborn cases the fish can be dipped in a fungus cure in the form of a dye which continues to work after the fish has been replaced in the aquarium.

Gouramis often develop dropsy which causes swelling to an extent in which the scales protrude from the body. Unfortunately there seems to be no easy cure for this disease and it is often kinder to destroy the affected fish.

Less common diseases occur which need specialist advice one of which is parasitic gill flukes; this condition yields to treatment with a mild acid: a teaspoonful of vinegar to a cup of aquarium water will cause the flukes to detach themselves.

Whatever problems related to disease may occur we strongly advocate reference to specialized literature. The hobbyist should not allow himself to be panicked into taking hasty actions which are irreversible before being reasonably sure of the nature of the problem.

One of the major advantages of freshwater fishes in comparison with marines is that they can be bred by the amateur aquarist, even by the absolute beginner. Indeed where live-bearers are concerned it is only necessary to put a male and a female in the same tank and they will do the rest. From there the aquarist can progress to more and more difficult species until, perhaps, he reaches those frontiers of the hobby where he applies himself to species not yet spawned or reared in tanks. Even then he is not likely to forget the day he first saw a minute pair of black eyes swimming on the surface of his tank – his first baby Guppy.

Methods of breeding differ so greatly from one family of fishes to another, or even from one species to another, that it will be easier to discuss them in the relevant chapters.

Blond Guppies *Poecilia reticulata* (below: female, right: male)

# Freshwater Plants and Tank Decor

Apart from their decorative function in the aquarium, the special importance of plants lies in their ability to assimilate the fishes' waste products. Without plants, toxic chemicals would soon contaminate the water and mechanical filtration would be needed. Many aquatic plants provide refuges where timid fishes can escape from aggressive varieties and young fishes can seek some protection. Most plants provide shade for the fishes from the glare of fluorescent tubes, while others are needed to receive the spawn of certain species.

The diet of most fishes includes some vegetation, and on those occasions when the aquarist is away from home at least some fresh food will be available if plants are present. Of course, there are some fishes that seem bent on destroying the vegetation, whether they need plant material in their diet or not. Cichlids figures largely in this category and should be provided with some other form of decoration and refuge such as rocks.

## Planting and Plant Care

The initial introduction of plants should be carried out about 48 hours after filling the aquarium with water. This will give time for any chlorine present in mains water to dissipate and the oxygen level to reach normal proportions. When the temperature is about right, 75°F (24°C), planting can start but first remove about a quarter of the water in the aquarium for topping up later. Plants bought as cuttings should be re-cut at the base

An effective centrepiece using bogwood, Water Palm and Wheat Plant

with a sharp knife and then simply insert the cut stem in the gravel to a depth of 1 inch (2.5 cm), lightly compacting the gravel around the stem. Cuttings should be planted singly, not in bunches. Dead roots should be cut off rooted plants, damaged or dead leaves removed, and then the roots spread out evenly in a depression in the gravel which is then firmed back into place. Gravel should not be heaped up round the crown as this could cause the plant to rot and pollute the aquarium water.

The rooting medium should be of mixed 2–5 mm mesh size. Colour is a matter of individual preference, but do not use light coloured materials; reflected light from below tends to discourage plant growth, and the fish and plants tend to show up better against a darker background.

There are several useful brands of planting media on the market which contain a slow-release plant nutrient. The granules are spread over the aquarium base as a thin layer and gravel placed on top.

The majority of popular aquarium plants are reasonably hardy, transfer well, and if they are given fair conditions will grow and even multiply. However, a list of some causes of plant failure may help ensure success.

1. Rough handling.
2. Extremes of temperature 57°F to 82°F (14° to 28°C) should not be exceeded.
3. Allowing surplus food to accumulate on the bottom of the tank, causing bacterial growth and rotting of plant stems at gravel level.
4. Inadequate illumination; allow about 20 watts for each square foot (1,000 square cm) of water surface.

An arrangement which makes good use of rockwork, with vigorous bushy plants such as *Cabomba* in the background, and long-leaved plants such as Twisted Vallis in mid-tank

5. Excessive illumination; adjust lighting to coincide roughly with daylight hours (or for about 10 hours).

6. Allowing plants to become dry.

7. Unsuitable water conditions; adjust water chemistry or try other species.

8. Competition from actively growing established plants too strong.

9. Excessive aeration which prevents the formation of carbon dioxide, essential for plants; it also causes aquarium detritus to settle on plant leaves.

10. Under-gravel filtration too active. Biological filtration relies on the cultivation of aerobic bacteria to break down waste products. If the bacteria do this job too well the plants are denied some of their essential nutrients. This can be avoided by planting in pots.

11. Aquarium base too cold which will retard plant growth. Insulation of the underside of the aquarium will prevent this problem.

12. Excessive growth of algae which can become an active competitor of the higher plants. Always ensure that your tank has some fishes that graze on the algae. Most live-bearing tooth carps, *Labeo* species, *Plecostomus*, *Xenocara* and related catfishes, *Otocinclus* catfishes, and Kissing Gourami will perform this function.

# The Plants

Aquatic plant classification is a confusing business, and there appears to be frequent disagreement between botanists over the correct nomenclature. In the following list of popular tropical freshwater aquarium plants, the scientific names are those most frequently used but vernacular names or corruptions of the generic name are often used instead.

***Vallisneria spiralis***–Straight Vallis or Twisted Vallis (var. *tortifolia*). This is probably the most popular aquarium plant of all. The long slender leaves, bright green in the spring, form a crown just above gravel level. The straight-leaved variety has longer leaves, up to 24 inches (60 cm) and is therefore suitable for the deeper aquarium. The twisted variety grows up to 20 inches (50 cm) and makes a perfect back-drop for the average home aquarium. It propagates from seeds and, more often, by runners and is a most adaptable plant as regards light, water and food requirements.

***Sagittaria*** The young stage is often confused with *Vallisneria,* but the older leaves are stiffer and crisper. It is not as popular as formerly, probably because of the emergent leaves which are difficult to accommodate under the modern aquarium covers.

***Echinodoras***–Swordplants. Many species of this genus are suitable for the home tropical aquarium. All have elliptical leaves, although the length to width ratio varies greatly. Some of the narrow-leaved species have attractively ruffled edges. All swordplants prefer soft water but will thrive in hard water. Properly fed in soft water, some species will grow too well and large leaves will extend far above the water surface, so feed sparingly.

Among the species available is the minute *E. tennellus* which can be used to carpet the foreground; a dwarf chain-sword, *E. magdalenensis*, which is best suited to the middle of the aquarium and a host of other species which are good for backgrounds, a particularly effective species being the popular Amazon Swordplant (*E. paniculatus*). The commoner species are not expensive but be prepared to pay the same for a species which grows to only 2 inches (5 cm) in height as for one which reaches 20 inches (50 cm).

***Aponogeton*** Three species are commonly available: *crispus*, *natans* and *undulatum*. A further two species, *ulvaceous* and *fenestralis*, are occasionally imported. They are available as tubers or as young plants. Their colours vary from light green (*ulvaceous*) to dark green (*fenestralis*). There is some resemblance to *Echinodoras* but the foliage of *Aponogeton* is soft and flaccid. All except *fenestralis* will adapt to depths down to 24 inches (60 cm).

*A. fenestralis* is the commonest of the three types of lace-leaf plants, so called because the leaves appear to have little tissue between the veins. The leaves are ovate, about 4 by 2 inches (10 by 5 cm) in size and are quite tough in texture. The plant seems to prefer to grow outwards rather than upwards, and consequently the leaves cover quite a large area.

*A. ulvaceous* is probably the most highly prized of all aquatic plants. Its pale green, wavy leaves are paddle-shaped and grow to 20 inches (50 cm) in length. This species needs plenty of room and, like all its relatives, very soft water.

All *Aponogeton* species require an annual rest period of about 12 weeks. After the winter flowering period in November and December, the plant should be removed and re-planted in an aquarium where the temperature does not rise above 68°F (20°C). *E. natans*, *crispus* and *undulatum* are relatively inexpensive plants; *E. ulvaceous* and *fenestralis* are expensive, but well worth having.

***Cryptocoryne*** In terms of permanency and decorativeness, plants of this genus cannot be excelled but they grow slowly and are quite expensive. There are many species, from the diminutive *C. nevilli*, 5.5 inches (12 cm) in height, to the giant *C. ciliata* which reaches 20 inches (50 cm). Both are pale green. There is a marvellous variety of colour and leaf forms in

An arrangement consisting largely of *Cryptocoryne*

*Cabomba aquatica*

pruning; any pieces removed will soon take root if planted in the gravel. Although they are always sold as cuttings, these are of sufficient length to make an instant show in the aquarium. They are among the least expensive of aquarium plants.

**Ceratopteris** One species, *C. thalictroides*, is available. It is known popularly as Indian Fern when planted and submerged, and as Floating Fern in its emergent form. The pale green leaves are deeply incised, forming a large number of lobes; the stem is very brittle. It is often referred to as a livebearing plant, because a single leaf broken from the plant will develop many baby plants before it decomposes. It is claimed that this plant has water softening ability.

**Synnema triflorum**–Water Wisteria. This is a relatively newly introduced plant which has become an established favourite. The leaf outline is like that of the Indian Fern but the bright green leaves grow axially from the stem, not from the base of the plant. It is a vigorous grower which must be topped when it reaches the surface. Individual leaves will form new growth if planted. It is favoured by many aquarists because of its large size and bushy proportions.

**Hygrophila** Only one species, *polysperma*, is available commercially. This is a light green plant with leaves about 1.5 inches (3 to 4 cm) long and 0.4 inches (10 mm) across growing axially from the stem. It is a rather limp species which damages easily and grows rapidly to the surface where the growth should be curtailed. It flourishes in hard or soft water. It can be used for backgrounds but also as a foreground plant if the stem is laid on the gravel and weighted down with small pebbles; new growth will sprout up from the length of the stem which if kept short will form a pleasing carpet-like effect. It grows quite well in poorly lit conditions. Prices for this plant are very modest.

**Ludwigia** Two species are regularly available. *L. natans* (=*mullertii*) has a dark green, oval, privet-like leaf with an attractive rosy under-surface. It is a tough plant which even vegetarian fishes leave alone. The second species, *L. arcuata*, sometimes known as Needle-

other species of this genus. Some species, *C. willisi*, for example, have attractively crinkled leaves. Some, like *C. becketti*, have leaves which are green on top and a rich copper colour underneath. Slow in growth, quite expensive to purchase, but very accommodating, the plants grow well in subdued light and though they prefer soft water will tolerate hard water very well. *Cryptocoryne* can be used as a foreground or background plant depending on the species. The smaller species serve well to break up the hard outline of aquarium rocks.

**Myriophyllum, Cabomba, Ambulia** (= **Limnophila**) The species of these three genera are similar in appearance. All of them have fine leaves in whorls arising from the stem at regular intervals from the base to the head. The commoner species of *Myriophyllum* are green, but a redbrown species is sometimes available. *Cabomba* has three species; two are a beautiful clear green and one a reddish hue. *Ambulia* is represented commercially by *A. sessiliflora* whose foliage is yellow-green to light green. All three genera make good spawning plants and later serve as refuge plants for the fry. They look at their best in a background position. Their rapid growth should be kept in check by regular

leaf Ludwigia, is a delicate and elegant plant with light green elongate leaves up to 15 mm (0.6 inches) in length radiating from a red-brown stem. Both species are available as cuttings and are inexpensive. Neither species likes the water temperature to be higher than 77°F (25°C) but they are otherwise tolerant of a wide variety of water and lighting conditions.

**Bacopa** *B. monniera* is the only species available to the aquarist. It has small, oval, light green, fleshy leaves about 0.4 inches (10 mm) across and 0.6 inches (15 mm) long, radiating from a rigid fragile stem. This is a useful plant which can be used towards the front of the aquarium without being obtrusive. Propagation is from cuttings.

**Temporarily aquatic plants** Of the several terrestrial/bog plants that can be used as temporary aquatics, two very striking species are gaining popularity and are worthy of inclusion in the furnished aquarium. The Wheat Plant, *Pleomela reflexa*, has cream and green striped, rush-like leaves which spring from a common base. The root system includes peculiar tuberous growths which resemble small potatoes. It is a rugged plant and is usually available as 8 to 10 inch (20 to 25 cm) specimens. Some confusion over nomenclature exists and this plant is also sold by aquatic plant nurseries as *Chlorophytum*.

The Water Palm, *Chamaedorea elegans*, usually has three to five stems of light green, tropical palm frond foliage. Specimens commonly available are 6 to 10 inches (15 to 25 cm) high. It will

Above: Water Wisteria *Synnema triflorum*
Left: Wheat Plant *Pleomela reflexa*

Malayan Swordplant *Aglaonema simplex*. The Firemouth Cichlids *Cichlasoma meeki* as they grew larger would make short work of these or any other plants

remain in reasonable condition, when fully submerged, for about eight weeks, after which it will slowly deteriorate unless moved into the air.

Another terrestrial species–the Malayan Swordplant, *Aglaonema simplex*–is also often used in aquariums. It has dark green, tough, glossy leaves of a broad spear shape, and could be confused with *Cryptocoryne* species. It will 'grow' for about 10 to 12 weeks when submerged but then growth stagnates and the plant must be removed to a temperate bog situation. It is a useful temporary plant and because of its toughness is recommended where boisterous fishes are housed.

All these species are particularly useful in the half-and-half aquarium.

## Tank Decor

The judicious use of rocks in the aquarium adds interest and creates depth, besides providing important cover for bottom fishes, but before choosing rocks the character of the aquarium water must be investigated. A hard limestone, which may be quite suitable in hard alkaline water, would drastically alter the chemistry of an aquarium containing soft acidic water. Generally, hard inert stones are found in areas of soft water and alkaline stone where mains water is hard, but this is not always the rule.

When rock collecting, mark out an area about the size of your aquarium on the bank of the river or on the beach, and arrange sets of stones within this area. This will help you decide what is needed and give you practice in the art of assembling suitable pieces. Avoid crumbling rocks and those containing veins of brightly coloured minerals. Freshly broken rocks sometimes leave very sharp edges, which should be dulled by rubbing with another stone; although a fish will not collide normally with an obstacle, it may do so if frightened.

Some impressive compositions can be created using driftwood, bogwood and cork bark. However, a prolonged soaking of six to eight weeks in frequently changed water is a wise precaution, and a check on the pH level should be made after installation. Any radical change should be corrected with partial water changes and the suspected item removed for further soaking. Aquarists living in soft water areas should be particularly careful.

Cork bark is often used to give a more natural appearance to the back panel of the aquarium and the result can be most effective. The buoyancy of the cork can be countered by attaching it to a piece of slate or glass with a silicone-rubber adhesive.

The use of decorative coral and shells should be restricted to marine aquariums where they help chemically to buffer the water. In the freshwater aquarium, their highly calcareous nature serves only to harden the water and render it more alkaline.

The guidelines for composing a visually attractive aquarium are few and simple. Never have a focal point in the centre of the aquarium or near the front. Groups, whether of plants or rocks, should be arranged in triangular form. A solid mass of rocks, or pieces of wood, should be relieved by planting low-growing plants in front of them. An impression of depth can be achieved by using foliage of contrasting colour and leaf shape. Do not plant fast-growing tall plants at the front of the aquarium and remember that water has the optical effect of bringing everything forward. Virtually all the decorative items should be placed towards the back of the aquarium, or at the sides where vegetation may be allowed to come to the front in diminishing height.

In the half-and-half aquarium, the water level is lowered to allow bog plants to be planted above the water line. Care has to be taken that loam introduced for bog growth is contained in pots and not allowed to contaminate the water. Obviously any plant with known toxic properties must be excluded. The surface area of the water is much reduced in these aqua-terra tanks and must be allowed for when considering the fish population size.

## Exhibiting at Shows

This fascinating branch of the hobby entails taking a tank to the exhibition, together with your chosen fishes, plants, rocks and gravel, and assembling everything on the show bench within a few hours. The completed aquarium should look as though it has been in place for several months. Water clarity is of paramount importance. A crystal-clear aquarium will always catch the judge's eye, whilst a murky-looking presentation, although it may be better designed, will be overlooked. Gravel and rocks should be washed thoroughly.

In this 'instant aquarium' competition, certain expedients are allowed, provided they are not patently obvious to the judge. For instance, plants can be anchored with lead strips, although exposure of a lead strip will, if spotted, involve a penalty, as would an uprooted plant or one with roots unnaturally placed. Plants need to be leaf perfect, with no sign of damage or algae growth. Pieces of broken plant floating on the water surface will not escape the judge's scrutiny.

Fishes should be chosen for their showing quality–if they hide they will not be judged. On the other hand, large active fishes, particularly barbs, can dislodge plants. Some judges prefer to see a small shoal of one species of fish. The use of plants or fishes which would ultimately outgrow the aquarium is likely to be penalized, as is the use of coldwater plants in a tropical aquarium.

Above: The grain of this bogwood gives great elegance to a very simple decor. The fishes are Pretty Tetras *Hemigrammus pulcher*
Below: A prizewinning furnished aquarium utilizing a great variety of plants, each correctly positioned ecologically and artistically

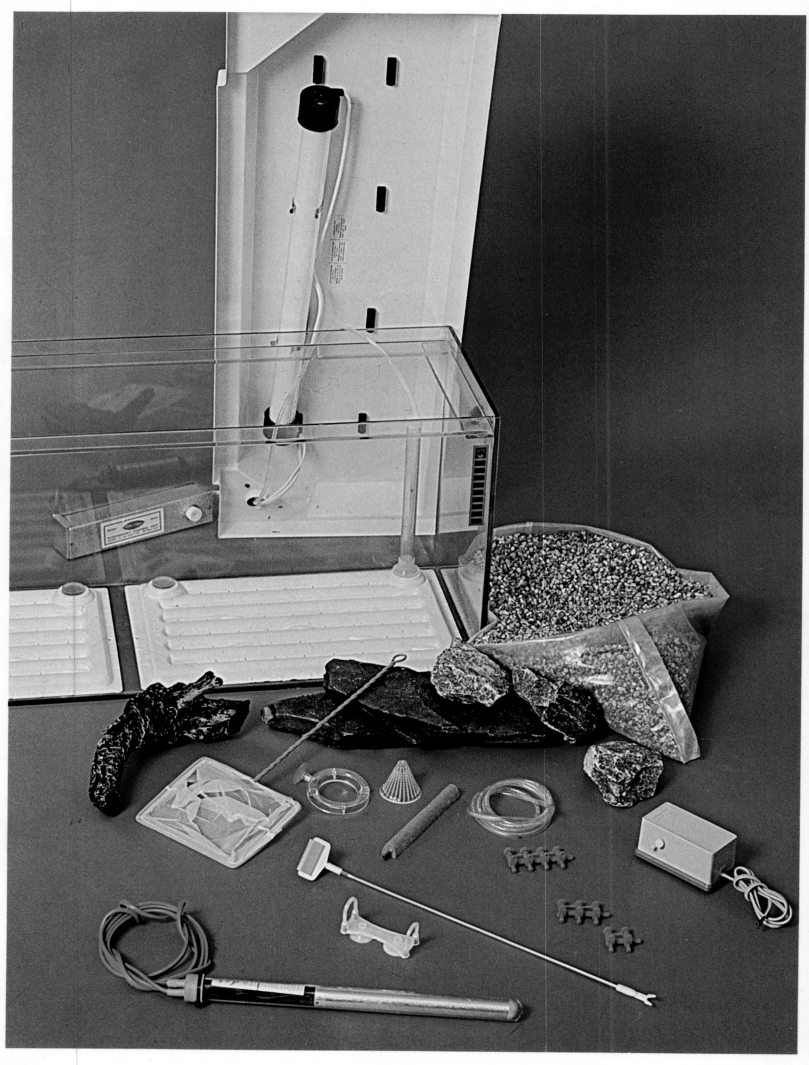

# Equipment

Many aspiring aquarists have been deterred by the bewildering choice of tanks, heaters and other accessory equipment available in their local aquarium shop. The basic requirements, however, are fairly simple: a tank, and suitable lighting, heating, aeration and filtration systems. The installation of the tank and its life-support systems is not difficult, as over a hundred million aquarists throughout the world have already discovered for themselves.

## Tanks, Stands and Cabinets

### TANKS

Until a few years ago, most tanks had frames made of angle-iron or plastic-coated steel. The majority of both freshwater and marine tanks are now made entirely of glass or a combination of glass with a metal or plastic bottom. These modern tanks have several advantages over the metal-framed types: they are aesthetically more attractive; they are bonded by a silicone adhesive and are much less likely to leak than a tank sealed with aquarium putty or cement; and as there is no metal in contact with the water in the aquarium there is no possibility of contamination from metallic ions. (Even metal bases should be avoided if you are thinking of setting up a marine system.) The table overleaf gives details of useful tank sizes.

Most glass tanks are made by specialist manufacturers and consequently the appropriate thickness of glass will have been calculated with considerable care. As a guide, however, to those who do wish to build their own tanks, the following thicknesses of glass should be regarded as a minimum.

the glass the more expensive it is and that it may be worthwhile obtaining quotations from more than one glass merchant. The trade price of glass is usually related to the volume purchased by the wholesaler, and his price to the retailer will affect the price you will have to pay. Do not try to economize by buying substandard glass. The size of tank will be determined not only by the cost but by the space available and by the type of fishes or invertebrates the aquarist intends to keep. Tanks holding 11 gallons (50 litres) are a popular size for freshwater aquariums. Smaller tanks are more difficult to maintain because it is not easy to install all the support equipment in a limited space. A tank of 22 gallons (100 litres) or larger is recommended for a marine system. Marine fishes are more territorial than freshwater species and will fight unless they have sufficient space. They also tend to grow to a larger size. The absolute minimum volume for a marine tank is 11 gallons (50 litres).

There are several very attractive all-plastic tanks on the market, usually one-piece mouldings. These are very satisfactory, especially for a beginner's first tank, but their drawback is that they can be scratched rather easily when being cleaned and therefore are not likely to have as long a life as a glass tank.

For reasons of decor or because of the space available for the aquarium, a high tank may be desirable, and it is important to note that the number of fishes the tank can support depends largely on the surface area of the water, not on its volume. This is because oxygen and carbon dioxide exchange takes place at the water surface. The following table of the fish-holding capacity of some popular sized tanks should be taken only as a rough guide and is dependent to a large extent on the efficiency of aeration and filtration systems.

| Tank dimensions in inches | Capacity in gallons | Thickness of glass |
|---|---|---|
| 24×15×15 | 20 | |
| 36×18×12 | 29 | 6 mm (approx. $\frac{1}{4}$") |
| 48×18×12 | 38 | |
| 48×24×12 | 51 | |
| 60×24×15 | 80 | 10 mm (approx. $\frac{3}{8}$") |
| 72×24×15 | 96 | |

| Dimensions of tank in inches | Recommended aggregate length of fishes in inches |
|---|---|
| 24×15×12 | 15 to 18 |
| 30×15×12 | 18 to 24 |
| 36×18×15 | 20 to 30 |
| 48×20×15 | 30 to 40 |
| | (these figures should be halved for marines) |

If your tank is to have a volume greater than 100 gallons (455 litres), you should seek the advice of the glass manufacturer. Some years ago the BBC ordered a 19ft (5.8 metres) tank for one of their studios, but the glass was too thin and during filming operations it burst, with disastrous consequences. Fortunately no one was hurt, but a tank which breaks under stress can send pieces of glass flying at lethal speeds in all directions. You will find that the thicker

The use of some form of cover glass (condensation tray) is strongly recommended for both freshwater and marine aquariums for the following reasons:
1. it effectively cuts down the amount of evaporation taking place and in so doing prevents damage to the electric lighting units which are usually positioned over the tank;
2. it effectively prevents certain species of fish, such as swordtails and hatchets, from jumping out of the tank;
3. it reduces the heat loss considerably and thus conserves energy and reduces running costs.

All the equipment necessary to set up a freshwater aquarium

# TABLE OF USEFUL TANK SIZES AND CAPACITIES

| IMPERIAL SIZES | | NEAREST METRIC EQUIVALENT | |
|---|---|---|---|
| length × height × breadth in inches | approximate capacity in gallons | length × height × breadth in centimetres | capacity in litres |
| 15× 8× 8 | 4 | 40×20×20 | 16 |
| 18×10×10 | 7 | 45×25×25 | 28 |
| 18×12×12 | 10 | 45×30×30 | 41 |
| 20×12×12 | 11 | 50×30×30 | 45 |
| 24× 8× 8 | 6 | 60×20×20 | 24 |
| 24×12×12 | 13 | 60×30×30 | 54 |
| 24×15×12 | 16 | 60×40×30 | 72 |
| 24×15×15 | 20 | 60×40×40 | 96 |
| 24×16×12 | 17 | 60×45×30 | 81 |
| 24×18×15 | 24 | 60×45×40 | 108 |
| 27× 8× 8 | 6 | 70×20×20 | 28 |
| 30×12×12 | 16 | 75×30×30 | 68 |
| 30×15×12 | 20 | 75×40×30 | 90 |
| 30×15×15 | 25 | 75×40×40 | 120 |
| 36×12×12 | 19 | 90×30×30 | 81 |
| 36×15×12 | 24 | 90×40×30 | 108 |
| 36×15×15 | 30 | 90×40×40 | 144 |
| 36×18×12 | 29 | 90×45×30 | 122 |
| 36×18×15 | 36 | 90×45×40 | 162 |
| 36×18×18 | 43 | 90×45×45 | 182 |
| 48×12×12 | 26 | 120×30×30 | 108 |
| 48×15×12 | 32 | 120×40×30 | 144 |
| 48×15×15 | 40 | 120×40×40 | 192 |
| 48×18×12 | 38 | 120×45×30 | 162 |
| 48×18×15 | 48 | 120×45×40 | 216 |
| 48×18×18 | 58 | 120×45×45 | 243 |
| 48×20×15 | 53 | 120×50×40 | 240 |
| 48×24×12 | 51 | 120×60×30 | 216 |
| 48×24×15 | 64 | 120×60×40 | 288 |
| 48×24×18 | 77 | 120×60×45 | 324 |
| 48×24×24 | 102 | 120×60×60 | 432 |
| 60×24×15 | 80 | 150×60×40 | 360 |
| 60×24×18 | 96 | 150×60×45 | 405 |
| 60×24×24 | 128 | 150×60×60 | 540 |
| 72×24×15 | 96 | 180×60×40 | 432 |
| 72×24×18 | 115 | 180×60×45 | 486 |
| 72×24×24 | 153 | 180×60×60 | 648 |

**USEFUL CONVERSIONS:** 1 inch=2.54 cm    1 gallon=4.55 litres    1 cubic foot=6.2 gallons (28.2 litres)
1 gallon weighs 10 lb (4.53 kg)    1 litre weighs 1 kg (2.2 lb)

The best modern tanks now have runners to take the cover glasses. The runners are strips of glass cemented to each end wall of the tank which allow the cover glasses to be slid backwards and forwards. The cover glass should be in two sections so that either the whole of the front or the whole of the back of the aquarium can be serviced at one time. Each section should have a small piece of glass fixed to the top with a silicone adhesive to act as a handle. Cover glasses are essential in marine aquariums where evaporation of water must be reduced to the minimum to prevent changes in the concentrations of the dissolved salts, light fittings and hoods must be protected from the corrosive action of salt water and the water protected from contamination by metallic ions.

## STANDS

Many aquariums can be displayed to advantage on some form of stand which can be a feature of the room or hall in which the aquarium is placed. You should ensure that the stand is an adequate support for the weight of water and for the tank, gravel and ancillary equipment which are placed on it. Many people have underestimated the weight of a full aquarium, with disastrous results. A gallon of water weights 10 pounds (4.5 kg) and the most popular tank holds 11 gallons; enormous weights are involved when larger tanks are installed. Large aquariums should not be installed without expert advice and it is obviously safer to distribute the weight on a plinth or cabinet than to concentrate the weight on the four legs of a stand. There are many types of decorative stand made of a variety of materials including wrought-iron and wood, as well as plain pressed steel. When installing the stand it is important to make certain that it is perfectly level by using a spirit-level, because a small deviation from the horizontal may cause its complete collapse when it takes the weight of the aquarium. A useful precaution is to place a half inch layer of polystyrene foam between the tank and the stand to even out any irregularities. A plastic surface to the top of the stand is essential if you are installing a marine system. It is almost impossible to avoid the odd drip of water when feeding the fishes or servicing the tank and salt water will quickly corrode most metals.

Your aquarium should be a showpiece in your home, so try to select a stand which not only shows it off to advantage but one which harmonizes with the decor of the room you have chosen for it.

## CABINETS

The most attractive housing for a tank is a cabinet with a veneer to match the other furniture in the room. There are many advantages to cabinets other than the aesthetic. Since only the front of the aquarium is exposed there is much less heat loss. The area beneath the tank can be utilized as cupboards, one of which can house the pumps, fluorescent control units and other electrics. Other cupboards can be used for anything from cocktail cabinets to hi-fi systems but can also function in a more practical way and house your nets, fish food and other accessories. If the 'window' or the 'picture frame' in the front of the cabinet is smaller than the front of the tank, the overlap will hide an unsightly airlift, gravelbed or heater. If the cabinet has greater depth than the tank, the area behind the tank can be used for decor and to create an optical illusion of limitless depth. It is very useful to have a piano hinge running the full length of the lid so that the front portion can be lifted for feeding or cleaning and the whole lid with its lights and wires need be disturbed only for a major re-arrangement.

# Lighting Systems

## LIGHTING

Without any doubt, fluorescent lighting provides the most popular and effective illumination for displaying the brilliant colours of aquarium fishes while at the same time enhancing the growth of most tropical aquarium plants. This type of lighting is also less expensive to run although it has a higher initial installation cost. The most popular types of fluorescent tubes are Grolux, Wotan and Trulite, but almost any kind will give good results when used properly. Grolux tubes give a reddish glow and probably enhance the colours of the fishes most dramatically but are not the best type of tube for encouraging plant growth. Trulite tubes which closely match natural daylight in spectral content are the first choice for plants. The best plan is to install one of each type of tube side by side over the aquarium. Trulite tubes are always recommended for use in marine aquariums because the light quality is essential for the maintenance of the minute plankton on which many of the invertebrates feed and it also encourages the growth of marine plants. The only problem to be aware of when using these tubes is that an essential part of the ultraviolet part of the spectrum is absorbed when it passes through normal cover glasses, thus reducing the effectiveness of the light. To overcome this, these tubes should be installed under the cover glass and have their contact ends coated with silicone to protect them against corrosion. The intensity and duration of illumination needed for a marine aquarium is considerably greater than that needed for a freshwater aquarium and the aquarist should purchase rather higher wattage tubes and run them for longer periods. Wattage is usually related to the length of tank, and the following is an indication of the size of tube and wattage needed relative to the length of a freshwater tank:

| Length of Tank | Length of tube | Wattage of tube |
| --- | --- | --- |
| 24 inches (60 cm) | 18 inches (45 cm) | 15 watts |
| 36 inches (90 cm) | 24 inches (60 cm) | 20 watts |
| 48 inches (120 cm) | 36 inches (90 cm) | 30 watts |

Five to ten watts should be added to these figures for a marine aquarium. The duration of artificial lighting should be about 10 hours for a freshwater aquarium and about 12 hours for a marine aquarium. This approximates to the natural lighting in the tropics where the fishes and plants originate. Many aquarists allow either too little or too much illumination which invariably causes problems with the plants—they waste away when there is too little light and develop an excessive growth of algae when there is too much.

A useful piece of equipment for the aquarist is a rheostat which can be connected to an ordinary domestic light bulb. By using the rheostat it is possible slowly to increase or decrease the intensity of light before switching on or off the fluorescent tubes. Most fishes are sensitive to sudden changes in illumination, an occurrence which seldom happens in nature. Some species of fish suffer from shock in such instances.

## HOODS

There are several forms of commercial hoods to contain the lighting arrangements on the market today. They are made from a variety of materials ranging from aluminium to plastic and fibreglass. Some are highly sophisticated in design and construction, and control not only the lighting but also many other items of electrical apparatus used in the aquarium. As mentioned earlier, it is important to protect the hood and electric cables from condensation to avoid corrosion and electrical problems. Wherever possible the hood should harmonize with the aquarium and give it a more tailored appearance. Many of the latest and most modern European tank manufacturers now build glass tanks with a formica or similar veneer which masks the upper part of the tank behind the hood; as well as producing a pleasant appearance this is essentially practical because the lighting units can be concealed.

# Gravel, Rocks and Backgrounds

## FRESHWATER GRAVEL

Many firms supply gravel without concerning themselves with its quality and this can lead to serious problems in freshwater tanks. The water in many areas is already fairly hard and if the gravel used contains a calcium salt then there is a slow but measurable increase in both the pH and the hardness of the water unless the tank is very crowded or overfed, conditions which in themselves are in any case undesirable. This increase in pH and hardness is detrimental to many characins and *Aphyosemion* species and to many other varieties. Many of our most beautiful aquarium plants are also adapted to soft and slightly acidic waters and so the use of a calciferous gravel is as harmful to fine plant growth as it is to some choice species of fish. Regrettably, many aquarium shops either cannot get a lime-free gravel or are unaware of how to test for lime and to compel their wholesalers to supply satisfactory gravel. A simple test for lime is to take half a cup of gravel and pour onto it a few drops of hydrochloric acid; if it effervesces, then there is lime present; if it does not react, your gravel is acceptable. A flint gravel is highly recommended, as nearly all are lime-free and many are attractively and naturally coloured. There are many forms of highly-coloured gravel and multi-coloured gravel which can help to create dramatic colour schemes for special displays, but in general look unnatural and do not enhance the overall effect. A one-eighth inch (3 mm) grain size is usually the best for the average aquarium. This size allows full filtration of the water through an under-gravel filter and does not become blocked easily, thus creating the optimum conditions for a natural biological filter. The amount of gravel needed is about 1 lb per 12 square inches of aquarium base area (450 grams per 77 sq. cm). Thus a $24 \times 12$ inch ($60 \times 30$ cm) base area tank would require 24lb (10.5kg) of gravel. This ratio can be used to calculate requirements of any other size of tank. Marine calculations are the same as above, although some aquarists prefer up to 15 per cent extra weight of oolite sand. All gravels should be thoroughly washed before use to remove superfluous dust and dirt, and should cover the aquarium floor to about 2 to 3 inches (5 to 7.5 cm) and slope upwards towards the back of the tank.

## MARINE GRAVEL

The gravel in a marine aquarium is fundamentally different from that in a freshwater aquarium. The gravel must be either oolite coral sand or dolomite sand to give a really good result. The reason for this is a little complex. In the marine aquarium the breakdown of waste nitrogenous products is absolutely essential because ammonia and nitrites are especially lethal at the higher pH values in a marine system. Essentially this breakdown is achieved by two broad groups of bacteria. The *Nitrosomonas* group which reduces the $NH_4$ (ammonia) radical to $NO_2$ (nitrite) and the *Nitrobacter* group which oxidizes the nitrite radical to $NO_3$ (nitrate) which is relatively harmless.

$$NH_4 + \textit{Nitrosomonas} + O_2 \text{ (oxygen)} = NO_2 \text{ (nitrite)}$$
$$NO_2 + \textit{Nitrobacter} + O_2 \text{ (oxygen)} = NO_3 \text{ (nitrate)}$$

Immense numbers of bacteria are required to produce these reactions. These bacteria grow primarily on surfaces of rock or sand and for this reason the oolite coral sand, because of its structural characteristics, has an infinitely greater surface area than any other, thus allowing far larger colonies of bacteria to grow and consequently enabling many more fishes to live in a given size tank. In addition, the oolite sand has an exceptional buffering capacity which helps keep the water at an even level of aklalinity and prevents sudden and disastrous drops in alkaline content.

## ROCKS

The choice of rocks for landscaping your aquarium is extensive. Sandstone, granites, slate and several others are eminently suitable. Rocks should be avoided, however, if there is any indication that they contain veins of metallic ores as this could lead under certain circumstances to undesirable leaching of metal ions into the water. Any rocks collected by the hobbyist from natural locations should be carefully sterilized and thoroughly washed before introducing them into the aquarium. This can be done by simply scrubbing them clean and then immersing them in boiling water for about ten minutes. Many fish require a subdued corner or cave in a tank where they can rest or hide and protect themselves from more aggressive species, so do take care to provide one or two places in the tank where the illumination is naturally reduced by rocks as this will give your fishes a choice of environments which they can select according to their individual needs.

## BACKGROUNDS

Many aquarists prefer to leave their aquarium in a natural state, relying on plants and rocks to provide an attractive background, but a great deal of rockwork and extremely thick cover of plants would be needed to obscure the back glass altogether if this is your aim. Others prefer to paint the back glass black, or green (or blue in a marine aquarium). Alternatively you can buy scenic

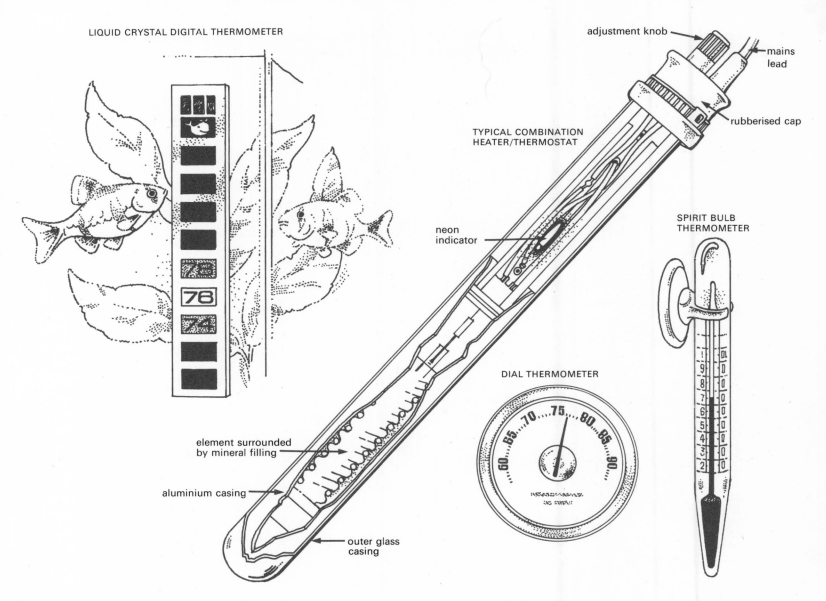

LIQUID CRYSTAL DIGITAL THERMOMETER

adjustment knob

mains lead

rubberised cap

TYPICAL COMBINATION
HEATER/THERMOSTAT

neon indicator

SPIRIT BULB
THERMOMETER

element surrounded
by mineral filling

DIAL THERMOMETER

aluminium casing

outer glass
casing

backgrounds which depict various underwater scenes, including rockwork, plants and even other fishes. Some scenes are reflective, often in metallized finishes which can create effects of appeal to some aquarists and can show off certain species of fishes to maximum advantage if used with discretion. Other scenes have very realistic three-dimensional effects which can help to produce a feeling of space in small aquariums. Try to choose a background which will harmonize with the effect you are trying to achieve and blend with your plants, rocks, gravel and fishes. The creation of natural scenes is the best way to achieve a harmonious and satisfying effect. Photographic backgrounds depicting rock formations and vegetation are much to be preferred to pictures of sunken galleons which even in a marine tank do little to improve its overall appearance.

# Heating Systems

### HEATERS AND THERMOSTATS

There are now very few separate heaters and thermostats made for the aquarium. Nearly all models of heater are combined with a thermostat, both of which are built into a glass or plastic tube, usually with an outside adjustment enabling the aquarist to vary the temperature up or down as required. The important points to look for are that there is no metal part in contact with the water, that the equipment conforms with electrical safety

regulations, that your dealer has found the equipment reliable, and that any faults will be rectified under a guarantee. Regrettably a few of the models which work on a simple magnetic make-and-break principle sometimes jam and cause your fish either to freeze or fry and all dealers have had the experience of an unfortunate hobbyist returning with this tale of woe. However, a fault of this kind usually reveals itself when the heater is first installed, so a certain caution during the first few days before any fish are introduced can pay dividends. New models based on solid state electronics are currently being introduced. These, while costing up to 70 per cent more than conventional designs, are almost foolproof, extremely reliable, and are a very good investment.

### THERMOMETERS

A thermometer is an essential item in all tropical aquariums. Here again there is quite a variety from which to choose. Until very recently the principal type was a spirit or mercury bulb thermometer consisting of a long glass tube filled with alcohol or mercury. The column of liquid rises or falls according to changes in temperature which can be read from a calibrated scale. This type of thermometer is usually stuck inside the tank by means of a rubber suction disc although there have been one or two floating varieties. Their great advantage is that they are cheap and fairly accurate, whilst their disadvantages are that being made of glass they are easily broken, and, because they are stuck on the inside of the tank and protrude inwards, they tend to get in the way every time it is necessary to catch a fish. Should one of these thermometers break in the tank, the contents can be very harmful, especially in marine aquariums.

Another smaller type of thermometer is circular in shape with an aluminium casing. Here a metal indicator arm is linked to the expansion or contraction of the metal case. These thermometers are attached to the inside of the aquarium by a suction disc which encircles the front of the thermometer. They are very accurate, neat, easy to read and of pleasing design; their cost is moderate in relation to their accuracy. The only fault with this type is the tendency of the rubber suction discs to fail. They are one of the few pieces of British equipment to lead in a field which is most often dominated by German, American and Italian manufacturers.

The most recent addition to the field of aquarium thermometers is in the form of liquid crystal digital units which are stuck to the outside of the aquarium by an impact adhesive. The vertical strip is divided into several boxes, each clearly marked at two-degree intervals from 70° to 86°F. The liquid crystals react so that the appropriate box lights up and can be read at a distance from the tank. If the temperature lies between two boxes both of them light up. The aquarist can see at a glance from the other end of the room whether the illuminated box is near the required range. These thermometers are both attractive to look at and simple to use. At the time of writing their cost is about double that of most spirit or mercury models, but they do overcome the disadvantages of the older types of thermometer. A drawback of the digital model is that the temperature range is somewhat limited on the models currently available, and in the event of the temperature going too high or low, the hobbyist may be at a loss to know what has occurred. Where heat treatment is necessary for disease therapy (for example when treating white spot) it could prove difficult to adjust the water temperature with any degree of accuracy if the scale is calibrated in two-degree intervals. As digital thermometers are fixed to the outside of the tank they are affected to some extent by the outside air temperature although there would have to be a significant difference between the temperature of the room and the water in the tank for this factor to be important. These new thermometers have a tremendous appeal to aquarists and seem to have become best sellers.

# Air Pumping Systems

There is probably no field where the aquarist is offered so wide a choice of equipment or is promised so much by the manufacturers. Each system has its particular uses and applications. Your requirements will vary according to the number and sizes of tanks in operation, the type of fishes or invertebrates you intend to keep and the degree of sophistication you are trying to achieve. This review of the available equipment should help you decide which system suits your needs and pocket. Reliability of the system is of foremost importance; an inadequate air supply at a critical time can be heartbreaking. The air pumps currently available fall into four principal categories: (1) diaphragm pumps, of innumerable models and

outputs; (2) piston pumps; (3) carbon blade rotary pumps; (4) low pressure air blowers.

## DIAPHRAGM PUMPS
This first category is the choice of probably the vast majority of enthusiasts and the reasons can be summarized quite easily. The performance and reliability of these pumps is good, they are neat and small, and are reasonable in price. All diaphragm pumps work on the principle of a small vibrating diaphragm valve which is caused to open and close by passing alternating current electricity through a magnetic coil. Each closing of the valve causes a bellows effect and the rapidity with which this occurs produces a continuous stream of air through the outlet. The simplicity of the design results in a degree of reliability unusual in a mechanical product and they can be left to run unattended for months and even years without any maintenance. The only part that wears out eventually is the diaphragm, but spares are inexpensive and readily available for reputable makes of pump. Diaphragm pumps do vary, however, in their capacity to produce air, and also in their price and the amount of noise they produce. As most aquariums are installed in a living room, this noise level is probably the over-riding factor to be considered when making a choice of pumps, a point which if ignored may cause more domestic conflict than any other! Always insist on listening to the pump operating under normal conditions in the dealer's showroom before

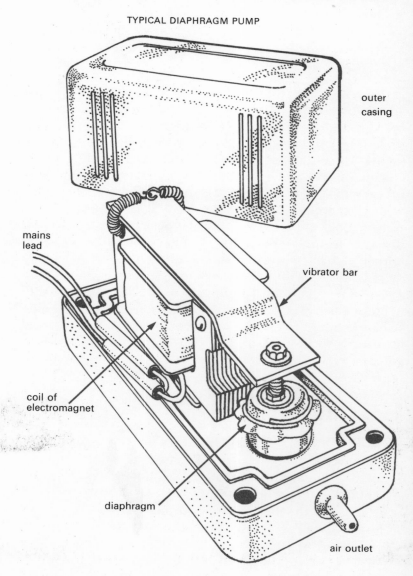

TYPICAL DIAPHRAGM PUMP

outer casing

mains lead

vibrator bar

coil of electromagnet

diaphragm

air outlet

making your choice; few shops will be willing to exchange a pump simply on the grounds that you have subsequently found it to be too noisy. Some aquarists find even the most silent diaphragm pump too noisy. It is often helpful to stand the pump on a small piece of sponge rubber which will help to deaden the vibrations. If this can be combined with placing the pump in a cupboard or box, it should be possible to reduce the noise to below normal audible levels. Many of the models offered today have more than one air outlet and this increased capacity is essential where a larger than average tank has been selected. Do bear in mind, however, that there are several high capacity models available which have only a single outlet and the simplest way to test the capacity of a pump's ability to deliver air is to place an air tube from the nozzle into increasing depths of water with an air diffuser attached. The weaker the model, the less able it is to displace the water and as the depth of operation increases so will the efficiency of the weaker pumps decrease. Do not select a pump which cannot push air through a column of water twice the height of your selected tank. Should you contemplate the possibility of later expanding to more than one aquarium, it is false economy to buy a pump which will serve a single tank. A really good pump can be used for several aquariums and will usually cost less than several smaller pumps.

To sum up, the intending purchaser should select a model which his dealer both recommends and is prepared to demonstrate; he should choose a capacity which is greater than that required rather than less, make certain that spare parts are stocked by his dealer, and compare the pump in price, design and noise output with other models. Finally remember always to place a diaphragm pump at the same level as the aquarium or above it because any interruption in the power supply may cause a siphoning effect to take place, with disastrous effects to the pump.

## PISTON PUMPS

This type of pump seems to be made only by two manufacturers, one in the U.S.A., the other in Britain. The advantages of piston pumps are that they are extremely quiet, very reliable and hardly ever wear out. Their drawbacks are that they are certainly not as cheap as diaphragm pumps and need an occasional application of oil to the pistons to maintain them in working condition. This lubricating oil must be prevented from entering the aquarium through the air line, because even the smallest amount of oil on the surface could cause major problems. A cotton wool plug filter placed in the airline will mop up minor amounts of oil or other dirt in the air. The major problem, from the point of view of the hobbyist, is the limited supply of piston pumps. You may have to pester your dealer to obtain one from his distributor. They also cost more but because of their reliability and low noise are highly recommended.

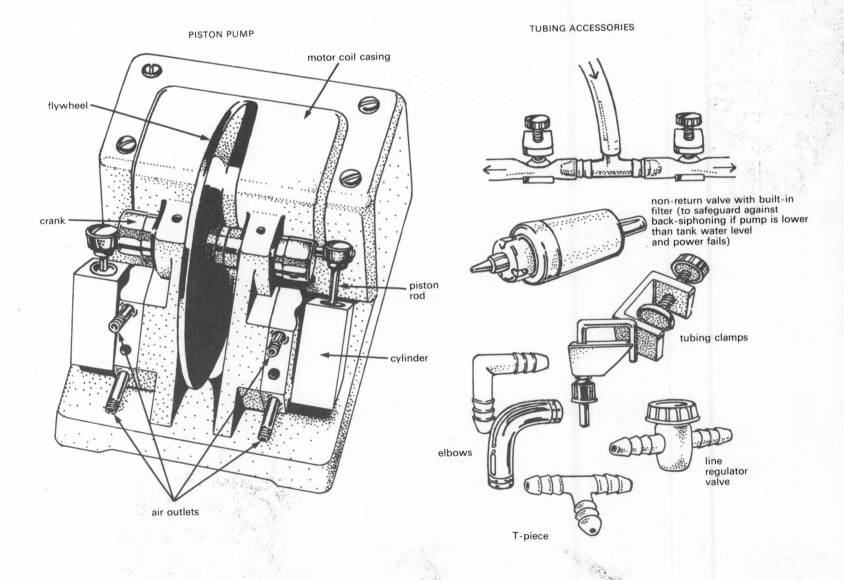

PISTON PUMP

motor coil casing

flywheel

crank

piston rod

cylinder

air outlets

TUBING ACCESSORIES

non-return valve with built-in filter (to safeguard against back-siphoning if pump is lower than tank water level and power fails)

tubing clamps

elbows

line regulator valve

T-piece

## CARBON BLADE COMPRESSORS

These pumps, which are used in many aspects of industrial and especially laboratory work, have found favour in recent years with some serious fish breeders and a few shopkeepers. They work by the rotation of three or four blades of carbon on a spindle at very high revolutions, producing a large volume of displaced air which is sucked through the displacement chamber. They are normally capable, therefore, of producing both positive pressure at the outlet pipe and a vacuum at the inlet pipe; great care must be taken never to connect the vacuum end with air lines leading to the aquarium or the pump will be ruined in seconds. Most of these pumps have a regulator which can alter the flow of air, and many have a small gauge for measuring the pressure of air being produced. They are very useful for the aquarist or shopkeeper wishing to service between 10 and 20 tanks (at which stage even the best diaphragm pump is inadequate) and where the demand does not justify the installation of a low pressure blower type pump. Carbon blade compressors have several drawbacks as they are usually quite noisy and are rather expensive. They also require periodic maintenance by replacement of the carbon blades and air filter pads which can be a modest but noticeable expense.

## LOW PRESSURE AIR BLOWERS

For the shopkeeper, wholesaler, fish hatchery, or really devoted aquarist, where 50 or more tanks are to be operated continuously at low cost and with absolute reliability, there is hardly any answer other than a low pressure blower of some kind. These pumps work by producing large volumes of air at a pressure of some 5 to 10 pounds per square inch (35 to 70 kilonewtons per square metre) by means of a rotary vane. They require a ring main installation of pipe of 1 inch (2 to 3 cm) in diameter to which plastic outlet connectors can be fitted by inserting them in fractionally undersized drilled holes. It is vitally important when installing these pumps to make certain that the first 6 or 7 metres of pipe is about 4 inches (10 cm) in diameter and that a valve is installed in this opening part of the run as any back pressure of more than 10 pounds per square inch will quickly damage the motor.

The only maintenance required is the occasional, usually annual, replacement of the pulley belt, yet these pumps can service from 50 to 400 tanks with ease. Although expensive and somewhat noisy, they are ideal for all installations where high performance, reliability and low maintenance requirements are the criteria. Most countries have at least one manufacturer.

## AIR STONES AND DIFFUSERS

An air line fitted to an air stone or diffuser is almost essential for any tropical tank not using undergravel or power-filtration. Not only does it provide a degree of oxygenation of the water, it also helps by driving out any excessive carbon dioxide gas by enabling diffusion to take place at the air and water interface of the bubbles. In addition, it generates a turbulence in the water which is beneficial to many varieties of fish and which they seem to enjoy swimming in if the flow is strong enough.

Air stones are made in various shapes, but are usually cubic, spherical or cylindrical. They are inexpensive and easy to keep down in the water because of their weight. They are made of a porous stone, but many do not give a particularly small bubble which is essential if maximum oxygenation is to be achieved. They also have a tendency to become clogged by salts suspended in the water over a period of time, especially in marine aquariums, and must be replaced. However, another useful type of diffuser is made of a fine balsa wood which produces very small bubbles. These are a little more expensive than air stones and have a tendency to float, especially initially, unless held down in some way until they become waterlogged. A new type of diffuser just on the market in Britain incorporates an elongated strip of porous plastic foam. These strips are available in various lengths from 6 to 24 inches (15 to 60 cm) and produce a curtain of fine air bubbles which create a pleasing effect coupled with a movement of water which the fishes enjoy. These new diffusers are fast becoming very popular indeed and can be recommended without hesitation even though they cost much more than the conventional air stones.

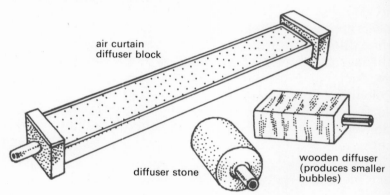

air curtain diffuser block

diffuser stone

wooden diffuser (produces smaller bubbles)

## CLAMPS, VALVES AND LINE DIVIDERS

The supply of air to an aquarium must be controlled in such a way that each part of the system receives an adequate but controlled supply, otherwise the air will take the line of least resistance, causing all of it to flow through just one outlet. The first thing for the aquarist to do is to count carefully the number of air line points he will require; for example, two lines for the uplifts of the biological filter, one for an air stone, one for a vacuum cleaner and one for an outside filter. Then according to whether the pump has a single outlet or twin outlets, he can purchase simple 3-way or even 4-way air line dividers which will distribute the air outflow as required. The flow can be regulated by placing on each air line a small valve or constriction which, by simple adjustment, will allow only the right amount of air to pass. These valves are sold in numerous forms and are made of plastic, steel, brass, or combinations of plastic and metal. They vary greatly in price; the more expensive models certainly give better control, and last longer, but for the average system the cheaper models are perfectly adequate. Some aquarists prefer a type of constrictor used in hospitals to control drip feeds. This type has a circular cut-out through which the air line is passed and the spirally controlled pressure is evenly applied around the tube ensuring that even some irregularity of the air supply will not cause problems in the aquarium. The author uses this type exclusively in his own breeding establishment but the cost of these restrictors is about five times that of the least expensive models and many aquarists prefer a simple plastic clamp.

# Filtration and Cleaning Systems

Two types of filtration are used in aquariums, both of which can be recommended but which function quite differently in maintaining high quality water in the aquarium.

## BIOLOGICAL FILTERS

This type of filter, now made by many leading manufacturers, is placed under the gravel which then acts as the filter bed. These filters are normally constructed of a large sheet of corrugated or indented plastic sheet perforated with fine holes or slots through which the water passes. At each rear corner of the filter plate there is usually a stand pipe or lift tube through which, by means of an air line, a venturi action of air causes a column of water to pass up the pipe; water thus pumped out of the filter plate is constantly replenished through the holes in its surface. It is most important to ensure that the filter plate fits firmly and exactly on the base of the aquarium so that an even flow of water is maintained and it is also necessary to choose a type of filter which has holes smaller than the grade of gravel selected. The water is drawn down through the gravel filter bed where excess food and waste products of the fishes are soon detoxified by enormous colonies of nitrifying bacteria which rapidly build up on the surface of the gravel. This neutralization of organic waste not only purifies the water but converts the impurities to substances which act as natural fertilisers. The major drawback of this system is that as the bacterial bed is highly aerobic the air pump must be kept running continuously; any shut-down will result in considerable mortality of the bacteria after only a few hours causing cloudiness and oxygen depletion in the tank. Despite this drawback, biological filters can be recommended for all types of freshwater aquariums.

At least two or three manufacturers offer this type of filter with a reverse flow system. In these units the water is drawn down through the corner tubes and then re-emerges into the aquarium upwards through the filter bed. The impurities in the water are neutralized in exactly the same way, but particles of debris and detritus, instead of becoming trapped in the gravel, are pushed up into the aquarium and can then be extracted easily by a mechanical filter.

Whereas biological filtration is useful in fresh water, it is essential in salt water where any accumulation of nitrogenous waste products will mortally poison your fishes in a matter of hours if they are not removed by an efficient filtration system. This is because ammonia, the first excretory stage of the nitrogenous wastes, is infinitely more toxic at the higher pH level of a marine system, which may be as high as 8.3, than at the pH of a freshwater system which is likely to be about 7. This mandatory biological filtration can be carried out either within the tank by means of a sub-gravel unit or by means of a large outside power filter unit with the filter gravel contained inside the box unit. In marine systems, the importance of continuous operation cannot be over-emphasized because the bacteria can start to die with frightening rapidity in as little as two or three hours, resulting in a sudden build-up of ammonia and highly toxic conditions for your stock.

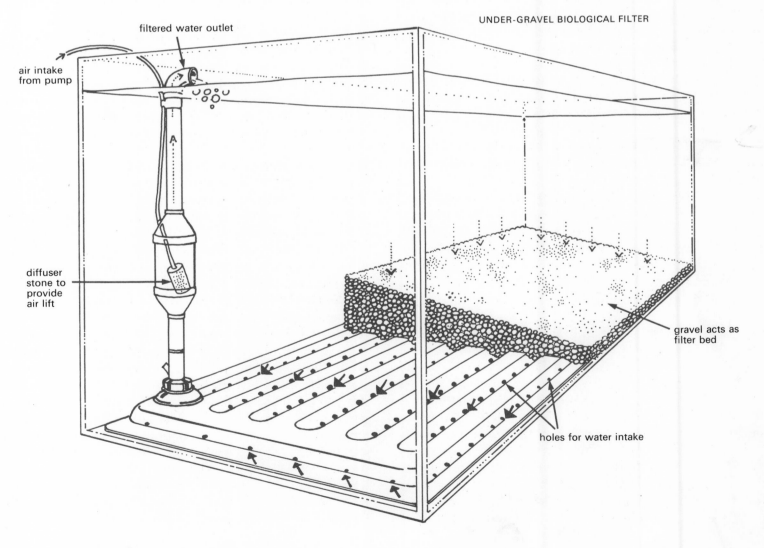

UNDER-GRAVEL BIOLOGICAL FILTER

filtered water outlet

air intake from pump

diffuser stone to provide air lift

gravel acts as filter bed

holes for water intake

## MECHANICAL FILTERS

This form of filtration is largely an optional extra. The purposes of mechanical filtration are to remove fine suspended particulate matter, to keep the aquarium clean and, in some instances, to alter the water chemistry. In a heavily populated aquarium such an extra will probably serve its purpose, but in the average aquarist's tank its merits are doubtful. The drawbacks of mechanical filtration are the cost of power filters, their bulky and often obtrusive appearance, and the considerable possibility of some small accident, mains electricity failure or other problem, causing the tank water to be siphoned out. However, the attractions of mechanical filtration to the serious aquarist and fish breeder are such that a survey of the field may be useful. Mechanical filters fall into two main categories: air lift filters, and power filters.

**Air lift filters** These are usually made of moulded perspex and are placed in the corner of the tank. Water is drawn through its filter unit by way of an air lift tube within the unit itself. They work well in small aquariums of up to 11 gallons (50 litres) but beyond this size they seldom have the capacity to cope. Here at least the failure of the air power will not cause any problems to the aquarist or the long-suffering members of the aquarist's family. The air lift filter should have the capacity to filter the volume of tank water once every three to four hours. Most manufacturers will give an indication of the capacity of the unit on the outside of the packaging, but your dealer will be able to advise you.

Filtration by the second group of mechanical airlift filters, of which there are numerous designs, involves the use of an outside plastic box. The water is drawn into the box usually by a siphoning action and returned to the tank in an air lift powered by an air pump. The larger and more sophisticated of these can effect a very large turnover of water but their great drawback is their unsightliness. It is most important that the air pump source for these units is situated above the tank, because otherwise a break in the power supply can, under certain circumstances, cause siphoning out of the tank down into the pump and onto the floor of the room with catastrophic results for all concerned, including the fishes. Advice from a reputable dealer should be sought before selecting a model, because some are far more prone to this problem than others due to basic faults in design. It is very difficult to get the siphon tubes of some models to start operating properly without great patience; swallowing quantities of aquarium water in your attempts to suck the siphon into action is a very real hazard.

**Power filters** The objective here is exactly the same as for air lift filters except that in order to get massive throughput of water into the filter system, an electrically driven motor is substituted for the less powerful air lift system. Two types are available. In the USA, the market is almost completely dominated by a model which has a filter box suspended on the outside of the aquarium and is driven by an electric motor of which many different ratings are available. These units are invariably ugly in appearance but have the merit of being able to push very large volumes of water through the filter box. There are models capable of driving up to 600 gallons (3000 litres) per hour

through the filter, and price for price they are much better value than the more sophisticated models made in Europe. The European power filter is made chiefly in Germany and Italy and is designed to be placed usually under or behind the aquarium so that it does not spoil the overall appearance of the aquarium. These filters usually consist of a cylindrical box with an electric motor on top which drives the water back up to the aquarium through an outlet tube. The drawbacks to these otherwise acceptable models are their high cost, the difficulty of seeing when the filter needs to be replenished and the difficulty invariably encountered when opening and closing the filter box. It is inevitable, however, that in the near future a manufacturer will produce a unit without these problems.

As well as keeping the water clear in marine aquariums, power filtration can remove excessive nitrates and phosphates by the use of ion exchange resins which are sandwiched between two layers of filter wool and placed inside the power unit. Before using any resin make sure that it has been tested extensively and that it has no harmful side-effects. Some of the resins now on sale not only remove undesirable waste products but simultaneously extract vital trace-elements as well and, in causing a massive physiological imbalance, can kill your livestock. In this respect, it is important to note that the excessive use of charcoal filtration in a marine aquarium can also reduce certain key trace-elements to an undesirably low level and it is best to avoid its use except to clarify the aquarium periodically and remove the yellow coloration called *gelbstopf* in Germany. It is also important to remember that all aquarium filter materials become exhausted eventually and should be renewed periodically. Unfortunately there is no simple way to determine when a resin or charcoal is exhausted, except by monitoring the quality of the aquarium water. The frequency of replacement will be related to the number of fishes kept in the aquarium, the original quality of the aquarium water and the amount and type of food offered to the fishes. A good rule of thumb, however, is to exchange the filtering media every four to six weeks.

**Diatomaceous power filters** These are relatively new types of power filter brought out during the last few years by an American company and now imitated by at least one European manufacturer. So far, having tried both, the author prefers the original version for ease of use and reliability, but the principle is the same in both systems in that the water is forced through a filter bag filled with diatomaceous earth. The advantage of these filters is that no interference with the water chemistry takes place and that particulate matter smaller even than 1 micron is removed from the water giving it a superlative clarity, usually within a very short time. They are particularly useful for removing from an aquarium 'green water', caused by small algae suspended in the water. The algae are quickly trapped and removed by these filters. Another great advantage of diatomaceous filters is that during any parasitic infection, the free-swimming stage of the parasite is removed before it can cause subsequent reinfection of the fish. Without a host, most parasites die within 24 hours. Anyone considering a power filter unit would be well advised to invest in a diatomaceous unit for their aquarium.

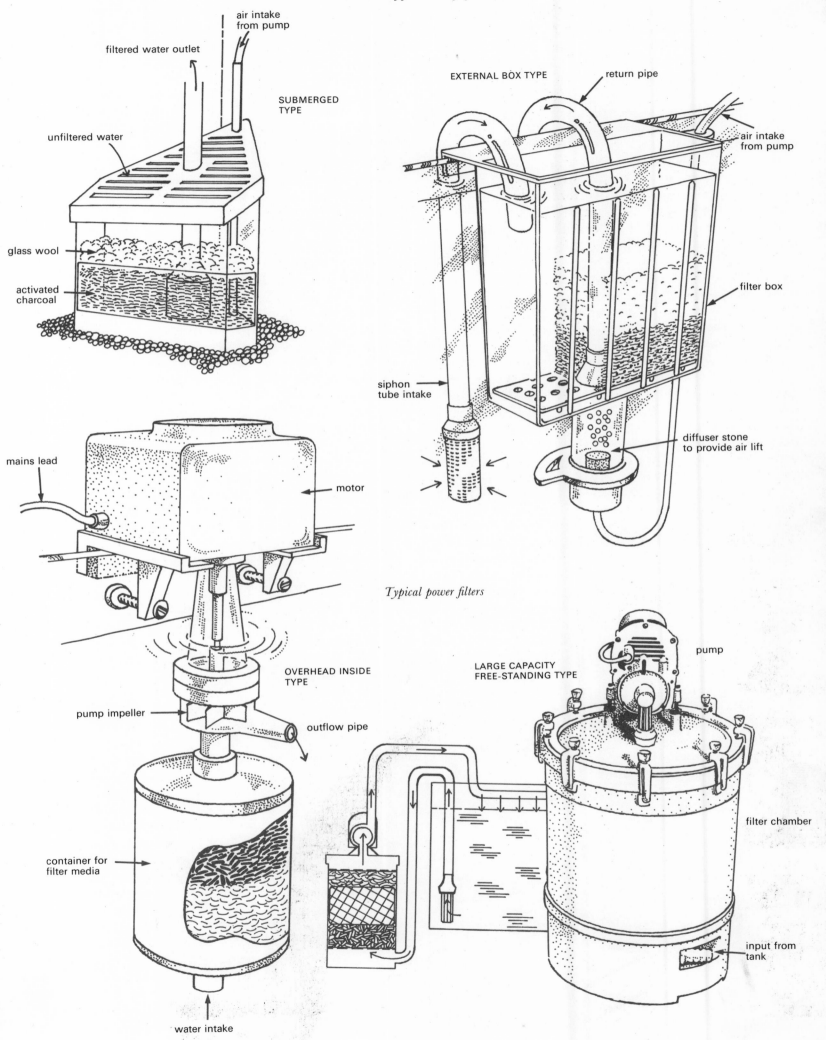

*Typical air lift filters*

**SUBMERGED TYPE**

air intake from pump

filtered water outlet

unfiltered water

glass wool

activated charcoal

**EXTERNAL BOX TYPE**

return pipe

air intake from pump

filter box

siphon tube intake

diffuser stone to provide air lift

mains lead

motor

*Typical power filters*

**OVERHEAD INSIDE TYPE**

pump impeller

outflow pipe

container for filter media

water intake

**LARGE CAPACITY FREE-STANDING TYPE**

pump

filter chamber

input from tank

## PROTEIN SKIMMERS

This comparatively new tool is useful for use in aquariums in which there is an above average number of fishes or invertebrates and where, for practical reasons, it is not possible to make the frequent changes of water which this situation normally calls for. Protein skimmers are especially useful for the marine aquarist who will be confronted with an excess of protein at more frequent intervals than the freshwater specialist. Proteins, usually in the form of amino acids, are produced by the aquarium animals and will pollute the tank if they are not removed periodically. Protein skimmers fractionate or collect these proteins by circulating the water through a column of vigorously bubbling air; the action of the oxygen in the air on the amino acids produces less soluble compounds which can then be skimmed off the top of the column. To be really efficient, the column of water inside the protein skimmer should be at least 2 metres in height as in professional aquaculture installations, but those available to the amateur aquarist are only 12 to 15 inches (30 to 40 cm) high. Some aquarists have solved this problem by building their own skimmers. The usefulness of the small units to the freshwater enthusiast is doubtful but they are better than nothing if a marine system is being maintained and they do allow a reduction in the frequency of water changes. If you do decide to build your own unit it is important to ensure that the size of the bubbles is as small as possible; the smaller the bubbles the greater the volume of air in contact with the water and the greater the degree of oxygenation. Thousands of tiny bubbles will produce a far more effective fractionation than a few large ones.

## ALGAE CLEANERS

There are two types of algae remover which have become standard equipment over recent years. The first and less expensive comprises a long rod with a plastic end into which a safety razor blade is inserted. This works exceptionally well and is effective until the razor blade inevitably becomes rusted or blunted by use. The other end of the rod is often modified to act as a planting stick which can be very useful especially as plants often become dislodged during the process of removing algae from the sides of a tank. Some models have a plastic blade and, to avoid scratching, these are the only ones which should be used in plastic tanks. A second type of algae cleaner on the market uses two magnets: one bar, which is covered with a rough cloth, is placed inside the tank; the other, covered with a soft cloth and usually bearing some form of handle, is placed opposite the first magnet but on the outside of the tank and the two are held together by magnetic attraction. By firmly, but not too rapidly, moving the outside handle up and down you can effectively remove the algae without wetting your hands or the carpet and at the same time polish the front glass. With a little practice the two magnets can be operated without becoming separated. Powerful magnets are essential and any worthwhile model should be very difficult to separate in the showroom. Those models which come apart easily in the hand will be useless when separated by the glass of the aquarium.

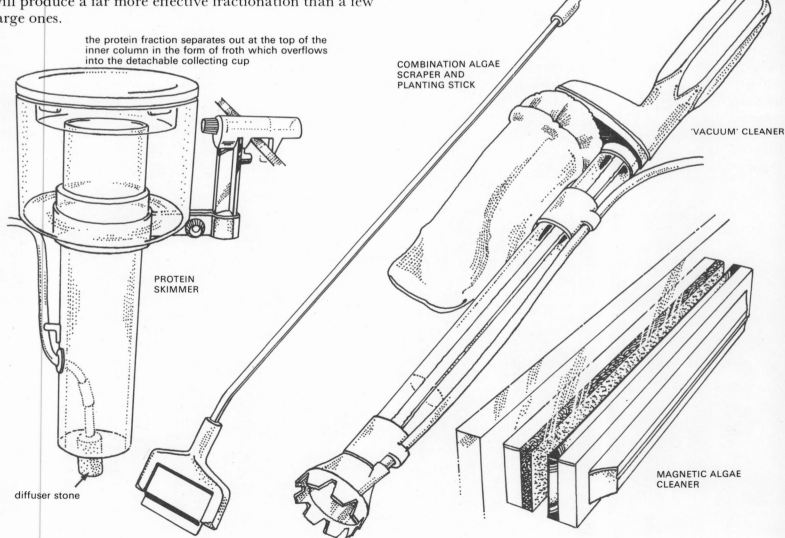

the protein fraction separates out at the top of the inner column in the form of froth which overflows into the detachable collecting cup

PROTEIN SKIMMER

diffuser stone

COMBINATION ALGAE SCRAPER AND PLANTING STICK

'VACUUM' CLEANER

MAGNETIC ALGAE CLEANER

## AQUARIUM VACUUM CLEANERS

Despite the best efforts of aquarium filtration, a certain amount of waste excretory matter will accumulate eventually in the aquarium. This is known in aquarium parlance as mulm and is composed principally of the breakdown products of fish excreta and to a lesser degree decomposed food. The simplest way of dealing with this problem is to make sure that your gravel slopes at a sufficient angle to the front of the tank, then with the aid of any one of the several aquarium vacuum cleaners you can siphon up the mulm into the vacuum bag which strains the aquarium water, the dirt being retained in the bag as in a domestic carpet vacuum cleaner. The power source for the siphon can be a simple rubber squeeze-bulb or an air jet supplied by your air pump, both of which will cause a column of water to rise through the cleaning unit. There are also one or two electrically powered models. Most models are effective but the filter bags eventually wear out and have to be replaced, so make sure your dealer stocks spares. Compare the price and quality of these cleaners as there is little to choose between the various models in terms of effectiveness.

# Miscellaneous Equipment

### OZONIZERS

A great deal has been written about the importance of ozone to the fishes' health in suppressing bacterial infection in the aquarium. Unfortunately there have been very few scientific studies to demonstrate the claimed advantages and the evidence to date is both conflicting and substantially unquantified. Ozone in the air can be a definite irritant to human beings exposed to levels above a certain threshhold value, and there is no known way of measuring precisely the ozone quantity in salt water where it forms a residue whose side effects may be undesirable. The indiscriminate use of ozone should be avoided except in the case of known bacterial disease, where in order to prevent a build up of contagious bacteria in the water, it may be introduced with the air supply for limited periods at a rate of approximately

1 milligram per hour. Papers presented at the 1977 International Ozone Institute Conference in Paris substantially supported the view that great care should be taken when using ozone. In particular, it should never be introduced where young fry or larvae are being reared, because even very low levels have been found to affect them fatally.

### BREEDING TRAPS

For those aquarists who are really serious about their hobby and who intend to breed fishes on a reasonably large scale, this section will be of only limited interest as the establishment of separate tanks for breeding and rearing, perhaps with custom-built traps for individual species, can be the only satisfactory system. Nevertheless, aquarists who are restricted to one or two tanks may find a commercially-produced breeding trap useful to protect the fry of livebearers. There are several models on the market. Some are constructed with a grill, above which the pregnant female is kept. After the fry are born they can swim down through the bars of the grill where the mother fish cannot follow. In certain models the fry find their way out into the tank proper by way of a slot in a V-shaped taper to the trap. Both these types are useful in a community tank if it does not contain other carnivorous fishes and has plenty of plant cover on the surface. In the type of trap which retains the fry in the underneath chamber, the female must be watched carefully to see when she has finished giving birth, because the young fishes may swim up again and then be devoured by their mother. This trap is often claimed to be useful for protecting newly-laid eggs but traps of this type are too small to have much chance of inducing most egglayers to spawn, and all claims to the contrary should be regarded as suspect, notwithstanding the drawings on the manufacturer's packet. A large breeding trap has another use which has nothing to do with breeding. It can be used to isolate a newly introduced fish for a day or two to give the established inmates, if they are aggressive and territorial, an opportunity to become used to the new fish and accept it. This technique is particularly useful with marines.

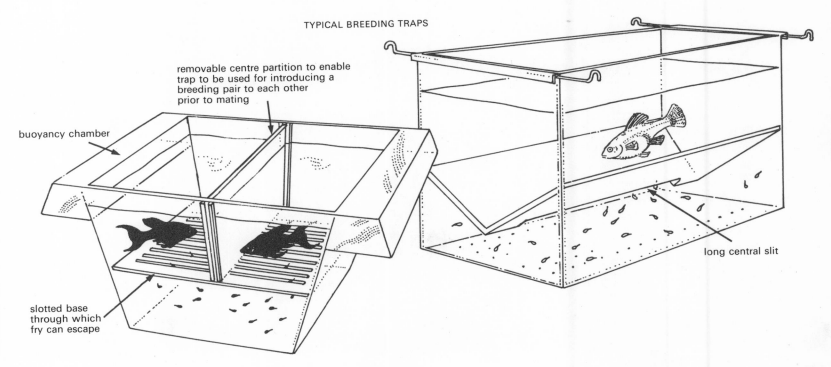

TYPICAL BREEDING TRAPS

removable centre partition to enable trap to be used for introducing a breeding pair to each other prior to mating

buoyancy chamber

slotted base through which fry can escape

long central slit

## FEEDING RINGS

Many aquarists feed live *Tubifex* and white worms to their fishes. If these are fed directly into the aquarium many will find their way into the gravel of the aquarium where they may die and consequently pollute the water. A floating conical worm-feeder with suitable slotted holes through which the worms can wriggle and be caught by the waiting fishes can eliminate this problem in a simple and inexpensive manner. There are several models on the market, including one which has an airline attachment to help oxygenate the worms and keep *Tubifex*, in particular, fresh and healthy. A large ball of *Tubifex* can last a few hours before it is consumed by the fishes and without some aeration or running cold water the worms can die swiftly, thus polluting the aquarium and giving rise to unpleasant odours. A feeding ring is sometimes advocated for general use to prevent excess food floating over the surface of the water or dropping down and fouling the tank. Although overfeeding is something the aquarist must learn to guard against, the restriction of food to one tiny ring will result in the weaker or more timid fishes being gradually forced out of the competition for food, with inevitably unfortunate results. For these reasons feeding rings cannot be recommended for general use

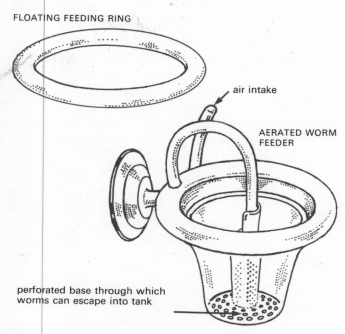

FLOATING FEEDING RING

air intake

AERATED WORM FEEDER

perforated base through which worms can escape into tank

# Placing and Setting Up the Tank

Having selected a tank, lighting system, heating system, filtration unit and air pump, the equipment has to be installed ready to receive the livestock; but you must first decide where to place the aquarium. Moving an aquarium once it has been installed is dangerous and, if you have already filled the tank with water, may be impossible because of its weight. Many beautiful aquariums are neglected and wasted by being placed in a narrow corridor where they receive only a passing glance. To gain the maximum benefit from the aquarium place it in a living room where it can act as a decorative accompaniment and be a source of relaxation. In houses without a fireplace the aquarium can be the focal point of the room. Another good location in some homes will be on a room divider where the aquarium can be seen from two sides and form part of the decor of two rooms. Easy access to a

source of electricity is an essential factor to consider; long leads of trailing cable are not only unsightly but are very dangerous, especially where there are children. Freshwater tanks are best placed away from a window to avoid an excessive growth of algae but marine tanks will benefit from some daylight, the increased algal growth contributing to a healthy fauna, especially of invertebrates. Some marine fishes need an almost entirely vegetable diet and will welcome a supply of algae.

An electrical distribution unit fitted to the side of the tank or beneath it has much to recommend it; owners of a cabinet can make use of one of the cupboards for this purpose. All the electrical requirements (for the heater, lights and pump) can be fed from this unit so that only one lead will be needed between the nearest electrical socket and the aquarium. Wherever possible reserve one socket solely for the aquarium, otherwise someone will inevitably leave it without power and effectively exterminate your fishes in a short time. Make sure also that a fuse of the correct rating is inserted somewhere in the circuit.

## FRESHWATER TANKS

When the tank is in place on its bed of polystyrene foam, take your undergravel filter and assemble it according to the instructions, ensuring that the airlift uprights are tightly and firmly in position—it is all too easy to fail to do this properly when installing some models. Having placed the filter in position the gravel should be washed thoroughly. This can be done by putting it in a clean plastic bucket or other non-metallic receptacle and running a stream of water through it, stirring constantly until the water runs absolutely clear. To ensure that all the gravel is really clean, it should be washed in several lots. Attempting to wash too much at a time usually results in only the top layer being properly cleaned. The gravel should be placed in the aquarium above the undergravel filter and should slope upwards from the front of the tank at about a 30° incline. The front of the tank should have about 2 inches (5 cm) of gravel, while the rear should be about 4 inches (10 cm) in depth. The next stage is to fill the tank slowly with water, placing a clean jug or bottle to catch the incoming stream of water so that it does not churn up the gravel. Do not fill to the very top of the tank, especially if you intend adding decorative rocks or other items. These will displace their own volume of water, so make appropriate allowances.

Now you should introduce your combined heater and thermostat by placing it in one corner towards the bottom of the tank and attaching it to the aquarium glass either with the supplied suckers or with an inexpensive holder unit to prevent it getting knocked and broken. Plug in the heating unit only after making certain that it is fully immersed. Do not make any alterations to the thermostatic control until at least 24 hours have elapsed, as nearly all models are preset to heat the water to an average temperature of 75°F (26°C). Should the thermometer which you will also have installed give a reading higher or lower than 75°F after this time, slowly and carefully adjust the thermostat according to the instructions until you achieve the desired temperature. 75°F is the optimum temperature for a community tank containing several species of fishes.

The air pump can now be plugged in and the air line

to the undergravel filter, outside filter and diffuser stones installed and allowed to start operating. Carefully check the air distribution system and make sure that the airlines are each receiving an even and steady supply. After 24 hours of aeration and filtration, and assuming the water temperature is correct, the aquarium is ready to receive fishes and plants though it is preferable to place plants in the tank a few days before introducing the fishes.

If you have bought cover glasses these should be placed over the tank and then the lighting can be placed over the aquarium. The fluorescent tubes, now virtually a standard item, are fitted into the hood you have chosen and the whole unit placed carefully away from any danger of splashing. Some models of aquarium covers have choke units built in to them, but the tubes are nearly always sold separately.

## MARINE TANKS

Unless you are using natural sea water, an artificial sea salt must be added to the aquarium water after you have brought it to the right temperature. Read the instructions on the packet and add the salt gradually, checking the concentration of salt water by measuring its specific gravity with a hydrometer. Hydrometers are sold by any good dealer and are an essential piece of equipment for the marine aquarist. When the salt has fully dissolved and the temperature has reached 75°F (24°C) the hydrometer should read exactly 1.022. You must now mature the

filter bed of the aquarium and this is best done by applying a dose of freeze-dried bacteria to the water and then feeding the bacteria with infusoria (see the chapter on feeding). In this way it is possible to mature a marine tank in eight to ten days; any other method will not only take several weeks but will allow the multiplication of unwanted competing bacteria which although not intrinsically harmful to the fishes or invertebrates will reduce the quantity of livestock the tank can maintain. To test the maturity of the tank you should use a standard nitrite testing kit which should be capable of measuring down to 0.25 parts per million (ppm) on its colour scale at which level it is safe to introduce the first fishes. At least two kits on the market do satisfy this condition but some do not. Any level above 0.25 ppm is dangerous for some sensitive species. You will find that the upward curve of the nitrite cycle will reach its peak at about 8 ppm and will then fall to 0.25 or less when the tank is mature. Do not rush to introduce several fishes at once and watch the nitrite level daily. The nitrite level often goes up a point or two after the first fish is placed in the tank so make sure that this fish is one of the less sensitive species such as a damsel. The nitrite concentration should drop after 24 to 48 hours and once this has occurred you may introduce further fishes, one or two at a time, but as a precaution continue to monitor your nitrite level for the first month. A well matured system should register a zero reading at all times after the first few fishes have been introduced.

*The assembly and connection of the basic equipment*

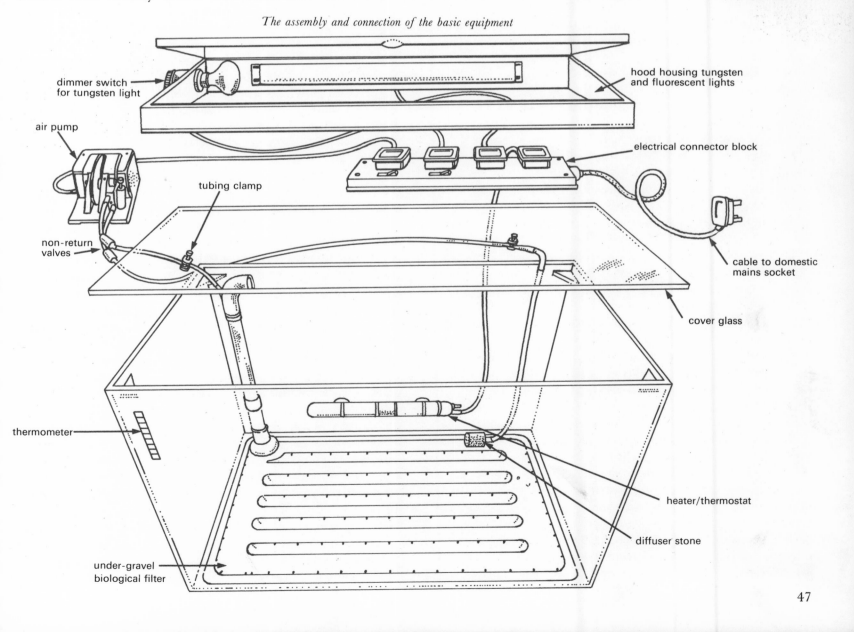

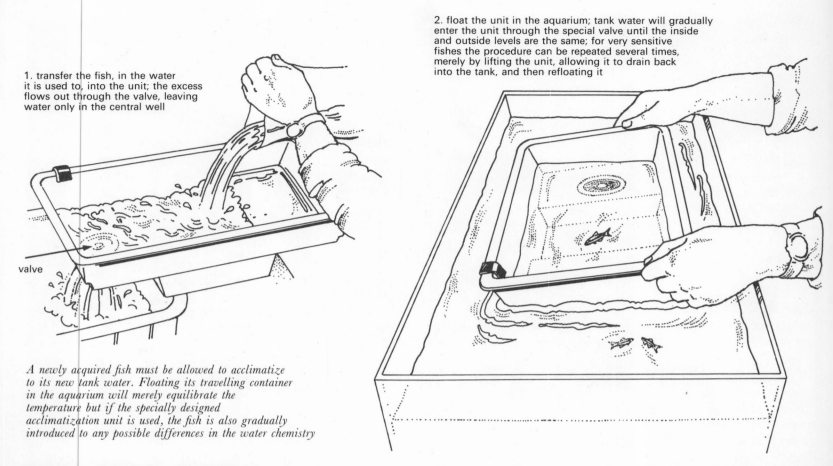

1. transfer the fish, in the water it is used to, into the unit; the excess flows out through the valve, leaving water only in the central well

valve

2. float the unit in the aquarium; tank water will gradually enter the unit through the special valve until the inside and outside levels are the same; for very sensitive fishes the procedure can be repeated several times, merely by lifting the unit, allowing it to drain back into the tank, and then refloating it

*A newly acquired fish must be allowed to acclimatize to its new tank water. Floating its travelling container in the aquarium will merely equilibrate the temperature but if the specially designed acclimatization unit is used, the fish is also gradually introduced to any possible differences in the water chemistry*

## INTRODUCTION OF FISHES

The transfer of the selected specimens from the dealer's tank to your own is a matter which needs careful handling as too sudden a change from one environment to another can cause your fishes unacceptable stress and can lead to the onset of possibly fatal disease, often in a matter of hours. Neon Tetras, for example, may die if transferred from soft to hard water too suddenly. Should you have the unfortunate experience of a major outbreak of disease in your tank and wish to eliminate it entirely and start again, a good household domestic bleach will totally disinfect your tank over 24 hours. Any chlorine which may still be present after changing the water can be removed either by aerating strongly for a few days, or by using any one of the several purifying products which are on sale at good aquarium dealers.

It is probably a truism to say that no two aquariums are exactly alike, and apart from small differences in temperature, there can be quite substantial differences in pH levels, degrees of hardness, nitrite and ammonia concentrations, and many other small and unquantifiable metabolic factors.

To monitor these parameters, reliable test kits should be purchased and used regularly as directed by the manufacturers. This will enable the aquarist to monitor his water quality and anticipate any drastic changes which can sometimes cause disastrous results for the inhabitants of the tank. When selecting any test kit it is important to compare the several makes available as many are difficult to use, and have poor colour definition in several cases; others measure only very large jumps in the parameter to be controlled, not allowing nearly enough fine monitoring, and one brand uses reagents which are notoriously unstable. When measuring nitrite and ammonia levels in either the freshwater or marine aquarium, it is most important to be able to measure

down to at least 0.25 ppm and the colour chart or alternative method should allow this measurement to be made accurately. One kit on the market has a colour chart which begins at 5 ppm—at this level all your fishes will be either dead or in a serious condition. Kits for measuring the pH level should allow readings as small as 0.2 to be made and the calibrations should be easy to read. Hardness can be determined in broader intervals, but as many kits for testing hardness have an inherent instability the aquarist should seek advice from his dealer about which type to buy.

The golden rule to observe is that transferences of fishes from your dealer's tank to yours should be as gradual a process as possible. The way to achieve this until quite recently has been to float the bag holding your fish in the aquarium and then slowly to add small amounts of the aquarium water to the bag. Although this does eventually achieve its purpose, it is a tedious and inexact process. An enterprising Italian company has recently introduced a device, now patented internationally, which resembles a floating breeding trap and has a well to receive the fish and the dealer's water. Very slow seepage of water takes place through a valve so that your aquarium water mixes at a controlled rate with the original water in this acclimatization unit. This reduces stress in the fish to a considerable extent, substantially reduces the chances of inducing disease, and greatly simplifies the introduction of new fishes to an aquarium. If there are very large differences in the quality of the water the process can be repeated by lifting up the unit, draining out half the water through the valve and replacing the unit in the aquarium. This device can also be used when transferring fishes from one tank to another.

This custom-built cabinet houses not only all the equipment for the tank, but also a hi-fi system

# Families of Freshwater Tropicals

## FAMILY POECILIIDAE
### Live-bearing Tooth Carps

This family originates from Central and South America. It includes Guppies, mollies, Swordtails, Platies, Halfbeaks and a few other little-known species. They vary in size from the Mosquito Fish which is less than an inch long to the Giant Sailfin Molly which can reach six inches. The life-span is from two to five years depending on size. In the aquarium they prefer well-matured, slightly alkaline water, but they are very tolerant. They are surface-feeding fishes with a wide diet which includes green food and live food. In the aquarium they will eat whatever is offered. They are peaceful in a community tank. They breed more freely than any other tropical fishes. In short, they are the ideal fish for the beginner.

The common name refers to the fact that live-bearers do not, like the vast majority of fishes, lay eggs, but give birth to free-swimming young.

For this reason they were long regarded as freaks of nature, like the Duck-billed Platypus, a mammal which lays eggs. In fact, there is little similarity between the reproductive systems of live-bearing fishes and mammals. The fertilized egg is simply kept within the female's body until it hatches.

At no time is the baby attached to the mother's blood-stream or dependent on her for food as in the mammal. Nor is there anything to compare with the maternal instinct in mammals. On the contrary, the live-bearing mother is likely to swallow her babies at one end as fast as they emerge at the other.

It is very easy to distinguish the sexes in this family. The female has a full, triangular anal fin, whereas that of the male is modified to the shape and function of a penis. The male is usually smaller than the female and more brightly coloured. The sexual drive is very strong in the male,

Right: Snakeskin Guppy *Poecilia reticulata*
Far right: Snakeskin Guppy *Poecilia reticulata*
Below: Multi-coloured Guppy *Poecilia reticulata*

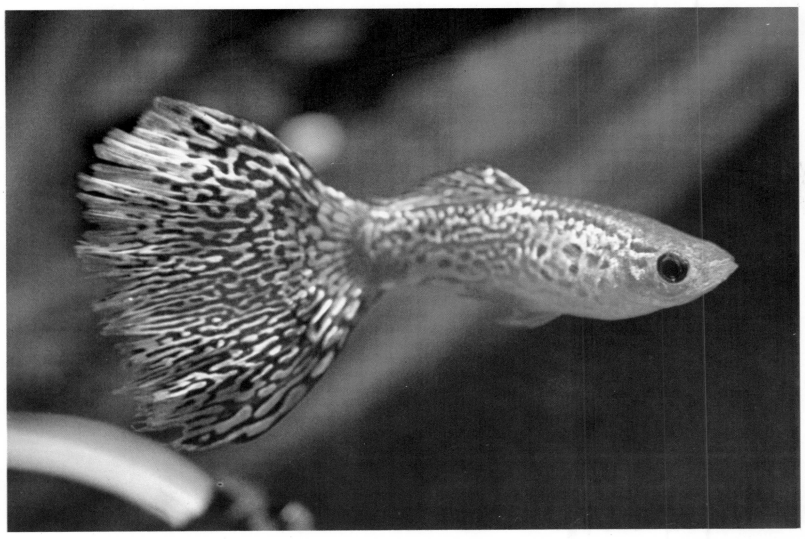

who pesters the poor female ceaselessly. It is therefore good practice to have several females to each male, especially since one fertilization can frequently sire three or four broods.

Females mature early and can reproduce at about four months. A mature female can drop a hundred or more babies at intervals of four or five weeks. The eyes of the unborn young are often visible as a 'gravid spot' near the anal fin of the mother. This is at its largest and darkest just before she gives birth. To save the young it is best to put the gravid female into a breeding trap, a device designed to allow the babies to fall through a small aperture into a nursery compartment.

The Guppy (*Poecilia reticulata*) is named after Dr. R. Guppy who first collected it in Trinidad in 1866. It is probably the world's most popular tropical fish, and it is not difficult to understand why. It has a remarkable ability to survive and reproduce in the most adverse conditions. The first tropical fishes I ever kept as a child were Guppies in an old accumulator jar with no heating but the coal fire and no live food. Nevertheless they lived and bred. They are plentiful and cheap and a good male is one of the most colourful creatures on earth.

In the wild, the female, which is silvery-green, grows to about $2\frac{1}{4}$ inches, the male, which has small splashes of several metallic colours, to about $1\frac{1}{4}$ inches. No two males are alike, and there are local variations in the domin-

Below: Red Wagtail Platies *Xiphophorus maculatus*
Right: Sailfin Molly *Poecilia latipinna*

ant colours. It is this wide palette and variability which makes the Guppy the perfect fish for experimental and selective breeding, and more has been achieved in the way of 'improving' on nature than with any other species. Some fanciers keep nothing but Guppies, and there are national associations striving to codify the latest developments and set appropriate show standards. There are now countless varieties, some classified by the shapes of their tails, some by their colours.

The possibilities of the male were so great that until very recently the female was completely neglected and remained a dull grey-brown without a hint of colour. Now she has been liberated from her drudgery as wife and mother and come into her own as an exhibition fish.

The Black Molly is one of the best known aquarium fishes. There is no such thing in the wild. All three species, which are found in brackish waters in the states bordering the Gulf of Mexico, are speckled. The Short-finned Molly (*Poecilia sphenops*), from which the Black Molly was developed by patient line-breeding, is a silvery-green with small black flecks. By selecting for more and more black, the Molly we all know – a sooty matt black all over – was produced.

Far more spectacular is the Black Sailfin Molly, which was produced by crossing a normal Black Molly with a Sailfin Molly (*Poecilia latipinna*) which is yellow with pale blue flecks. The

adult male possesses an enormous flag-like dorsal fin which runs almost the length of his body. It is held erect during the mating display. Another colour variety has recently been achieved, the Golden Sailfin Molly. Its intense orange body speckled with gold brings a blaze of colour to the tank and is a most welcome addition to the live-bearer range.

Most spectacular of all is the Giant Sailfin Molly (*Poecilia velifera*) whose dorsal fin is even larger than the Sailfins. But *P. velifera* is rather large for the aquarium, growing to six inches. Black specimens are very rare, the normal colour being dark orange flecked with pale blue. There is also an attractive smaller molly called the Lyretail which exists in both black and albino forms.

Mollies are extremely tolerant, but to do well they really need slightly salty water with a high pH, plenty of space, and plenty of green food, preferably algae. They will also take lettuce or spinach.

Mollies are easily damaged or shocked by netting and transportation. Moving gravid females will often result in the premature birth of babies which have not digested their yolk sacks or are too heavy to swim. Unlike other live-bearing toothed carps, mollies do not eat their own young.

For the serious breeding of mollies a pair should be given a large well-planted and well-lit tank to themselves and left alone.

The Red Swordtail (*Xiphophorus helleri*) is another famous fish which does not exist in the wild. In Mexico Swordtails are all a drab green. Selective breeding has lengthened the 'sword' (sported only by the male) and produced several handsome colour varieties, but, as always happens with line-breeding, the species has been reduced to about half the size of its wild ancestors, which grow to about five inches, excluding the 'sword'. The 'sword' is not a weapon, merely an extension of the tail.

Swordtails are very easy to keep and breed. When excited, as he usually is, the male shoots backwards and forwards near the female at amazing speed. He is the Casanova of the aquarium, frantically pursuing every female in sight, including those

of other species as well as his own. He is also a great leaper and the glass cover must not be left off with swordtails in the tank.

The first colour varieties were green (with a red line down the length of the body) and red. Both have yellow 'swords' edged with black. Then came the Red-eyed Red, which also has a red 'sword', and the Albino. Now there is the Red Wagtail, with a black tail and sword, the Tuxedo, which sports a black waistcoat as well, the All-black and the Golden. The finnage has also been developed to produce Hi-fins, Lyretails and Veiltails.

The Platy belongs to the same genus as the Swordtail, but is smaller, more chunky and, of course, lacks the 'sword'. The Variegated Platy (*Xiphophorus variatus*) has some colour (the male at least) in the wild, but the Common Platy (*X. maculatus*) from which most of the colour varieties have been developed is a dark bluegreen. Now we have Red, Black, Yellow, Blue and Spangled, and several more elaborate markings such as Sunsets and Bleeding Hearts. Hi-fin varieties have also recently appeared.

Platies are even more hardy than Swordtails and have really no drawbacks at all as a beginner's fish.

## FAMILY CYPRINIDAE
## Barbs, Danios, Rasboras and Minnows.

This is the largest family of fishes in the world, with about 1,500 species. Almost all have scales but none of the family possess teeth or an adipose fin. This family is found all over the world in tropical and temperate climates with the exception of South America and Australia. The smallest of this family is the *Rasbora maculata*, which is less than one inch, (2.5 cms) and the largest, the Mahseer of India which is over six feet in length. Most species have one or two pairs of barbels, sensitive whiskers which help them to locate worms and other delicacies among the gravel.

The Bitterling has a unique method of reproduction; it is the cuckoo of the fish world, utilizing the freshwater mussel as the keeper of its eggs. The female has a remarkably long ovipositor which she carefully inserts into the mussel and lays a few eggs, the male

Far left: Golden Sailfin Molly *Poecilia latipinna*
Left: Hi-fin Red Swordtail *Xiphophorus helleri*

Far left: Albino Tiger Barbs *Barbus* or
*Capoeta tetrazona*
Left: *Barbus bimaculatus*
Below: Checker Barb *Barbus* or *Capoeta oligolepis*

then releases his sperm which is drawn into the mussel during its process of filter feeding. The process is repeated, often for three days until the spawning is complete. The mussel then looks after the eggs and the fry until they become free-swimming.

Most of the other cyprinids are egg scatterers, and the eggs are non-adhesive. The easiest of the cyprinids to breed are the Zebra Danio and the Mountain Minnow. The technique of spawning is standard for the home aquarist. The sexes should be separated for several days and fed on a diet of live food to bring them into condition. The parent fish, in a ratio of two males to one female, are introduced at dusk to a clean aquarium filled to only two or three inches. The floor of the aquarium should be covered with clean pebbles or marbles or a raft of glass rods bound together so that the eggs can pass between them but the fish cannot. The following dawn will usually bring about spawning. The females dash around the aquarium with the males in hot pursuit. The eggs are scattered wildly and usually sink to safety, after being fertilized, between the marbles or rods. The parent fish

should be removed on completion of spawning, but many species would not harm the minute fry, which hatch in two days, were they left in the aquarium with their offspring. One female will usually lay two to three hundred eggs, so the breeding of this type of fish is a good commercial proposition. The fry are usually free-swimming within five to seven days, and should be fed sparingly on a liquid fry food.

Barbs are hardy, active, boisterous fishes, which like plenty of aeration and vegetation. They will live from two to eight years according to size. These fishes are found in rapid, shallow streams throughout tropical Asia and Africa, but not in the New World. They will eat anything and are tolerant of most water conditions, providing the water is clean. Barbs are naturally shoaling fishes and are seen to best advantage in the aquarium in small shoals which will always stick together. The classification of barbs is currently under review, the genus *Barbus* being split into three – *Barbodes*, *Capoeta* and *Puntius*.

The most popular barb has always been the Tiger Barb (*Barbus* or *Capoeta tetrazona*) from Sumatra, with its broad, black, vertical stripes on gold and its bright red fins. Its main failing is that toothless or not it has a terrible habit of nipping the fins of other fishes. To keep them with any fish which has long flowing fins is to court disaster. The Tiger Barbs are better kept in a shoal where they chase each other and leave the other fishes alone. The females are fuller in the body and the males have a tendency to develop a very red nose when they become excited. There is now also an Albino Tiger Barb. These look very attractive with their pale bodies and pink eyes, but it could be argued that the breeder was striving hard to breed the colour out of an already beautiful fish.

Another popular and hardy little fish is the Rosy Barb (*Barbus* or *Puntius conchonius*) from north-west India. This fish has the colour of beaten silver (with gleaming edges to the large scales), which turns to burnished copper in mating condition. Outside of the breeding season, when his rosy hue has faded, he is still identifiable by the dark tip to his dorsal fin. This is the easiest of the barbs to breed.

A barb which retains his bright colour irrespective of his mating inclinations is the Checker Barb (*Barbus* or *Capoeta oligolepis*) which is found in Sumatra. The scales along the body

Below: Zebra Danio *Brachydanio rerio*
Far right: Giant Danios *Danio malabaricus*

are alternately black and gold, hence the name, but the main feature is the large, black-bordered, orange dorsal fin, which grows darker in the male when mating. They are quite easy to breed in the standard way and the females lay a lot of eggs for their size. They seldom exceed a length of two inches but are very hardy and will survive amazingly low temperatures. Many other barbs are suitable for the beginner and for the community tank, particularly long-standing favourites being the Nigger and Cherry Barbs. A much rarer but very peaceful and attractive barb is *Barbus bimaculatus*.

The danios are a very popular group, presenting no problems to the beginner. The favourite is undoubtedly the small distinctive Zebra Danio (*Brachydanio rerio*) from Bengal, with its blue-black horizontal stripes on silver, always zipping about the tank and practising its quicksilver turns. Equally active and streamlined is the Pearl Danio with its mother-of-pearl shades of pink and mauve which change with the light. The largest of this group is the Giant Danio (*Danio malabaricus*) from the Malabar Coast. They grow to a length of five inches but are still quite peaceful with smaller species. The sexes are almost identical and during spawning they lay adhesive eggs in very large numbers. The parents usually make no attempt to eat the fry, but there is no point in tempting providence, and as the parents do not have a role in the upbringing of their young, they should be removed

Below: Silver Shark *Balanteocheilus melanopterus*
Bottom: Flying Fox *Epalzeorhynchus kallopterus*
Right: Cardinal Tetra *Cheirodon axelrodi*

from the nursery aquarium.

Very similar in shape and habits to the danios are the White Cloud Mountain Minnows (*Tanichthys albonubes*) from Canton, China, where they were first discovered by a Chinese boy-scout called Tan. Baby White Clouds have a neon-like blue light running down the almost transparent body. This fades as they grow, but the adult, which reaches only 1½ inches, remains colourful.

Again with the rasboras there is a clear favourite, the Harlequin (*Rasbora heteromorpha* and *hengeli*) which comes from the Malay Peninsula. The Harlequin has a deeper body than other rasboras. The body colour is a glowing reddish-gold with red fins, but the really distinctive feature is the long,

Silver Shark (*Balanteocheilus melanopterus*). Though obviously not a true shark its dorsal fin and general body shape give it that appearance. This species came from Thailand in the early sixties and proved an instant success. It has always been quite expensive but the fish has no bad habits. The Silver Shark is ideally suited for the very large community aquarium. It likes plenty of space. It will grow to a length of fifteen inches yet remains peaceful. Smaller and very dramatic is the Red-tailed Black Shark (*Labeo bicolor*). Another recently discovered fish in this family is the Flying Fox (*Epalzeorhynchus kallopterus*) which has many physical similarities to the pencil fish. This fish is found in Sumatra and is an excellent scavenger. It is also peace-

black triangle in the centre of the rear half. The *R. hengeli* is a smaller fish with a narrower triangle, but is not in my experience paler, as most books claim. Unfortunately it is extremely difficult to breed Harlequins in the aquarium. They are imported in very large numbers.

The most attractive of the other rasboras are the Red Line Rasbora (*R. pauciperforata*) which is like an elongated Glowlight Tetra, and the Redtail Rasbora (*R. steineri*), one of the few fishes to come from the temperate zone of China. All the rasboras prefer soft acid water.

Another member of the family is the

ful, even towards the smallest of fishes. It requires a large amount of green food, so spinach or lettuce must be given if algae are not present.

## FAMILY CHARACIDAE
### Tetras, Pencil Fishes and Piranhas

It is one of the largest families in the world — 1,300 species, and new ones are still being discovered. These fishes originate mainly from tropical America with a few from Africa. The major external difference from the cyprinids is that all the characins have an adipose fin and teeth. The great majority of characins are colourful, friendly fishes, undemanding in their diet and perfect for a community aquarium. There are of course exceptions such as the notorious Piranha and the plant eating *Metynnis*. Most of the tetras prefer soft acid water with plenty of cover and soft lighting. The heavy tropical rainfall of the Amazon basin, where many of them are found, continually freshens the streams and pools. Some aquarium water should therefore be replaced with rainwater at frequent intervals.

The breeding habits of this family are similar to most egg scatterers but the eggs are adhesive. They frequently spawn in shoals, but certain members have very interesting characteristics.

The Splash Tetra (*Copeina arnoldi*), although not the most beautiful of fishes has the fascinating breeding technique of leaping out of the water with its mate and depositing its eggs on a leaf above the water line. The parents then spend their time keeping the eggs moist by splashing them, using their well developed tail fins. Glow-light Tetras (*Hemigrammus gracilis* or *erythrozonus*), when mating, will swim alongside each other, lock fins and execute a 'barrel roll' that the most accomplished pilot would admire, scattering their eggs.

Probably the most popular of the characins is the Neon Tetra (*Paracheirodon* or *Hyphessobrycon innesi*) named after W.T. Innes, the author and aquarist, in 1936. This little fish was given international acclaim and is still to this day one of the fastest selling

Below: Lemon Tetras *Hyphessobrycon pulchripinnis*
Right: Congo Tetra *Micralestes interruptus*

Right: Glowlight Tetra *Hemigrammus gracilis* or *erythrozonus*
Below: Rosy Tetras *Hyphessobrycon rosaceus*
Bottom right: *Hyphessobrycon rubrostigma*

aquarium fishes. In spite of the popularity of this species and years of experience that aquarists have enjoyed, it is still very difficult to breed. The fish will readily accept dry foods, but sifted daphnia is a firm favourite. The Cardinal Tetra (*Cheirodon axelrodi*) was first introduced to the aquatic world in 1956 as a sort of 'Super' Neon Tetra. The deep red underparts run the full length of the body and the fish grows considerably longer. The life expectancy of the Cardinal is also greater than that of the Neon, but it is even more difficult to breed.

One tetra that is relatively easy to

spawn is the Lemon Tetra (*Hyphessobrycon pulchripinnis*). They love to spawn in shoals, but also love to eat their own eggs. It is, therefore, desirable to encourage the spawning to take place in an aquarium densely planted with feathery plants of the Cabomba and Ambulia type; these will provide maximum protection for the adhesive eggs. This is an attractive little fish with a translucent, yellowish body and red eye. The dorsal and anal fins are black, edged with lemon and the Latin name, *pulchripinnis*, means 'pretty fin'. They are quite hardy, very peaceful and grow to a length of $1\frac{1}{3}$ inches.

The Rosy Tetra (*Hyphessobrycon rosaceus*) is one of the larger fishes in this family, growing to a length of 2 inches or more. The fish sports a beautiful black flag of a dorsal fin edged in enamel white. The adult male develops a longer dorsal fin and the female has a red tip on the point of hers. A shoal of these fishes is a beautiful sight in any aquarium. They are relatively easy to keep but very difficult to spawn.

The Black Phantom Tetra (*Megalamphodus megalopterus*) is identical to the Rosy Tetra in shape, but smaller and altogether darker. It is also more difficult to breed, and is one of the less common tetras. A more colourful species is the Serpae Tetra (*Hyphessobrycon callistus* or *serpae*), a real jewel of a fish with a bright red anal and tail fin, black dorsal and deep orange body. They were first imported into Europe in 1931 and have grown in popularity ever since. Peaceful yet not afraid of larger species they are far easier to breed than *H. rosaceus*. The male is smaller and slimmer than the female but more brightly coloured.

The Rummy Nosed Tetra (*Hemigrammus rhodostomus*) is longer and slimmer than most tetras. His nose is a vivid red. This colour seems to vary in intensity with the mood of the fish. The species was first introduced into Europe in the early thirties. It is peaceful and highly recommended as a community fish, or, since it will tolerate very acid water and high temperature it is a good fish to keep with Discus. Probably the most attractive of the African species is the Congo Tetra or Congo Salmon (*Micralestes interruptus*) which has metallic rainbow colours and a tail with uneven and rather

ragged extensions of the middle rays.

After considering the other members of the family it is difficult to imagine that the dreaded Piranha (*Serrasalmo nattereri*) could be related to the Neon Tetra. The Piranha's ability to reduce a large animal to a skeleton within a few minutes is not exaggerated. Millions of us have seen it on television. The Piranha has powerful jaws and needle-sharp teeth and an appetite for fresh flesh (including fingers), which is frightening to witness. A rather morbid interest has given this fish a certain popularity as a 'pet', although it can claim a certain beauty with its beaten silver, upper half and rosy, lower body. It is the bulldog jaw that spoils the effect. The usual length of a fully grown specimen is twelve inches (30 cm) and its body is eight inches (20 cm) in depth. It cannot of course be kept with other species.

## FAMILY GASTEROPELECIDAE
### Hatchets or
### Freshwater Flying Fishes
These fish obtain their name from the shape of the body, this great depth of 'chest' accommodating the powerful muscles which enable the fish to fly several yards, skimming above the surface of the water. Unfortunately this is rarely observed by the aquarist. In their natural habitat they feed on small insects, either airborne or surface swimming; in the aquarium they seem to take readily to live daphnia. There are Marbled and Silver species both from the Amazon region. Their colour is not exciting but their shape makes them a very interesting novelty in an aquarium. They are, however, rather delicate and very short-lived, and they have rarely been bred.

## FAMILY ANABANTIDAE
### Labyrinths
Anabantids have the remarkable ability to 'breathe' in two ways. Not only do they possess conventional gills, they are also equipped with a 'labyrinth' (a cavity in the head), which enables them to absorb oxygen from the air. The labyrinth is a rather complex structure comprising a mass of capillary tubes which bring large surface areas of blood into close proximity with the air. The oxygen is absorbed directly into the blood-stream and waste gases are given off. When the oxygen is exhausted in the labyrinth, the fish surfaces and takes a gulp of fresh air, whilst simultaneously expelling the waste gases through the gills. This auxiliary breathing system enables the fish to be independent of oxygenated water, thereby enabling it to live in a very small volume of water. When male Siamese Fighters (*Betta splendens*) are shipped from Singapore, they are packed in small plastic sachets barely large enough to

Right: Blue Gourami *Trichogaster trichopterus*
Far right: Dwarf Gourami *Colisa lalia*

hold the fishes, with only sufficient water to keep them wet. Amazingly, they will live for days under such conditions. In the mid-sixties male Siamese Fighters in goblets were used as a table decoration in the dining room of a well known New York hotel.

Anabantids are often referred to as 'Bubble Nest Builders'. The male of the species mixes his saliva with air and blows hundreds of tiny bubbles in the form of a raft. This raft is usually anchored and in the case of some of the gouramis is interlaced with plant leaves and algae. The male then displays himself under his nest and awaits a female who is in breeding condition (if he has not been fortunate enough to procure one earlier). The male is often very impatient when a female reveals her willingness to mate. Should the female be rather slow in moving under the nest, he will probably attack her. Should both parties be agreeable, the mating embrace begins. The male wraps his body round the female and they enter a euphoric, trance-like state. As the male squeezes the female, hundreds of eggs fall from her and are instantly fertilized. In the case of gouramis the eggs float upwards into the bubble nest, but the eggs of the Siamese Fighter are heavier than water and sink after fertilization. The male Fighter recovers from the mating before his partner and quickly dives gathering the eggs in his mouth, then blows them into the nest. When spawning is completed, the nest must be constantly repaired and the eggs cared for. In the case of the Fighters this is a task purely for the male and the female is driven away. As the eggs hatch, about two days later, the movement of the fry often breaks the bubbles and the fry fall from the nest. It is the unceasing task of the father for many days to catch or pick up the youngsters and replace them in the nest. When they become free-swimming they follow the father round the aquarium in a dense little shoal and he gently shepherds them. Shortly, however, his paternal instinct may begin to lapse and, if not removed, he will start to eat them.

Gouramis are handsome fishes with a stately manner of swimming, often holding out before them their long pelvic feelers, which were presumably evolved to help them to navigate and identify objects or creatures in very muddy water. By far the handsomest is the Pearl Gourami (*Trichogaster leeri*). This fish originates from the Malay Peninsula and obtains its name from the pearl-like, lacy pattern that covers its body. The male develops a beautiful orange breast, which is very intense during mating. The length of the adult is approximately four inches. Both male and female will care for the young. This species has an unusual appetite for the Hydra, which is a small stinging member of the Coelenterate family and an enemy of most fishes. It is therefore a useful member of a community aquarium.

The Dwarf Gourami (*Colisa lalia*) is as the name suggests, one of the smallest fishes of the gourami family, with a maximum length of approximately 2½ inches. The male is a very colourful and beautiful fish, whilst the female is very drab. They originate from northern India and are accustomed to rather high temperatures, their optimum breeding temperature being 85°F. 29°C. This species is particularly fond of utilizing plants in the bubble nest and both parents will tend the eggs and fry.

The Blue or Three Spot Gourami (*Trichogaster trichopterus*) acquires its second name from the two spots on the body, the third being the eye. They are quite large fish, growing to a length of six inches and can become very aggressive when adult. The male is not very accomplished when it comes to building bubble nests, but this is of no great consequence as both the eggs and the fry float. Like the Pearl Gourami, this species has a taste for the Hydra and occasionally small fishes (including their own young). The males of the Three Spot are of similar coloration to the females, but can be identified by the longer and more pointed dorsal fin.

The Siamese Fighter (*Betta splendens*) was first bred in 1893. Since then it has been developed from a rather dull nondescript creature to a colourful, flamboyant and much sought after aquarium fish in a wide range of colours. The male fighter with his deep rich colours and full flowing fins is always at his best when displaying himself to a female or squaring up to an adversary. The female of the species is relatively insignificant; with dull colouring and small fins but she is quite peaceable and rarely lives up to her name. The male however, has only two reasons for living; fighting and

Left: Siamese Fighters *Betta splendens*

breeding. It is impossible to leave two males together in an aquarium without the certainty that their lovely fins will be tattered rays within minutes.

Most males are peaceful towards any other species, but become enraged by the presence of another male fighter or even by their own reflection in a mirror. In Malaysia large sums are

changes will be beneficial. Earthworms and maggots are good food.

The breeding pattern of this family is worthy of a special mention, and it is a pattern which is closely adhered to by almost every member. Cichlids do not like forced marriages and will sometimes kill the mate carefully chosen by the aquarist.

wagered on fights, staged much as cock-fights were once staged in England. They rarely grow beyond three inches and the rearing of them is a long process. The young take approximately six months to mature and at least eighteen months to reach full size.

## FAMILY CICHLIDAE
### Cichlids

Cichlids originate in Africa and South America. The family includes some of the largest species kept as aquarium fishes. They are carnivorous and often aggressive and only the dwarf species (which are in any case more beautiful) should be considered for a community tank. Young Angels are almost irresistible and will be good members of a community for many months, but eventually they will reach a size where they can no longer be kept with very small fishes such as Neons. Also many of the larger cichlids habitually pull up plants and make great holes and trenches in the ground. They really need a large tank to themselves with decor mainly in the form of rocks. Heavy filtration and frequent water

If several young fishes are kept together they will pair as they mature. The selection of a partner takes place with what appears to be a wrestling match or trial of strength. The male will lock mouths with a female and 'wrestle' with her for several minutes. Should either partner then retreat, that is usually the end of the romance. If however, the pair continue for several bouts they are likely to become permanent partners. The nesting site selected may be a leaf, a piece of stone, a cave or even a hollow in the gravel, but it is always meticulously cleaned. The cleaning process is carried out by both parents, mouthing and grazing on the site until all traces of algae or dirt have been removed. Often more than one site is prepared. The actual laying of the eggs is often preceded by a further bout of mouth-wrestling before the serious business is commenced. It is at this stage that the female lowers her ovipositor, and the male lowers his sperm tube, which is considerably thinner and more pointed. The female glides slowly over the nesting site, brushing it with her ovipositor and laying a line of adhesive eggs, then she is quickly followed by the male who fertilizes them. Several hundred eggs are laid in this fashion and when the female is emptied of eggs the routine of cleaning begins immediately. The 'mouthing', as the cleansing process is called, takes the form of the parents collecting a few eggs in their mouths, rolling them round, then spitting them back onto the nesting site. Any infertile or ones growing fungus are eaten. The oxygen supply to the eggs is maintained by the parents who create a constantly moving current of water over the nesting site by fanning the water with their pectoral fins. The fanning and mouthing process is maintained until the young become free-swimming. Frequently the parents will decide to 'move house' and take their young with them. This can pre-sent the problem of leaving some of the young unguarded. This is overcome by one of the parents taking a mouthful of young across to the new nesting site, whilst the other also collects a mouthful and stays on guard. As if by some pre-arranged signal, the parents then dash to the opposite site, passing midway, and prepare to perform the reverse process. When the young become free-swimming they will swim in a shoal around their parents who shepherd them about, protecting them from predators.

A typical cichlid in all respects is the Severum or Deacon (*Cichlasoma severum*). It will grow to a length of eight inches and is one of the really aggressive cichlids. This fish has the ability to change colour very rapidly, either to blend in with its background

Left: Siamese Fighter *Betta splendens*
Below: Ram *Apistogramma ramirezi*

or to express anger. The young of this species look remarkably like the Discus, but as the fish matures it loses its round appearance and the body becomes more elongated. The adult is easily recognizable by the vertical 'dumb-bell' marking in front of the tail. Two handsome smaller cichlids are the Jewel Cichlid (*Hemichromis bimaculatus*) from Africa and the Fire mouth (*Cichlasoma meeki*) from S. America, which grow to about 5 in. The former cannot be trusted in a community aquarium, but the Firemouth is usually well-behaved. He has a vivid orange-red throat with loose folds of skin which he blows out when angry.

The best known member of the family is undoubtedly the Angel (*Pterophyllum scalare*) – this common and most graceful fish has a very romantic scientific name – *Pterophyllum* means the winged leaf; and *scalare* refers to the dorsal fin and means, 'like a flight of stairs'. The species originates from the Amazon and Guyana and grows to a length of five inches. The body is extremely compressed, the dorsal and anal fins very long, and the ventral fins even longer so that they look like feelers, though they do not use them as such as the gouramis do. Consequently the Angel is taller than it is long. Its breeding habits follow the cichlid pattern, and the young, when hatched, grow very rapidly. A shoal of baby Angels at an age of five weeks (by which time they have developed to adult shape) following their parents is a wonderful sight. They can easily be frightened during spawning or whilst tending their young, and will eat their brood. Many new varieties have been produced in recent years, including Golden Angels, Half-blacks, Black Veiltails and Marbled Angels.

The dwarf cichlids, especially those of the genus *Apistogramma* are very beautiful and highly coloured and can safely be kept with other small species. But they are delicate fishes which often succumb to disease and which require soft, very clean, and slightly acid water. The apistogrammas are all natives of the Amazon Basin and South America and the largest never exceed three inches. Typical of the genus is Ramirez' Cichlid (*Apistogramma ramirezi*), commonly known as the Ram. This lovely little fish rarely exceeds two inches and has a vivid jewelled body. The male can be easily identified by the elongated rays at the front of his dorsal fin. A golden variety has been developed which is very beautiful, but it is debatable whether the original Ram can possibly be improved on.

The nearest rival to the Ram among the African dwarf cichlids is the Krib (*Pelmatochromis kribensis*) or (*Pelvicachromis pulcher*), which gets its name from the Kribi River in equatorial west Africa, where it was discovered. This placid fish sports a vivid pink waistcoat, and the smaller female often outshines her male counterpart. When in breeding condition the colours of this fish put it almost on an equal footing with its marine cousins. The Krib is a cave-dweller and prefers to lay its eggs on the roof of a cave-like structure, but once the eggs are

Left: Common and Golden Angels
*Pterophyllum scalare*
Below: Black Angel *Pterophyllum scalare*
Bottom: Golden Ram *Apistogramma ramirezi*

Right: Krib *Pelmatochromis kribensis*
Bottom right: Firemouth *Chichlosoma meeki*
Far right: Discus *Symphysodon aequifasciata* or *discus*

hatched, they seem to move house two or three times a day. The female spends most of her time looking after the young whilst the male finds and prepares new nesting sites.

The most exotic of all freshwater fishes is the Discus (*Symphysodon aequifasciata* or *discus*), so named because of its shape. This large, showy fish originates from the Amazon and was 'discovered' as an aquarium species in the early thirties. Though basically brown in coloration, the extremities of the fins are often tinged with red and orange and the body is lined with a filigree pattern of azure blue. When Discus are in breeding condition, the intensity of the coloration is considerably increased, the male being brighter. The minimum breeding size is approximately four inches, but adult fishes grow to more than double that size. Discus are fastidious in their feeding habits and seem to prefer a high percentage of live foods of the cyclops, daphnia and fly larvae type. Water for Discus must be extremely clear, soft and acid. It will tolerate an incredibly high temperature. In the wild Discus are frequently trapped in a dry spell in pools where the temperature may reach 110°F. (43°C.). When the rains come and a flush of fresh cool water sweeps into the pools, that is the signal to the Discus to begin spawning.

The newly hatched Discus fry obtain their first food from a mucus or slime which is secreted from the bodies of the parent fish. This 'milk' seems to give all the nourishment required by

the babies until they are fully free-swimming. Discus are prone to a rather odd disease which attacks only this species; it takes the form of deep abscesses about the head and usually proves fatal. Selective breeding has developed many colour strains within this species.

## FAMILIES CALLICHTHYIDAE, SCHILBEIDAE AND COBITIDAE
### Catfishes and Loaches

These are the cleaners and scavengers of the fish world. They are equipped with whiskers or barbels round their mouths with which they stir up the sand and gravel, and root out any food scraps which may be present. They are primitive fishes which have remained unchanged for millions of years. They are tolerant of worse water conditions than any other family.

The genus *Corydoras* are the smooth armoured catfishes that originate largely from South America. The corydoras usually have two rows of large horny scales running down the length of the body, hence the name 'armoured' catfish. They are relatively peaceful fishes, very hardy and long-lived, ideally suited to aquarium life, and they obtain almost all of their food from the sand or gravel. Most species of the genus have unusually large heads and eyes in relation to the size of their bodies. This gives them an air of innocence which is very endearing.

The corydoras have somewhat unusual breeding habits. After the female has laid her eggs and had them fertilized, she continues to clasp them in her ventral fins until she finds a suitable spot to deposit them. This is usually under a broad leaf which will provide shade for the eggs. On hatching, the young fry are totally self-sufficient and hide in any mulm which is available.

The Leopard Cat (*Corydoras julii*) is a typical example of the smooth armoured cats. It originates from the regions of the Amazon and grows to a length of 2½ inches (7 cm). It is basically silver with black spots like a leopard and a black flag dorsal fin similar to the Serpae Tetra. This species is very peaceable. They spend most of their time hunting for food. Other fishes rarely acknowledge their presence.

Several families are covered by the term catfishes. Some are very different indeed from the corydoras. Many would be considered ugly, or at least an acquired taste. The Pangasius Catfish (*Pangasius sutchi*) belongs to a small family, the Schilbeidae. Most of the species in this family are native to Africa, but Pangasius comes from Thailand.

It swims in a very shark-like manner and, unusually for a catfish, in the middle of the tank. It can be seen from the size of the eye that it is a nocturnal fish. Its food is mainly scavenged from the floor, but it will take any free-swimming insect life. This fish will grow to a length of twelve inches.

Loaches (Cobitidae) have a very wide distribution. They are closely related to the cyprinids but differ from them in never having jaw teeth and possessing three pairs of barbels. Some loaches are like whiskered worms, and only one species, the Clown Loach (*Botia macracantha*), from Sumatra and Borneo, can be described as beautiful. The Clown Loach has two sharp spines in his gill-plate which can be erected when he is handled, to cause his owner a painful jab. He is rather shy, but otherwise an excellent aquarium fish, peaceable and long-lived.

## FAMILY MONODACTYLIDAE
### Monos and Scats

There are many species of fishes living in the brackish water of estuaries which seem to have the ability to live either in seawater or freshwater. Some of these fishes are very attractive and are kept by both freshwater and marine aquarists. It would seem on balance that the marine aquarist has a greater chance of success with these fishes, as they often contract fin rot and fungus diseases when kept in soft freshwater with a low pH. However, a little aquarium salt added to the freshwater aquarium usually enables the brackish water fishes to feel 'at home'.

Scats (*Scatophagus argus*) are sometimes kept in freshwater aquariums, but they grow very large and are liable to eat the plants. They can be aggressive with smaller fishes at feeding time.

Monos are better fishes for the freshwater tank, especially the Malayan Angel (*Monodactylus argenteus*) from Africa and South East Asia. But even this hardy fish would probably be happier and healthier in brackish or even salt water. Malayan Angels have voracious appetites and quickly grow to a maximum of five inches (12 cm). The silver body reflects the light, and

in a healthy specimen the dorsal fin glows a rich orange. They look particularly effective in a shoal. Neither Monos nor Scats have been bred in captivity.

Top left: *Hemichromis bimaculatus*
Bottom left: Armoured Catfish *Callichthys callichthys*
Above: Clown Loach *Botia macracantha*
Below: Malayan Angel *Monodactylus argenteus*

## FAMILY CYPRINODONTIDAE
### Egg-laying Tooth Carps

The egg-laying tooth carps, or killi-fishes as they are more commonly called, belong to a family which contains some of thé most beautifully coloured freshwater fishes in the world. They are relatively small, rarely longer than 3 inches (8 cm), and therefore need close inspection to appreciate their beauty fully. Killifishes are found in every continent except Australasia, but the most spectacular species are from Africa. Species of the genus *Aphyosemion* live in pools, irrigation ditches, small streams, and almost any depression which regularly holds shallow water, in tropical West Africa. *A. australe* is one of the most commonly kept species, and also one of the most striking, its long slender green body speckled with blood-red and its large lyre tail edged with orange and white. *Nothobranchius* is another brilliantly coloured genus, the large scales picked out in vivid blue, and with bright red tails in most species.

There are over 500 species of killi-fishes, and no generalisations will cover them all. Bruce J. Turner and John W. Pafenyk in their little book '*Enjoy Your Killifishes*' give invaluable details of 95 species tabulated accòrd-ing to size, temperament, water re-quirements, tank stratum occupied, temperature and lighting require-ments, breeding habits, and suitability for the community aquarium.

Most killifishes can be kept in a community aquarium, contrary to common belief, provided there is plenty of shade, slightly acid water, and a temperature of about 72°F (22°C). The peaty dark water enjoyed by tetras and rasboras is particularly suitable. The aquarist would be well advised to use Black Water Tonic or a similar 'ageing' preparation for tap-water which is to be used for killifishes. Their large fins indicate that they are strong jumpers and any aquarium in which they are to be kept should have secure and close-fitting cover glasses. Killifishes are particularly suitable for the kind of 'total environment' tank or vivarium/aquarium now becoming popular in Europe, with shallow water, the upper part being landscaped with marginal and terrestrial plants, and occupied by amphibians, reptiles and butterflies.

The large mouths of killifishes in-dicate that they are predators. They enjoy live food, including small fishes. They will, however, usually accept frozen foods and occasionally freeze-dried foods. Their life-expectancy is very short in comparison with other families. This is a necessary part of the adaptation of the family to its habitat. In the hot summers of tropical Africa drought is commonplace, with the frequent drying up of the waters in which the killifishes live. The Lung Fish has adapted to these extreme conditions by evolving the ability to live without water. Killifishes have evolved a different method, harsher on individuals, but just as effective in perpetuating the species. The killi-

*Nothobranchius guentheri* male

fishes grow extremely quickly, reaching sexual maturity in as little as 12 weeks. Then they spawn and bury their eggs in the mud, where they remain, often quite dried out, throughout the dry season. As soon as the rains come, they hatch, and the cycle begins again. The parents rarely survive to a second season, though they will sometimes do so in captivity. Not all killifishes are substrate breeders. Some lay their eggs on but not under the mud; some species, which live where there is water all the year round, spawn in the roots of surface plants.

Killifishes are relatively easy to breed in captivity. A small, shallow aquarium is required, with a layer of boiled peat on the base of the tank, which will help to keep the water slightly acid. There should be no artificial lighting. The temperature for spawning should be rather higher than the fishes have been used to, about 76 to 80°F (25 to 27°C). If the male and female have been kept together, if is often helpful to separate them for a few days before putting them into the breeding tank. The sexes are very easily distinguished in killifishes, the male being larger and much more colourful. His colours become brighter still during mating. Immediately before and during the mating, the pair should be fed exclusively on live foods such as *Daphnia*, *Cyclops*, bloodworm and *Tubifex*. When the eggs have been laid, the parents should be removed. The eggs may then simply be left to hatch. The time taken to hatch is very

unpredictable and can be anything from 8 to 30 days. Since the eggs will have been laid over a period of several days, the hatching will be spread over the same period, and there is some danger of the earliest fry, which grow very fast, eating the latest. This can be avoided by the method of removing the peat containing the eggs, draining the water from it, and keeping it in a plastic bag in a warm place for several weeks. Returned to water, the eggs will hatch simultaneously within hours.

All members of the *Nothobranchius*, *Cynolebias* and *Pterolebias* genera, and some *Aphyosemion* species are substrate breeders. Most other species, including the popular panchaxes (*Aplocheilus* species), spawn in 'mops' suspended from the surface. These are easily made by winding nylon yarn round the hand to make a skein, then tying one end to a cork and cutting the other. The cut ends will then hang from the surface like the roots of a floating plant. Several females may be introduced to the breeding tank with one male. Over several days each will lay hundreds of eggs. A breeder who wishes to raise a high proportion of these must remove the eggs daily from the mops into separate small aquariums or plastic boxes containing similar water to the breeding tank. There the fry will be safe from the predations of their older brothers. The fry will quickly progress from infusoria to microworm and brine shrimp larvae, and within a week will be eating *Cyclops* and fine *Daphnia*.

*Aphyosemion gardneri* male

# Breeding Freshwater Tropicals

## Water

Perhaps the single most important factor in modern aquarium fish breeding has been the recognition of special water requirements, in particular hardness.

The scale of hardness is indicated in parts per million (ppm) of calcium carbonate ($CaCO_3$). From 0 to 50 ppm is considered soft, while 200 to 300 ppm is accepted as hard. Another scale uses milligrams per hundred thousand. A scale frequently used is that of German degrees of hardness (dH,) approximately 18 ppm = 1 dH, which, without recourse to decimals, makes a rather coarse scale. Reference to hardness throughout this section will be in parts per million. The hardness test kits generally available for aquarium work rely on the interaction of indicators giving a positive colour change.

One reads of 'ordinary tap water' being used in aquarium keeping, but there is of course no such thing. Water issuing from the domestic tap differs from town to town and sometimes even within a town. The chemistry of the water in one particular household can change as the water authority draws on different sources, so even if you intend to restrict your breeding interests to the species that will breed in your particular tap water some effort should be made to establish at least its hardness and pH. This information will then be of use to other aquarists, or even to yourself if you move from that particular source.

Many desirable species of freshwater tropical fishes remained unbred in captivity until their water requirements became known. This is particularly so of species which rely on soft water, such as the Discus (*Symphysodon discus*), Cardinal Tetra *(Cheirodon axelrodi)* and Chocolate Gourami *(Sphaerichthys osphromenoides)*.

For an aquarist living in a hard water area supplies of soft water can be difficult and expensive to obtain; distilled water, de-ionised water and rainwater are the most convenient sources. Collecting soft water from another area should also be considered if it is available within a reasonable distance. Domestic water softeners are of little use as the treated water has as much mineral in it as it had before treatment, the difference being that the calcium present is exchanged for sodium. Water softened by a de-ionising apparatus is most often used simply because of the availability of commercial outfits which are specially marketed for the aquarist; water obtained in this way must be well aerated before use, as a good deal of carbon dioxide is present, and a low (acid) pH will be evident until this gas has been dissipated.

Rainwater is a perfectly good source of soft water, but the earth's atmosphere is far from clean, and isolated showers are unlikely to produce suitably clean water. Heavy rain should fall for perhaps 20 minutes before collecting can safely begin. Filtering dirty rainwater is not a successful method, as although dirt solids are removed, dissolved impurities are virtually impossible to eliminate. Using distilled water is the most expensive way to obtain water of pure quality. Commercial producers tend to store it in lead containers and minute amounts of lead, which is poisonous, may dissolve. It is therefore safest to use water of medical quality.

Storage of very soft water must be carefully considered. Glass, polythene, PVC and stainless steel containers may safely be used for this purpose. Soft water not only has the ability to dissolve minerals, but will also absorb gases very readily, so adequate covers are required on storage containers.

When altering the character of soft water it is important that measurements of pH are accurately taken. There are many pH testing packs available and they are very easy to use, relying on colour indicators in a way similar to those in hardness test kits.

Soft acid water is frequently required. The best way to achieve a naturally acid reaction is to use sphagnum moss peat in a container–a large aquarium is most suitable–and add soft water. The amount (in bulk) of peat can be between 10 and 20 per cent of the volume of the receptacle: the more peat there is the quicker the acidifying process will be. Even so, the process will take about a month to produce clear, amber-tinted water; during this time the temperature should be kept at 72–77°F (22–25°C). Progress will be speeded up if floating lumps are squeezed under water until they become saturated. Some breeders use oak leaves to good effect to acidify water, but the use of sphagnum moss has the additional value of introducing beneficial trace elements and hormones. Some successes have also been reported using pure chemicals to achieve a given pH reading. Acid sodium phosphate and hydrochloric acid are two such chemicals; great care must be exercised and only very dilute quantities should be used. In case of accidental overdosage, such chemicals should never be added to an aquarium containing livestock. While fishes have the capability to adjust from one water type to another, they do not all have the same degree of adaptability. It is possible to kill specimens by subjecting them to too great a change.

## Choosing Suitable Tanks

### BREEDING TANKS

The size and shape of a breeding aquarium depends upon a number of factors: for example, the physical proportions of the fishes, the degree of activity during spawning, and the number of fry expected from the spawning. Aquarium size may also be affected because of a lack of space or perhaps a shortage of suitable water. An aquarist breeding soft-water fishes in a hard-water area will need to exercise economy, and smaller tanks do mean less water.

Typical examples would be the Zebra Fish *(Brachydanio rerio)*, which requires shallow water and a good run, suggesting an aquarium not less than 24 × 8 × 8 inches (60 × 20 × 20 cm) in size, half full of water. (In all sizes length and breadth are given first.) Angel Fish, *Pterophyllum*

Discus *Symphysodon discus* guarding its eggs laid on a vertical slab of slate

*scalare,* and other species do well in breeding tanks of 36 × 15 × 15 inches (90 × 40 × 40 cm), full of water. Opaline Gouramis (*Trichogaster trichopterus*) are not very large fishes and are not particularly active during spawning; however, the female needs plenty of room to escape the attention of the male during spawning breaks, and in addition a thousand fry could be expected, so that something in the order of 30 × 15 × 12 inches (75 × 40 × 30 cm) would meet the requirements both for spawning and for a few weeks afterwards, until the fry have grown to a size that makes overcrowding inevitable.

### NURSERY TANKS

The size of this aquarium will depend on the number of young fishes to be accommodated. Assuming a brood of one hundred, 24 × 15 × 12 inches (60 × 40 × 30 cm) would be suitable. This aquarium should have filtration of a fairly vigorous type, either sub-gravel or a large box filter containing gravel. Water condition at this stage can be allowed to be more arbitrary (up to 150 ppm) and just slightly acid (pH 6.5). One must be on the lookout for cannibalism all the time. Certain individual fishes will grow more quickly than others, and the larger will start consuming those that have been slower to develop; a second aquarium is required to accommodate the larger specimens.

## Factors Influencing Spawning

### TEMPERATURE

It is quite usual to arrange for the breeding tank to be a little warmer than the stock holding tank, and this will often induce spawning. With river fishes (that would normally experience fast-flowing well-aerated water) a sudden slight drop in temperature—accomplished by adding cold water—will frequently start off the spawning act; typical examples would be *Brachydanio* and *Danio*. The aspect of the breeding aquarium can have an effect on when a pair of fishes decides to breed. The early morning sun, indeed the sun's rays at any time of day, can have a triggering effect, as the temperature will probably rise at the same time.

### AERATION

Aeration can stimulate the spawning act with many species, especially those from fast-flowing rivers. Fishes building bubble nests, however, do not appreciate the surface disturbance as it makes the nest-building quite difficult.

### SEASON

An interesting phenomenon, and one which it is wise to observe, is the preference of some species for breeding at specific times of year. This applies particularly to wild-caught species, in which the breeding urge coincides with the rainy season, when the rivers swell and overflow, thus providing copious amounts of fresh food for both parent fish and fry. The so-called annual fishes, on the other hand, are urged by nature to spawn as the dry season approaches. As the last vestige of water is about to evaporate, eggs are laid that will withstand a protracted period of drought. Because fishes, like all creatures, are equipped with a biological clock, this impulse to breed at a time best

suited to conditions in their natural habitat does not wear off in the aquarium until several generations have been bred in captivity.

## Spawning Media

Although aquatic plants are the first natural choice when the spawning medium is being considered, there are good alternatives, some natural, some artificial. Though aquatic plants will be readily accepted by brood fishes, they are difficult to sterilize without damage and are rarely fit for repeated use. One of the most popular natural alternatives is coir or coconut fibre. This material can be teased out to form a good spawn-receiving clump, which is sterilized by being dropped in boiling water; it may be used for three or four occasions. Man-made fibres are being used successfully; the yarns available for knitting are of many different textures and plys, and experiment will prove the suitability of one mixture or texture over another. Colour does not appear to matter so long as the feel is right to the fish. Yarn-type media can be in the form of bunched strands approximately 4 to 5 inches (10 to 12 cm) long, either attached to a float of cork or polystyrene, or simply left as a bunch on the aquarium bottom. The choice of an artificial spawning medium is sometimes dictated by circumstances; for instance, certain characins have transparent hook appendages on the anal fins which are apt to catch in the fine filaments of man-made fibres, so an alternative has to be used.

When it comes to fishes that place their eggs on hard, firm surfaces (substrate spawners), quite a few domestic materials can be used effectively, and have the advantage of being easy to sterilize. Inverted flower-pots, both ceramic and plastic, make good spawning sites for the larger cichlids, while smaller cichlids find the same object more acceptable lying on its side, so they can use the interior. Lengths of PVC drainpipe, 3 inches (75 mm) in diameter or more can be usefully employed for similar species. Plastic aquarium plants are useful as they can be cleaned in hot water, and they tend to give a more natural look to an otherwise barren breeding tank. Certain bubble-nesting fishes would favour a lily pad to spawn under; as an alternative the lid from a polythene tub has been used successfully.

## First Live Foods for Fry

Success in fish breeding comes more easily with careful planning. One important aspect of this is arranging to have a good supply of the right kind of food ready when it is required. First food will be needed as soon as the fish's yolk sac (nature's rations for the first two or three days) has been absorbed.

Microscopic live foods—usually called infusoria—take time to culture. Between three and ten days should be allowed, depending on temperature. Two to three days after reaching an optimum infusion the organisms will be too large, or a larger order of infusorian will have taken over. All too frequently young fishes die with a surfeit of food all around them—food that is too large to swallow.

Of the various infusoria probably the most useful is one called *Euglena viridis*. This is correctly termed a flagellate—a creature of difficult animal/vegetable dis-

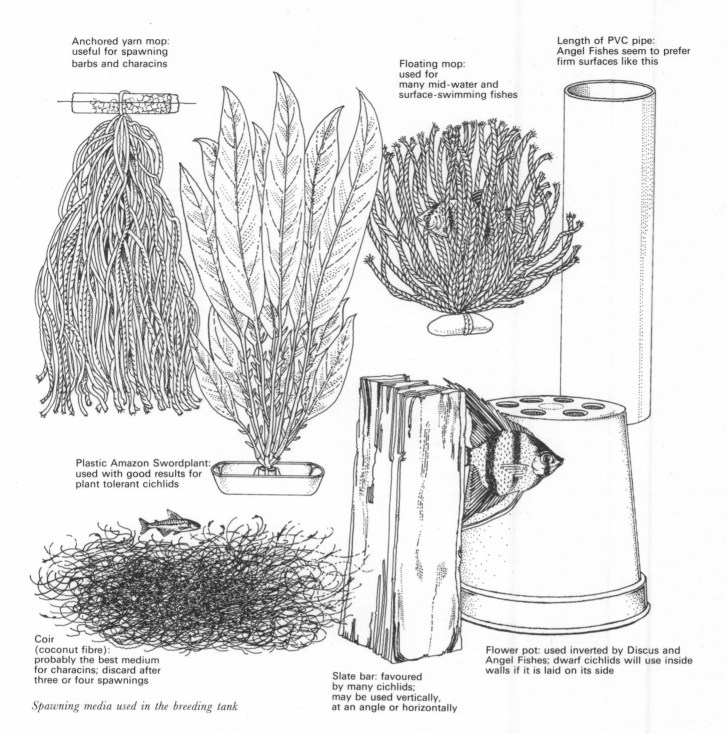

Anchored yarn mop: useful for spawning barbs and characins

Floating mop: used for many mid-water and surface-swimming fishes

Length of PVC pipe: Angel Fishes seem to prefer firm surfaces like this

Plastic Amazon Swordplant: used with good results for plant tolerant cichlids

Coir (coconut fibre): probably the best medium for characins; discard after three or four spawnings

Slate bar: favoured by many cichlids; may be used vertically, at an angle or horizontally

Flower pot: used inverted by Discus and Angel Fishes; dwarf cichlids will use inside walls if it is laid on its side

*Spawning media used in the breeding tank*

tinction but of proved worth as a first food for the smallest fry. Seed cultures are bought in a pure state and need careful attention to propagate successfully. Care needs to be exercised to avoid contamination by higher order organisms, ever present in airborne form, so the cultures have to be kept covered. The culture medium is usually of a wheat germ infusion. Cultures have the advantage of a good life in optimum conditions, but will rapidly deteriorate at temperatures over 75°F (24°C); 68°F (20°C) should produce the best results. Other infusoria are less critical in propagation, but quicker to reach saturation point. An open-topped vessel is filled two-thirds full with tap water and one thin slice of raw potato per gallon added. In the course of the next seven to ten days this will produce small infusoria which make a good follow-on food after *Euglena*. Other larger infusoria will soon invade the culture, and these in turn will serve as another intermediate stage of food. Crushed lettuce leaves added to this culture medium encourages a build-up of the larger organisms.

A low-powered microscope is invaluable when checking cultures, which should always be done immediately before they are fed to the fry. The concentration of the culture will vary enormously from day to day and it is most important that live infusoria are fed and not just dirty water; surprisingly the difference is almost impossible to see with the naked eye. Remember that to ensure a continuous supply of the right size of food, new cultures must frequently be set up.

It is difficult to advise on the amount and frequency of feeding; the question can only be satisfactorily resolved by trial and error, remembering always that too little food will lead to starving fry but too much will quickly lead to a polluted nursery tank. Close observation at this time with both hand lens and microscope may reveal a situation that would otherwise escape notice. Observe the stomach of the fry – they should always be obviously full. If they are not, either the food is unsuitable (perhaps too large) or it is suitable but the fry are sick. Commercial breeders feed four or five times a day, and as in their natural habitat fishes are able to feed all day long this frequency is not excessive. Pipettes or small syringes are suitable devices for feeding minute live food to the fry.

During the first few days the nursery tank can be equipped with a simple internal filter (the type which uses a sponge is very suitable) and the diffuser switched off. In addition to active filtration, it is beneficial to make partial water changes, of one-third of the aquarium capacity, twice a week.

The young fishes should be able to take newly-hatched brine shrimp when they have grown to just under half an inch long (about 10 mm). Since they were discovered, brine shrimp larvae–the newly-hatched *Artemia salina*–have been a boon to the breeder, whether commercial or amateur. At the moment of hatching, which takes about thirty-six hours at 77°F (25°C) the shrimp is soft and very tiny and is suitable as a first food for many newly-hatched fishes. But be warned: the growth of the brine shrimp is rapid, and the second-day growth may be too large for the same batch of fry–another batch of brine shrimp eggs should have been arranged to hatch so that newly-hatched shrimp is available every day. Natural sea water, or sea water made of proprietary salt mixes, should be used as the medium for hatching brine shrimp eggs. Always aerate the hatching container vigorously. It is important that brine shrimp bodies (they die in less than an hour in fresh water) are removed, as they will very quickly pollute the small volume of water in the breeding tank. A siphon of 3 mm air-tubing is useful for this purpose. Another larva, that of the crustacean *Cyclops* is available at certain times of year. These have to be caught with very fine nets from freshwater ponds. In size and shape they resemble the brine shrimp, but have the advantage of living longer in the warm fresh water of the nursery aquarium though there is always the danger of introducing parasites or diseases with them.

# Breeding Livebearing Fishes

Members of the family Poeciliidae, the livebearing tooth carps are largely responsible for making the hobby as popular as it is. The fact that the more common livebearers–swordtails, mollies, platies and Guppies–can be bred in limited quantities in the community aquarium has done much to encourage the novice towards greater breeding achievements. Generally, livebearers prefer hard water, but all except mollies will thrive in soft water. Strains that have been bred and raised in soft water areas should if possible be chosen by breeders whose own water is soft.

Sexing of all livebearers is made easy by the fact that the male has the modified anal fin, forming the gonopodium, which it uses as an intromittent organ. However, some fishes, particularly platies, hold this fin close to the body and it is not always clearly defined. Another peculiarity, which is shown particularly among Lyretail Black Mollies, platies and in Simpson Swordtails, probably because of the use of hormones by commercial breeders, is the apparent formation of a gonopodium in a female. In these cases it is best to consider behaviour rather than physical characteristics.

On reaching maturity, females form eggs inside them which the male fertilizes using the gonopodium. One such fertilization can persist for several broods–a fact that makes line breeding an exacting task.

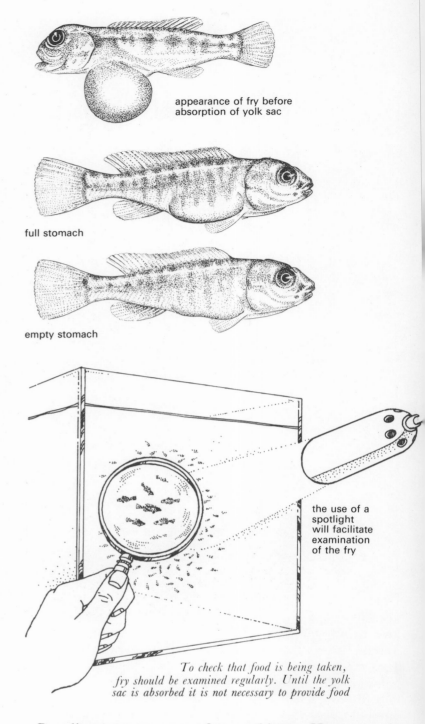

appearance of fry before absorption of yolk sac

full stomach

empty stomach

the use of a spotlight will facilitate examination of the fry

*To check that food is being taken, fry should be examined regularly. Until the yolk sac is absorbed it is not necessary to provide food*

Breeding presents very few problems. However, the gestation period (usually three to five weeks) cannot be predicted exactly because temperature affects the cycle and also the female can delay the birth if conditions are unsuitable. The number of fry in each brood increases as the female grows in size.

All livebearing fishes have a cannibalistic tendency, which varies not only with the genus but also between individuals. To ensure the safety of the offspring some form of trap is therefore necessary. A net trap, consists of a box framework covered on four sides and the base with a 2 mm mesh fabric. The size of the trap will depend on the species–for Guppies the minimum requirements are 12 × 8 × 8 inches (30 × 20 × 20 cm), for platies 14 × 9 × 9 inches (35 × 22 × 22 cm), and for Swordtails 18 × 10 × 10 inches (45 × 25 × 25 cm). These traps should be used in conjunction with breeding tanks having twice the cubic capacity of the trap. The female should be removed from the holding tank when the swelling of the abdomen indicates an advanced stage of egg development, and

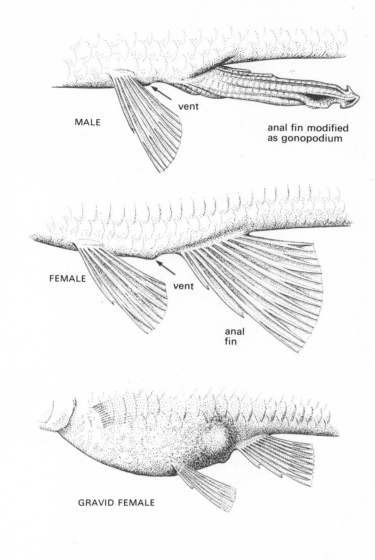

MALE

vent

anal fin modified
as gonopodium

FEMALE

vent

anal
fin

GRAVID FEMALE

*In livebearers the form of the anal fin is different in the two
sexes. When the female is close to producing the young her abdomen
becomes swollen and darkens in the region near the vent*

transferred carefully into the trap. The temperature in the
two tanks should be the same. Clumps of refuge plants
should be provided outside the trap; this will encourage the
fry to swim out of the trap and stay out of harm's way. The
temperature should be increased by 3.5°F (2°C) and a small
box filter installed in the nursery. Swordtails and platies are
jumpers, and can easily jump out of the confines of their
trap unless a restrictive cover is fitted.

Mollies, possibly because they are almost wholly
vegetation eaters, rarely eat their young, however, and
with them the best yields are obtained in large aquariums
of 13 to 17½ gallons (60 to 80 litres), containing hard
water with a light salt content. Males are best kept out of
the way once the female has been fertilized. As with all
young fishes, first foods should be given at frequent
intervals. Contrary to general opinion, livebearers do
benefit greatly from the feeding of brine shrimp larvae
during their first week.

The four types of livebearer considered so far are all
popular and widely available. Good colourful strains have
been established and finnage has been developed to a
high degree, but, because of the ease with which they
breed, much good work can be undone by allowing
different strains to interbreed. So, if you must keep red,
yellow, blue and black platies together either make sure
they are all of the same sex or accept the fact that you will
surely have some non-conforming types when the young

arrive. Guppies, in particular, reach sexual maturity
very early, and males are capable of fertilizing a female
almost before its sex can be distinguished, so aquarists
keen on perpetuating a certain strain have to be particularly vigilant and segregate the sexes as soon as it is
possible to do so. Other livebearers occasionally available
but not as attractive commercially are the Mosquito Fish
(*Heterandria formosa*), the Merry Widow (*Phallicthys
amates*) and various *Limia* species. These species seem to
respond to thickly planted nursery aquariums rather than
traps, but the rule should always be to remove males once
they have done their job and leave the females in peace.
Several females may share a nursery, the larger fry being
removed periodically and transferred to growing-on
aquariums.

# Breeding Egg-laying Fishes

Probably the greatest challenge to the fish breeder is
presented by the smaller characins—tetras, as they are
popularly known. Almost without exception characins
breed more easily in soft to moderately soft water; that is,
water of hardness under 100 ppm. It is possible to breed
quite a number in hard water, but in soft water they
respond better and the yields are always higher.

The eggs of these tiny fishes are, not surprisingly,
extremely small; they are usually almost transparent too,
which makes detection even more difficult, at least until
one has learnt to recognize them. Many spawnings have
been thrown away through ignorance. A torch and low-
powered hand lens used in the same plane—that is viewed
as close to the bottom of the tank as possible—during the
hours of darkness, is one way of ascertaining the presence
of eggs or young fishes. If the spawning tank is small and
the bottom clear, lifting the tank aloft and gazing from
below (assuming that there is good lighting above) will
make egg spotting easier. However, this method does tend
to scare the brood fish.

### AN EXAMPLE OF TYPICAL PROCEDURE
The following account would apply to the popular Neon
Tetra (*Paracheirodon innesi*).

**Water source** Use clean rainwater or de-ionised water
that has had sphagnum moss peat soaking in it for a
month, the layer of peat to be one-fifth of the water depth.
De-ionised water should always be well aerated before
use and the receptacle covered with a glass lid.

**Brood fishes** These should have been kept, sexes apart, at
about 72°F (22°C) and fed on a diet including some live
food.

**Breeding tank** The tank dimensions should be 18 × 10 ×
10 inches (45 × 25 × 25 cm) or 18 × 12 × 12 inches
(45 × 30 × 30 cm), half-filled with water, prepared as
above; the water should be clear and filtered preferably
through polymer wool. A trap of 2 mm mesh net, made
from nylon, PVC or some other inert man-made fibre,
should be inserted so that the base is approximately half
an inch (12 mm) above the glass bottom of the tank. The
other dimensions of the trap should be just slightly less
than the inside dimensions of the tank.

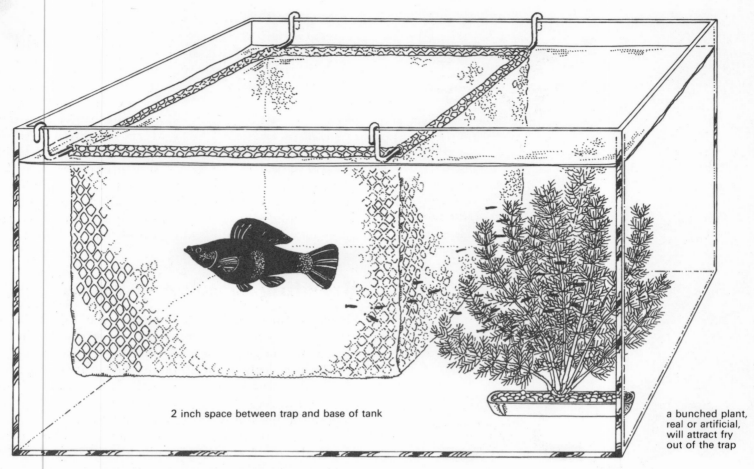

2 inch space between trap and base of tank

a bunched plant, real or artificial, will attract fry out of the trap

*A suggested set-up for breeding livebearers. It is advisable to cover the tank with a sheet of glass to prevent the female jumping out.*

**Spawning medium** Some commercial breeders favour coir (coconut fibre) for this purpose. A small amount is teased out and boiling water poured over it; it is then washed in de-ionised water, clean rainwater, or soft tap water and placed in the net trap.

**Temperature** The temperature should settle at around 73.5°F (23°C); gentle aeration using a suitable stone diffuser, which may be under the net trap or within it, should also be provided.

**Breeding procedure** Select a male and female: the female should not be too plump, and both fishes should be young adults (around 6 to 9 months old). Place them within the net trap in the breeding tank. It is best to choose a time to do this which coincides with a period when you will be able to give maximum surveillance – perhaps a Friday evening would be the most convenient. Introducing the pair at nightfall is considered desirable because they will become accustomed to the new surroundings gradually by dawn light, instead of being subjected to strange surroundings in the brightness of day, when they would spend most of the day in a very nervous state. With luck your chosen pair will spawn on the Saturday, but generally the real activity starts on the second day, the first day being taken up with typical tetra courting behaviour – male displaying to female, female chasing male away, male leading paths through the spawning medium, and finally driving the female through the medium. Several practice runs are made before eggs are actually released.

The act of spawning is accomplished with the male and female quivering side by side over or within the spawning medium. Eggs are ejected in short bursts of about twelve, the actual moment of release being triggered by a sudden sideways push from the male. The eggs are supposed to be semi-adhesive, but the majority fall through the mesh to the glass bottom of the tank; without the trap many of these eggs would be eaten. The period of spawning cannot be stated accurately, as much depends on both the number of eggs the female has formed, and on the virility of the male. Several pauses in the spawning act occur and these can quite easily be mistaken for the end of the spawning. The completion of the spawning is indicated when the brood fishes lose interest in each other; they should then be removed with a sterile net and returned to their individual quarters.

Hatching takes place 18 to 24 hours later, and the newly hatched alevin can be seen making short hops from the bottom of the aquarium. It is not unusual to find fungused or white infertile eggs at this stage, and in a quantity which may tempt the amateur fish breeder to abort the exercise, but it pays to be patient; what often appears to be a whole batch of infertile eggs is in fact only a proportion. It is a question of the bad eggs being very obvious, and the good fertile ones being almost invisible.

In presenting breeding details of the popular families, the general breeding pattern is explained and any species varying radically from the norm is dealt with separately.

## FAMILY CHARACIDAE

Characins are among the easiest species both to keep and to breed, available to the aquarist. There are also some

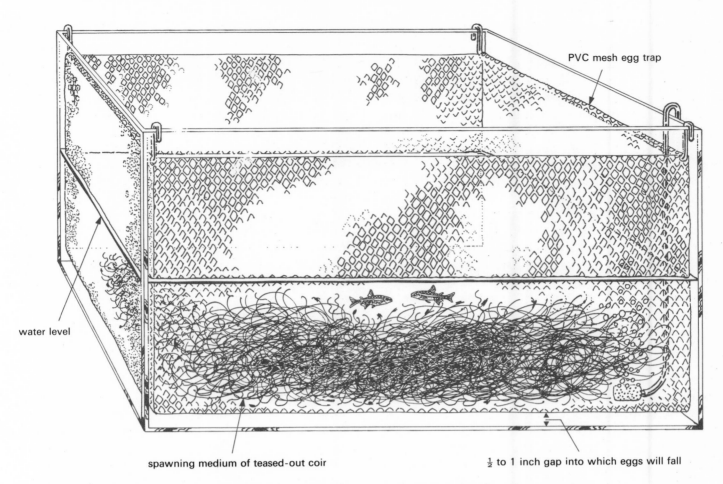

PVC mesh egg trap

water level

spawning medium of teased-out coir

½ to 1 inch gap into which eggs will fall

*A suitable arrangement for spawning characins. Some species are said to have light-sensitive eggs and so the tank should be shaded from direct light when the parents have been removed after spawning*

very desirable species which demand particular environments and are not easy to breed. The majority of characins breed in much the same manner as the Neon Tetra discussed above, so it can be said to behave typically of the family; other species however, may not require the same precise attention to water condition and temperature.

One of the less frequently available, but nevertheless much sought after characins is the Emperor Tetra, *(Nematobrycon palmeri)*. Although the majority of breeders use one pair in their breeding tanks, polygamous breeding is probably more successful. The Emperor Tetra is not easy to sex when immature. In mature specimens the male has the greater extended spike to the caudal fin, and it is also larger, age for age, than the female.

For a breeding attempt use an aquarium $36 \times 15 \times 12$ inches $(90 \times 40 \times 30$ cm) with soft $(40$ ppm) water acidified to pH 6, no gravel present, gentle aeration, sterilized coir making quite dense spawning areas over much of the aquarium, and temperature fluctuating between 77 and 81°F, $(25$ and $27°C)$. The fishes are put in the breeding tank in the ratio of one male to three females, three such quartets being used together. They are left for seven days and then removed to another, similarly equipped tank. At this stage the eggs are seldom seen, but this does not matter because the process assumes spawning to have taken place. Seven days later feeding commences. Fry are very inactive, so the observation of two or three is no indication of the number present, which could quite easily be 150 to 200. Parent fishes seem to spawn over an extended period which, together with the fact that several females may have spawned, will result in a multitude of differently sized young, all requiring different

sizes of food. Small infusoria, larger infusoria and newly-hatched brine shrimp will therefore have to be fed at the same time.

Ten days after the adults have been removed most of the spawning medium can also be taken away, and not until then will the aquarist know the true extent of the spawning. A small amount of coir can be left strewn about the bottom of the aquarium to serve as cover for the younger fish. In employing this continuous 'conveyor' method of breeding, the adult fishes are fed in the usual way while in the breeding aquarium.

With the Characidae one can breed with fishes two-thirds grown, and sometimes smaller. Mistakes have been made in the past, when it has been said to be vital that the adults are fully grown before breeding can be attempted. When particular pairs of 'difficult' characins are found to spawn well and produce good quantities of young, it is recommended that the pairs are kept identified, if necessary by keeping a single specimen in a tank. This is particularly important in the case of Cardinal Tetra and Congo Tetra, where the percentage of fertile males seems to be low.

## FAMILY CYPRINIDAE

Within the family Cyprinidae we find some very popular genera, *Barbus* (also known as *Puntius* and *Barboides*) having established themselves under the common reference 'barbs'. Of generally larger size, they require larger breeding tanks and as the brood is usually 500 or more, growing-on tanks need to be of 13 to 17½ gallons (80 to 100 litres) capacity; a good spawning of an average-sized species will need several of these.

**Barbs** Assuming that one of the popular barbs is to be bred, such as the Rosy Barb, Ruby Barb or Tiger Barb, the size of breeding tanks should be 24 × 15 × 15 inches (60 × 40 × 40 cm) – larger if possible. Water should not be hard – 100 to 150 ppm would be about right; pH would be best at about 6.5. As barbs lay adhesive eggs net traps do not work so effectively – the eggs adhere to the mesh and are picked off by the parents. Some rather dense spawning medium is therefore required, which can be natural plants like bunched *Cabomba*, *Myriophyllum* or *Limnophila*, plastic plants of similar leaf shape, nylon yarn mops weighted to the bottom, a few handfuls of coir – in fact, anything that needs a little effort to drive through. Water depth need not be greater than 10 inches (25 cm) and the water temperature set at 79°F (26°C); mild aeration should also be provided. The majority of the barbs are relatively easy to sex, especially when in breeding condition. The males are the more brightly coloured, and female barbs in roe show a very distended outline.

A brood pair should have been conditioned in separate aquariums and fed on a good fresh diet including chopped garden worms, live *Daphnia* and fly larvae where obtainable. As with characins, the pair should be brought together on an evening preceding a day when the breeder is free to observe the spawning – or at least the preliminaries. The morning after the introduction should bring some preliminary movement, especially if it is bright and sunny. The male begins the courtship with a display in which all fins are spread and the colours deepened. This showing off is accompanied by nudging by the male, who then 'pushes a path' through the spawning medium, as if to show the female what is required of her. The courtship may develop the same day or it may take until the second or third day to get going in earnest, when the male will pursue his mate very vigorously all over the aquarium, diving through the spawning medium, where momentarily they cease chasing to come in close contact, flank to flank, while eggs and milt are discharged from the trembling pair. The chase continues until, exhausted and empty of roe, the pair rest on the bottom. As soon as they are rested they go hunting for the precious eggs and undo all their good work unless the aquarist removes them. There will be no difficulty in identifying the eggs. Many will be seen adhering to the spawning medium, and as many more again will be found on the bottom. They take about a day and a half to hatch but the transition from eggs to alevin does not at this stage indicate mobility. The newly-hatched fry will hang suspended tail down, either attached to the side of the aquarium or on the medium on which they were spawned. A further 24 hours will see the fry in a horizontal position, swimming in a very jerky fashion close to the bottom and keeping concealed using whatever cover is at hand. At this stage the numbers will appear to have dropped drastically; this is only because of their hiding instincts and within the course of a further day most of the fry will be massed immediately below the water surface. They will be looking for food, which the aquarist must now provide. Newly hatched brine shrimp and proprietary fry foods can be given at this time. The spawning medium should be carefully removed and an internal box filter fitted. Water condition is critical for barbs and even slight pollution will result in multiple deaths; as well as good observation it pays to have a keen sense of smell, trained to detect aquarium water that is not quite right. Barbs generally become unbalanced and even distressed when fed certain dry foods, but pre-soaking will help to overcome this problem. Live foods and fresh foods do not seem to have the same effect.

**'Sharks'** Within the same family Cyprinidae are the popular aquarium sharks: the Silver Shark (*Balanteocheilus melanopterus*), the Red-tailed Black Shark, (*Labeo bicolor*), the Red-finned Shark, (*Labeo erythrurus*), and that popular bottom working fish, *Epalzeorhynchus kallopterus*. Regrettably, apart from a report of spawning following surgical interference with the male pituitary glands, these fishes have not been bred by amateur aquarists. Size could be a limiting factor, for they all grow large, larger than some authorities would have us believe; diet could also have some effect, as not all natural foods can be substituted satisfactorily. However, as long as a fish remains unbred in captivity, the challenge to breed it remains to urge the keen aquarist on.

The huge family of Cyprinidae includes some of the smaller, more popular community fishes such as species of *Rasbora*, *Brachydanio* and *Tanichthys*. Within these genera are several beginner's fishes, ideal in the fact that they are easy to breed – fishes like the Zebra Fish (*B. rerio*) and the White Cloud Mountain Minnow (*T. albonubes*).

**Zebra Fish** Taking the Zebra Fish as being fairly typical of the *Brachydanio* species, breeding may be accomplished in the following manner. Take a small shoal of six to eight fishes, separate males from females, place them in separate tanks and feed them well for ten to fourteen days. Sexing is no problem, as the female swells considerably with roe and the body lines become distinctly bent, whilst the slimmer male has almost straight lines. Prepare an aquarium for spawning. This should be long, shallow and narrow; 30 × 8 × 8 inches (75 × 20 × 20 cm) would be fine. Fill with water to 4 inches (10 cm) deep. The water hardness can be literally anything up to 300 ppm and at neutrality – pH 7. Layer the bottom with pebbles about 0.5 to 1 inch (12 to 25 cm) in size, adjust the heating to about 84°F (29°C) and introduce quite active aeration with a diffuser-stone. The shoal can then be introduced to its new quarters; an ideal ratio would be three males to two females. Zebra Fishes are egg scatterers and also avid egg eaters, the gaps between the pebbles are to trap eggs and hide them from the brood fishes.

In a long narrow aquarium Zebra Fishes will be seen to traverse the swim room without turning until they reach the end. The advantage in having a long aquarium is that the eggs laid at one pass will not be eaten on the return, as they will have had time to sink to the bottom, to the safety of the pebbles. Spawning occurs on the run, and the males present will give prior attention to any females that are ready to spawn at that moment. It is quite safe to leave the breeders in the breeding tank for three days, after which time all parent fishes should be removed back to their usual quarters. A particular spawning can take to four to six days to hatch and become free-swimming; allowing for spawning over three days, all eggs should have become free-swimming young by the tenth day. The fry are small and require microscopic live food which may be supplemented by proprietary dry or liquid food.

Another novel way of collecting the eggs is to place a receptacle – a cereal bowl or soup bowl will do – just below the water surface so that the parent fish can just swim over the rim. The bowl is filled with fine-leaved plants, and parent fishes will drive over the spawning medium and deposit their eggs – they do not return to eat them with this arrangement.

The advantage of this method is that a conventional breeding aquarium can be used, for example one measuring 24 × 12 × 12 inches (60 × 30 × 30 cm) and the eggs can be removed at will to be hatched in another aquarium. As these fishes produce non-adhesive eggs, the use of a net trap will also produce good results as long as at least 24 inches (60 cm) of swim room is provided within the trap.

**White Cloud Mountain Minnow** This species has a wide temperature tolerance of 50 to 86°F (10 to 30°C), a fact of which advantage may be taken in breeding them. For this species a permanent breeding tank can be set up, with a gravel bottom and plenty of fine-leaved and floating plants. Care should be exercised to exclude snails and snail eggs which could later devour fish eggs. In this breeding aquarium, which can be anything from $5\frac{1}{2}$ gallons (25 litres) capacity upwards, a small shoal is introduced, preferably with an equal number of each sex. In a fairly warm house the aquarium used need not be separately heated but just allowed to fluctuate with the ambient temperature. When the time comes to breed from the fishes a heater is introduced to bring the temperature up to 75 to 77°F (24 to 25°C) when they will begin to spawn amongst the plants. After four to five days the fry will be seen swimming at the surface amongst the floating plants, when they can be removed with a large spoon and transferred to raising quarters.

Parent fishes are not difficult to sex when of equal age, as the male is always smaller, more slender and more highly coloured in both body and fins. In the permanent breeding tank described, the adult fishes are fed in the normal way on proprietary foods, and even the fry can be reared on suitable proprietary foods.

**Rasboras** Finally from the family Cyprinidae, we consider the beautiful species in the genus *Rasbora*. These are all lovers of warm, clear, soft water with an acid tendency. They are intolerant of polluted water conditions. The majority of rasboras are egg scatterers, producing semi-adhesive eggs that are strewn about in fine-leaved plant clumps. The procedure for breeding follows very closely that of the characins; the main difference is in the size, as popular aquarium rasboras are generally larger than the popular characins, and breeding aquariums consequently have to be larger. Distinguishing the sexes is difficult, although in adult fishes ready to spawn the female is appreciably deeper, and when viewed from above will be seen to be broader. In all specimens the adult males are marginally shorter.

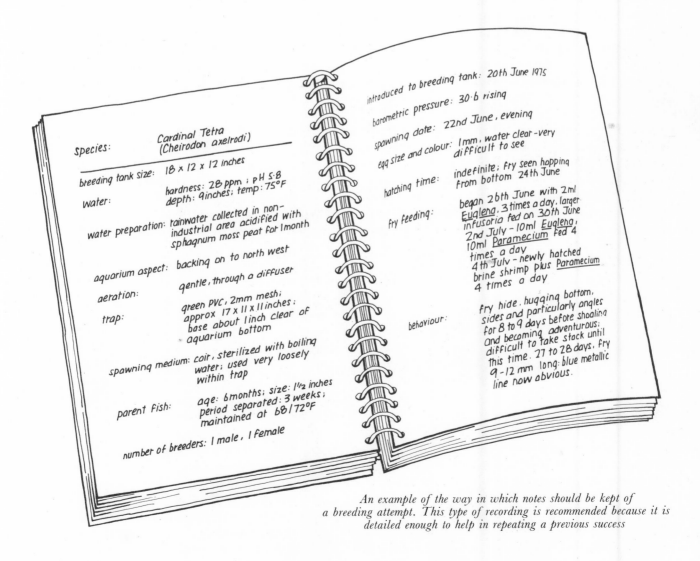

*An example of the way in which notes should be kept of a breeding attempt. This type of recording is recommended because it is detailed enough to help in repeating a previous success*

The Harlequin Fish, *R. heteramorpha*, is not only the most popular species, but is also a non-conformist, as its reproductive behaviour varies from the norm. It is an egg placer, and produces adhesive eggs which it prefers to attach to the underside of wide, firm-leaved plants. Harlequin Fish are not easily sexed, neither are they easy to encourage to breed. For this smaller species, aquariums of $18 \times 12 \times 12$ inches $(45 \times 30 \times 30$ cm) will suffice. A layer of non-calcareous gravel, sufficient to anchor plants, should be installed, and soft, peat-acidified water with a hardness not greater than 20 ppm is then introduced; finally, the aquarium is planted with good specimens of *Echinodoras*, *Cryptocoryne* or *Aponogeton* plants. The aquarium temperature should be in the region of 81°F (27°C).

The parents should be separated between spawnings. Distinguishing the sexes is best accomplished by viewing from above, when the slimmer outline of the male will be noted. At breeding time a line above the triangular body mark becomes more brilliant in the male and stays a dull creamy yellow in the female. The female is introduced to the breeding tank first, and 12 to 24 hours later the male may follow. The period of separation and good feeding should increase the urge to spawn. Courting begins with the male flaunting before the female, with colours accentuated and finnage at maximum spread. Occasionally the show will cease and a short chase will ensue, first the female in pursuit and then the male chasing the female. This love-play culminates in both fishes coming together under an overhanging plant leaf, when the male folds his body around that of the female and they roll so that the female vent is uppermost, in

contact with the leaf, where about 20 eggs may be deposited.

When all the eggs are laid the parents must be removed, or the eggs will be eaten. The eggs will hatch in one day, but will remain hanging from the leaf for fully 24 hours more, becoming free-swimming on the third day. The recommended first food is *Euglena*, and a good supply should have been prepared well in advance. After a week, larger infusoria may be fed, and at the end of the second week brine shrimp larvae may be offered. Once the fry are accepting brine shrimp, growth will be rapid.

## FAMILY CYPRINODONTIDAE

The family Cyprinodontidae, the egg-laying tooth carps, includes some fascinating miniature fishes, groups of which have been loosely called killifishes, annual fishes and top minnows. Almost all prefer soft acid water that is not too tropical in temperature – 68 to 73.4°F (20 to 23°C). They breed naturally where mosquito and similar fly larvae abound, their preference being for live food. According to species they will be found spawning at the surface, in mid-water, or within the base material which should be of dead vegetable matter (peat). Breeding of much of the family is accomplished using what can best be described as egg farming techniques, because the eggs are removed literally individually by the aquarist and treated as experience has proved most satisfactory. Generally, aquarists specializing in breeding egg-laying tooth carps keep one species to an aquarium, but have several pairs together. For the smaller species an aquarium size of $15 \times 8 \times 8$ inches $(40 \times 20 \times 20$ cm) is ample and

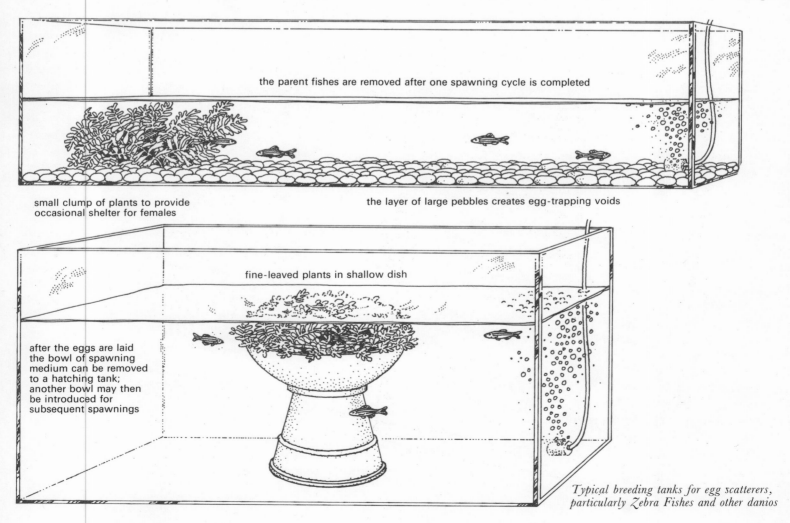

the parent fishes are removed after one spawning cycle is completed

small clump of plants to provide occasional shelter for females

the layer of large pebbles creates egg-trapping voids

fine-leaved plants in shallow dish

after the eggs are laid the bowl of spawning medium can be removed to a hatching tank; another bowl may then be introduced for subsequent spawnings

*Typical breeding tanks for egg scatterers, particularly Zebra Fishes and other danios*

even larger species are comfortably housed in $24 \times 12 \times 12$ inches ($60 \times 30 \times 30$ cm). Surface or near-surface spawning species need floating plants like Water Lettuce *(Pistia stratoides)* or Floating Fern *(Ceratopteris thalictroides)*, as the roots of these make admirable spawning places. Floating mops or bundles of nylon yarn attached to a float make a convenient substitute. The spawning medium is lifted daily and inspected for eggs, which are removed (fingers are best) and transferred to small hatching boxes. Plastic sandwich boxes are often used for this purpose; any plastic box approximately $6 \times 6 \times 3$ inches ($15 \times 15 \times 7$ cm) will do; covers with minute ventilation holes should be used. The water in these hatching boxes should be the same as that used in the breeding tank, and a small amount of waterlogged peat may be included to keep the water acid, which helps to prevent egg funguling; some breeders prefer to use a pure chemical fungicide, such as acriflavine. As the eggs hatch—and this process takes from 12 to 21 days—great care has to be exercised in feeding the fry in the hatching boxes. Newly-hatched brine shrimp is an ideal food, but as it dies very quickly in soft acid water, pollution can soon occur in such small quantities of water.

The above brief account applies to a whole range of genera, including *Aphyosemion, Epiplatys, Aplocheilus, Pachypanchax, Roloffia, Rivulus* and *Fundulus*. Some species, including those in the additional genera *Nothobranchius, Cynolebias* and *Pterolebias*, and certain species from the previous list, spawn on the bottom and in the bottom vegetable layering. Aquarists breeding these fishes have a peat layer on the aquarium bottom approximately 1 inch (2.5 cm) thick. Pairs of some species dive into the peat to deposit their eggs; others lay their eggs on the surface of the peat and bury them afterwards.

The harvesting procedure is usually begun when spawning has been observed and is estimated to have gone on long enough (these fish often spawn over several days). The parents are removed, the peat is scooped up in a fine net and most of the water squeezed out. The peat and the eggs contained within are then placed in a waterproof container—a polythene bag is quite often used—which is set aside at a temperature of 68 to 72°F (20 to 22°C) for a period of one to four months' incubation. At the end of the period, which will vary from species to species, the peat is put back into the aquarium and water of a similar nature to that in which they were spawned is added; and in a very few hours the eggs will start hatching.

Distinguishing the sexes is easy for most species in the family, as the male is in almost every case the more highly coloured and has greater fin development; in fact the difference is often so marked that the two sexes have been thought to be different species.

## FAMILY CICHLIDAE

Within the family Cichlidae will be found fish in an enormous variety of colour, size, temperament and habit. They have also highly developed nurture habits. The larger species could quite easily be termed family pets, for they can become very domesticated. Species of this family all produce adhesive eggs and are egg placers; the sites they choose for depositing their spawn vary between flat level stones on the bottom, the underside of cave-like structures, vertical or near-vertical surfaces, and on firm aquatic plant leaves.

The accepted way of obtaining a true breeding pair is to obtain six young fishes and grow them on together, allowing them to sort out their own mates when they become mature. Cichlids have a very wide distribution, and water and temperature requirements can vary between the opposite ends of the hardness and pH scales. Nor can their diets be described in general terms, as they include carnivores, vegetarians, plankton feeders and even scale eaters.

Four species with diverse methods of reproduction are those of the *Apistogramma, Pterophyllum, Symphysodon* and *Labeotropheus* genera, and these will be described.

***Apistogramma*** Species of the genus *Apistogramma* number about twelve, all of them under 3 inches (7.5 cm) when fully grown; hence the popular name of dwarf cichlids. They have a preference for soft water on the acid side, and for a temperature of about 79°F (26°C). They abhor murky water and any sign of pollution, so crystal clear, well-aerated water suits them best. Some species have obvious differences between the sexes, the males being more colourful and with more developed finnage than the females; however, a few can only be truly sexed when ready to breed, when the males will always outshine the females in brightness of colour. The females begin to show egg fullness which starts behind the pectoral fins and extends to the anal fin.

The breeding tank may be of a permanent nature, that is it may be set up for one pair only, which may stay in residence permanently, the eggs or young being removed as they arrive and transferred to another rearing aquarium. An aquarium about $24 \times 12 \times 12$ inches ($60 \times 30 \times 30$ cm) should first be cleaned and the base covered with non-calcareous gravel. The gravel must be lime-free or the water will become hard and alkaline, which will allow unfavourable bacteria to exist and egg development to be affected. Water, preferably clear rainwater suitably acidified with peat, should be added, and several pieces of flat stone provided. These may lie flat on the gravel and also form caves. A little plant growth should also be provided, especially *Echinodoras* species. The temperature should be set at about 77°F (25°C) rising to 81°F (27°C) and gentle aeration will help. Introduce the selected pair and be prepared for some beautiful love-play. When they have settled down in their new home the male will make advances to the female. A showing-off parade will follow, and at times the male may peck at suitable spawning sites and then return his attention to the female. The courtship often culminates in a trial of strength, with the pair locking jaws and proceeding to push and pull each other all over the aquarium and at times rolling over completely in the tussle. After the rough and tumble, the pair combine their exertions in cleaning a spawning site, quite often a flat stone surface or under the roof of a cave, or occasionally on a firm plant leaf. Whatever spawning site is selected, some practice passes will be made before spawning begins, when both male and female will pass over the spot with vents in close contact with the site. At this time the female ovipositor will be quite obvious as a projection from the vent about 1 mm wide and 1.5 mm long—a short blunt tube. The male sperm tube will be seen to be shorter and more pointed. Spawning begins with the female traversing the site, laying a continuous line of eggs which the male will fertilize by quickly following the line with his sperm tube in close contact with the eggs. The spawning continues until all the eggs are laid; numbers will vary depending on the species and the age of the parents, but an average would be 150 to 200 in the case of young adults. Now the parents will take turns to fan the eggs, which they do with a combination of fin movements, mainly with the pectoral fins. This action ensures a constant passage of moving water over the eggs. An ideal pair will share this task amicably, but ideal pairs are not common in nature and some squabbles may result from one or other parent shirking the responsibilities. Such domestic upsets are often of a trivial nature, and no harm is done; occasionally the upset gets out of hand, one or other parent starts eating the eggs, and soon they are all gone. Because of this many aquarists remove the eggs and hatch them artificially, safeguarding the brood but giving up the possibility of witnessing a marvellous example of parental care. Such upsets are less likely to occur when mates are self-selected.

If all goes well the eggs will hatch in three days, when the once-immobile egg mass now becomes a mass of tethered movement, as the developing young are fixed with an adhesive thread to the spawning site, and will be so placed for a further three days while the egg-sac is absorbed. During this second three-day period, the parents may transfer the wrigglers to another site or even deposit them in a depression in the gravel. The exercise is one that enables the parents to do some cleaning up, because inevitably some debris gathers around the hatching eggs and not all eggs hatch; some become fungused so their removal is apparently for reasons of hygiene. The transfer is made by either parent picking up a developing baby in its mouth and spitting it out at the new site. It is claimed that whilst being transported the young are also cleaned. By the sixth day the parents are fully occupied: the young will be breaking away from their 'anchors', to be caught by the parents and made to rejoin the mass. The seventh day usually sees the brood free-swimming, but very much under the command of the parents, who will shepherd them to safety at the least sign of danger. At this moment the young begin searching for food, and the larger infusoria – *Paramecium*, for example – will be accepted eagerly, as will fresh, newly-hatched brine shrimps – but only the first day's hatching. Once this state is reached and the young are eating well, there is no point in keeping the parents with them. The brood fish should be carefully removed and an efficient box filter installed. Carry on feeding progressively larger food, remembering always that these are fishes which will not tolerate anything other than absolutely clean water.

The aquarist who removes the eggs, preferably on a convenient piece of stone, will witness the development of the eggs up to day six. The eggs should have been put in a similar-sized aquarium, with water of a similar composition, and a gentle flow of air bubbles allowed to play near the eggs. This is a poor substitute for the active attention of the parents, but it helps. Without the orderliness of the parents things may seem to get out of hand at times, with fry becoming detached or stuck together, straying everywhere but where they should be. However,

all comes right when they become free-swimming, and this method does leave the parents undisturbed in their permanent home – all ready to spawn another time, which during a spawning spell can be as often as every ten days.

**Angel fishes** These, which can be any of three or four species of *Pterophyllum*, behave in a similar way to the *Apistogramma* species. However, there are some differences. A pair is usually placed in a bare aquarium approximately 36 × 15 × 15 inches (90 × 40 × 40 cm) with a large capacity box filter and a spawning pot (inverted flower pot), a 16 inch (40 cm) length of 4 inch (10 cm) diameter PVC pipe, or a near-vertical piece of slate, glass or ceramic; whatever is used, the material must be inert. The fishes are not fussy about water type, especially if the stock is of many generations' aquarium development. Nevertheless the best results will be achieved with water no harder than 100 ppm, and at pH 6.0 to 6.6. Sex differences in angel fishes are not easily discernible until they are in spawning condition; then, when viewed head-on, the female and male will display a similar difference to the printed letters U and V in the area immediately behind the ventral fin attachment. The incubation of the eggs in an artificial set-up is sometimes accompanied by the use of a mild fungicide, methylene blue being the most popular. If the water is sufficiently acid, however, this should not be necessary. Young angel fish will feed on newly-hatched brine shrimp immediately and as they grow the larger shrimp will also be appreciated, until at approximately four weeks live *Daphnia* will be taken. Despite reports claiming that *Daphnia* is of little nutritional value, young angel fish will grow apace on it.

**Discus** The genus *Symphysodon* is said by some authorities to have one species and a number of sub-species, but this assertion is not accepted internationally.

Until 1956 the Discus was very much a mystery fish. Some claims of successful breeding had been made, but no details were published. In 1956 the writer published a full account of the breeding of these magnificent cichlids and revealed for the first time that here was a fish with unique nurture habits.

Breeding is as for angel fishes, with the following differences: the water must be very soft – under 20 ppm; pH must be acid, at 5 to 5.5 – de-ionised water, acidified with sphagnum moss peat is used to achieve this condition; the temperature should be not lower than 81°F (27°C); the aquarium size should be 36 × 18 × 18 inches (90 × 45 × 45 cm); non-calcareous gravel may be used on the bottom – or nothing. *Echinodoras* plants should be planted in the gravel, or in pots if the bottom of the aquarium is bare. Some tall pieces of slate should be set at a slight angle and power filtration should be incorporated, filled with polymer wool and occasionally with peat to correct the pH. A compatible pair should be left in sole charge permanently once installed. Pairs that have self-selected are more likely to be successful parents but even so, the success rate for a good brood pair is, at a conservative estimate, about one in five. At this point it would be as well to emphasise an important fact of the Discus anatomy – the mouth. It is small, very small considering the fish's bulk, which will indicate to an observant aquarist that it requires many small meals of small food. The condition of brood fish can be enhanced using chopped earthworms, fly larvae (especially glass worm), and scraped ox-heart.

Sex differences are difficult to discern, and the only sure way is when the female's ovipositor and the male's counterpart are seen. The female's is 2.5 mm wide, 4 mm long and blunt; the male's is approximately 3.5 mm long and pointed, and is more easily hidden by the pelvic fins. Good Discus breeders can grow their offspring to maturity in ten months, but this is only possible with dedicated attention to feeding and general welfare.

Courtship starts with a little jaw-locking but this is neither particularly violent nor of great duration. It is followed by a shuddering movement that both sexes perform quite frequently, which begins with a head shake that passes down the body, and indicates a spawning within 24 hours. Eggs are laid in similar fashion to those of angel fishes, on near-vertical surfaces—quite often the glass panels of the aquarium, occasionally the heater tube, plant leaves, larger flower-pot sides, and slate bars. At least 400 eggs are laid in a good spawning by experienced parents. Development to the free-swimming stage takes eight days, and in the meantime the fry are transferred frequently from plants to rocks, rocks to plants and so on. Immediately before free-swimming, the whole spawning seems to stick together in a large cluster—rather like a swarm of bees. Within hours the young take off and surround their parents in a cloud, feeding from the back of both male and female on a highly nutritious food that oozes through the parents' epidermis dorsally, gradually being produced all over the flanks. The young Discus feed

on their parents' food for seven days before accepting introduced foods, of which the first and most readily accepted is brine shrimp larvae. Very soon the young fishes will take dead foods, scraped ox-heart being particularly favoured. The young are removed at about two and a half to three weeks old, and raised in separate growing-on tanks.

**Labeotropheus**   Species of the genus *Labeotropheus* behave in a manner typical of the cichlid fishes found in the lakes of the Rift Valley of Africa. The water condition required must be very hard, 400 ppm, and alkaline at pH 8. For breeding, a very large aquarium, 48 × 18 × 18 inches (120 × 45 × 45 cm) or larger is recommended, using a gravel base and containing considerable rock-work, possibly amounting to 25 or even 30 per cent of the cubic capacity of the aquarium. Many caves should be formed by the aquarist from the rocks and several specimens of each species of *Labeotropheus* may be introduced. Each will find a home of its own, and if this condition prevails harmony too will prevail. The brood fishes are easily sexed, the males being very much brighter in colour and often with different body and fin markings. A power filter is recommended to maintain water cleanliness.

In this commune the males will court the females of their choice and obviously the female full of roe will receive prior attention. Preliminaries seem to be considered unnecessary; the colouration of the male will intensify, and other males showing an interest in the female are butted and chased away once a male has

*Typical set-up for breeding small cichlids such as* Apistogramma, Julidochromis *etc. The same arrangement, but without plants, could be used for a pair of larger cichlids such as species of* Cichlasoma, Aequidens *or similar sized fishes. A community breeding selection of certain Rift Valley cichlids—* Labeotropheus, Pseudotropheus, *for example—could also be accommodated in this type of arrangement, which is essentially one of generous rockwork forming numerous cave-like retreats*

assumed his dominant dress. Just prior to spawning the male will pursue the female relentlessly all over the aquarium, through caves and gullies and out in the open. Suddenly the female will pick out a spot on the bottom, quickly fan a depression and lay her eggs. The male immediately fertilizes them. The whole process is conducted at speed, not a bit like the leisurely spawning of the South American cichlids. The female scoops up the eggs in her mouth and retires to her chosen retreat, while the male, already losing interest in his latest mate, goes off to see if his services are required elsewhere. The female must now be removed, which is not an easy task in an aquarium full of rocks. A nursery aquarium should be provided for the female: 20 × 12 × 12 inches (50 × 30 × 30 cm) is adequate for the purpose, and some gravel, a few small rocks and even a few plants can be added; the temperature should be in the region of 77 to 79°F (25 to 26°C).

The eggs may be expelled or swallowed by the female while she is being caught, but a really good female will hold on to her eggs whatever happens. The incubation period is approximately three weeks during which time the female eats no food. The mouth swells considerably as the young fish develop, and if one is fortunate enough to be able to look into the mouth some of the embryos will be seen. When the fry finally leave their cramped home they are alert, perceptive and adventurous, seeking food immediately. They are approximately 10 mm in size – large enough to be able to tackle brine shrimp larvae and pulverized ox-heart. The female needs to be well fed to help her to recuperate; chopped earthworms are fine for this purpose. She should not go back to the 'commune' for at least 14 days, during which time she will do no harm if left with her offspring. In fact she will shepherd them away from imagined danger, and attack any inquisitive person who peers too close to the aquarium glass.

## FAMILY ANABANTIDAE

This family contains such favourites as the Siamese Fighting Fish *(Betta splendens)* and the various species and varieties of gourami. All species require warmer than normal water, 79°F (26°C) or more, and do better (that is, produce more fertile eggs) in water of hardness under 150 ppm. Generally the sexes are not difficult to distinguish when mature. In most gouramis the male finnage is more highly developed, with dorsal and anal fins more pointed; in all species the male is the more colourful, and in most the difference is marked, although in some it is only discernible when the fishes are in breeding colour – notably in kissing gouramis *(Helostoma* species,) Chocolate Gourami *(Sphaerichthys osphromenoides)*, and Moonlight Gourami *(Trichogaster microlepis)*.

Sexes should be conditioned in separate tanks; diet should, where possible, contain some live fly larvae. Females become very much distended with roe when ready to breed. The breeding tank should be 18 × 10 × 10 inches (45 × 25 × 25 cm) for small species up to 1.5 inches (3.5 cm) long, and 24 × 12 × 12 inches (60 × 30 × 30 cm) for those up to 2 inches (5 cm) long, and 30 × 15 × 12 inches (75 × 40 × 30 cm) for those up to 3 inches (7.5 cm) long. The water in the breeding tanks need be only 6 inches (15 cm) deep and some Floating Fern *(Ceratopteris thalictroides)*, or fairly fine-leaved plants, left to float on the surface. The female is transferred to the breeding tank

first, and left for 24 hours to become accustomed to her new surroundings – if the male is the first occupier he will become too dominant. The male may be put in with the female on the second day; usually his colours will heighten within minutes, and if all goes well he will begin building a nest of bubbles. This is accomplished by taking a large gulp of air at the surface, and converting it into thousands of small bubbles which pour from the gill opening having been coated with an 'anti-burst' preparation *en route*. At various times the male will cease nest-building to engage in preliminary courtship, which entails displaying with all fins spread and colours accentuated. With a really compatible pair, the female will join in the nest-building. Depending on the species, the nest may be large and elaborate, with or without plant reinforcement, or at the other extreme a half-hearted affair with bubbles scattered untidily in every corner of the breeding tank. The aquarist can assist at this point by ensuring that the aquarium is covered, thus keeping the air above the nest humid and preserving the bubbles.

When he is satisfied with the results of his labour, the male will set out to court his spouse in earnest. The usual displaying is followed by a 'come and see what I have built' invitation, and a more active chasing may well ensue. If the fishes are compatible and ready, it will not be long before the female allows the male to escort her to a position under the nest where he will encircle her body with his own, visibly exerting pressure to squeeze the eggs from her. During this manoeuvre the female is positioned under the nest upside down so the eggs are projected upwards. At the instant of ejection the male releases sperm to fertilize the eggs. This embracing takes from five to ten seconds and is accompanied by much trembling and fin fluttering. The pair then break away to collect the eggs that are falling to the bottom with their mouths and, with infinite care, blow them into the bubbles at the surface. The performance is repeated again and again until all the eggs have been persuaded from the female. Apart from the spawning act the male takes time off to reinforce the nest with more bubbles and to return any eggs that may fall out of it. At this stage the male may resent the female's presence, doing his best to chase her to the furthest corner. The time for intervention has come, and very carefully the female should be netted and removed for recuperation in other quarters. Great care must be exercised not to disturb the nest while using the net.

The eggs, of which there are usually several hundred, are quite difficult to see among the bubbles, at least for the first twelve hours or so. They darken while developing and can then be spotted more easily. What happens next depends on the temperature. At a temperature of 81 to 86°F (27 to 30°C) between 36 and 48 hours are required for the eggs to hatch, and a further 40 to 60 hours to become free-swimming. The young fish is a semi-mobile egg about the size of a comma. The male parent, still at present in the nursery will be constantly blowing errant offspring back into the nest and forming more bubbles to replace those that have burst. At what stage the male is removed largely depends on how well you can trust him. There is no need for his presence once the fry are free-swimming; as the temptation to eat the whole spawning

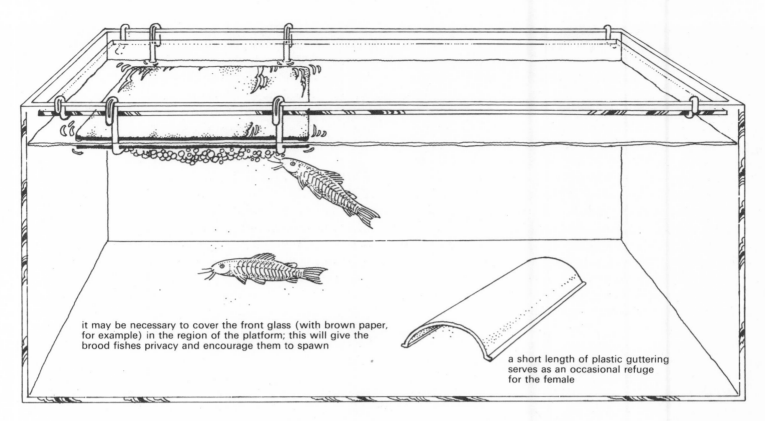

it may be necessary to cover the front glass (with brown paper, for example) in the region of the platform; this will give the brood fishes privacy and encourage them to spawn

a short length of plastic guttering serves as an occasional refuge for the female

*Breeding tank arrangement for* Hoplosternum *species (bubblenest catfish). Aeration should not be provided during nest building as surface disturbance would disperse the nest bubbles produced by the parents; mild aeration may be used when the fry are free-swimming*

is ever-present, many breeders remove the male as soon as the eggs hatch (that is after 36 to 48 hours) and still manage to raise many hundreds of young.

The free-swimming stage coincides with the exhaustion of the yolk sac. Very fine live food, preferably *Euglena*, should now be given, fed every three to four hours for the first four days, followed by a slightly larger live food for a further week, when newly-hatched brine shrimp should be fed. An internal filter of the sponge type should be installed at this time and serviced at least once a week. Between two and three weeks (assuming optimum growth) the young anabantids will start developing their labyrinth organ and they will be seen making frequent trips to the surface. At this time, particularly if the air temperature is colder than the water temperature, adequate aquarium cover should be provided. Every two or three days the larger fry should be transferred to a separate tank as they may eat the smaller ones.

**Chocolate Gourami** Of all the species of anabantids, the one that differs most from the foregoing general breeding account is probably the Chocolate Gourami. This somewhat delicate fish requires very soft acid water 10–20 ppm, a pH of 5 to 6 and a temperature of 81 to 86°F (27 to 30°C). Sexing of the adult fishes is not easy, but males in breeding colour show a brighter gold edge to the anal fin, and the outer rays of the caudal fin become pale gold. The female does not appear noticeably fuller when ready to spawn.

The female lays eggs over gravel, rock or other hard substrate and, after fertilization by the male, eggs are collected and incubated in the mouth of the female. Incubation takes 14 days, during which time the parent makes no attempt to feed. A critical period is reached on the third day when the eggs may be consumed; if she carries them over this period you are more than likely to

be successful. On the fourteenth day the young are released one at a time. They have no further contact with the parents, who should be removed from the breeding tank, the male as soon as the first fry appear and the female when she has released all her family. If the male appears to worry the female he can be removed earlier.

The fry can be fed on newly-hatched brine shrimp straightaway. However, frequent feeding with this food does tend to effect the pH of the water, and remedial measures should be taken to keep it acid by careful water changes. As with all mouth-brooding fish, the spawnings are quite small in number–around forty being usual.

## CATFISHES

The many tropical freshwater catfishes suitable for the amateur's aquarium are included in several families. Unfortunately not many have been bred, possibly because aquarists tend to use these bottom fishes as scavengers–a term that is not favoured by the writer, because it leads fanciers into believing that the fishes are self-sufficient. In a well-populated community aquarium, catfishes can have a lean time, because they are literally living on leftovers. Catfishes, like any other sort of fish, require a specific diet and water conditions similar to that found in their natural habitat. The inclusion of worms and fly larvae in their diet will do much to bring them into breeding condition.

*Corydoras* The most popular genus of catfishes, and certainly the most attractive, is *Corydoras*. Species in this genus have the added advantage of remaining small, 3 inches (7.5 cm) being about the largest. They come from fairly fast-flowing waters, and therefore prefer the aquarium water to be well aerated; the soft to medium-soft water should be of neutral pH. They are not easy to sex, especially as immature specimens; in a few species the male has a higher dorsal fin, but this is not general, and it is far better to be guided by body outline. When the female is in spawning condition, she will be seen to be much broader when viewed from above; she also acquires a decidedly pink abdomen.

It is customary to use the services of two or more males to one female in the breeding aquarium, which may be 24 × 12 × 12 inches (60 × 30 × 30 cm.) It should be set up with fine gravel (2–3 mm mesh), several stones and a few large-leaved plants—*Echinodoras* or *Cryptocoryne* being the most suitable. The water temperature is set at 79°F (26°C) and well aerated before the introduction of the fish, aeration being reduced to a gentle flow at the time of their entering. In their newly set-up home the fish should be fed well on white worms, bloodworms, and thoroughly cleansed *Tubifex* worms; scraped raw ox-heart may also be used. The period of maximum breeding activity occurs between November and March, so serious attempts should be made during this time.

Unlike other fishes, it is the female *Corydoras* that selects the mate, and she alone cleans the spawning sites, which she does most laboriously–taking up to ten minutes to clean one site. Next she goes to her selected male, grips him with her mouth in the region of his vent and proceeds to shake him violently, evidently extracting sperm. She then conveys the sperm in her mouth to one of the prepared sites and places four to six eggs on the same spot. When the eggs are produced they are caught by the paired anal fins, which enclose them until they have been safely deposited. Numerous spawning sites on plants, rocks and the aquarium glass are cleaned. From young adults 150 to 200 eggs can be expected, the spawning usually being spread over two days.

The pair will not seem interested in devouring their eggs, but it is usual to remove all parent fishes when the spawning is complete. The eggs hatch in five days; the young catfishes may be fed on newly-hatched brine shrimp and micro-worm. Great care should be exercised in feeding, as if food is left uneaten it will find its way into the gravel, die, and pollute the aquarium. One notable *Corydoras* breeder arranges for a trickle of fresh water to run through the nursery tank, which helps to overcome this particular hazard. After a week on the brine shrimp and micro-worm, grindal worm and chopped white worm may be fed.

***Hoplosternum littorale*** This catfish, which is bred quite often, grows to a little over 5 inches (13 cm). Distinguishing the sexes is made easy by the fact that the male has a marked difference in the pelvic fins, the leading rays of which are considerably thicker and yellow-brown (sometimes red) in colour. The male grows larger than the female.

An aquarium 36 × 15 × 15 inches (90 × 40 × 40 cm) is filled with water of about 100 ppm hardness and neutral pH and the temperature adjusted to 81°F (27°C). Sexes should have been conditioned in separate aquariums for a period of 14 days, before being brought together in the breeding aquarium. A rigid platform of slate, about 12 inches (30 cm) square, should be fixed at the water surface. Maintenance of water level on the slate platform is critically important and the tank should be covered with an all-over sheet of glass to reduce water loss through evaporation.

The fishes build a nest of large bubbles under the slate platform and lay their eggs among the bubbles. The young hatch in three days and become free-swimming in five days. The fry do not take to the bottom until the third week. Once free-swimming they will take newly-hatched brine shrimp, sifted *Daphnia*, or *Cyclops* larvae as well as micro-worm. Parents should be removed once the young are hatched.

## FAMILY ATHERINIDAE
This family contains three of the popular aquarium 'rainbows': Australian Rainbow *(Melanotaenia maccullochi)*, Madagascar Rainbow *(Bedotia geayi)* and Celebes Rainbow *(Telmatherina ladigesi)*. Conveniently, all can be bred in a similar fashion using nylon spawning mops in a bare aquarium.

The Australian and Madagascar Rainbows grow to 4 to 5 inches (10 to 12 cm) and require a breeding aquarium of 36 × 15 × 15 inches (90 × 40 × 40 cm). The Celebes Rainbow being smaller, will make do with 24 × 12 × 12 inches (60 × 30 × 30 cm). The procedure for breeding is quite simple, and similar water conditions suit all three: a hardness of 80 to 100 ppm, with neutral pH and a temperature of 79 to 81°F (26 to 27°C). Fill the aquarium with water and add a large capacity box filter. Alternatively use a bed of small gravel and under-gravel filtration with fast turn-over. Make up nylon mops using about 20 double strands 8 to 10 inches (20 to 25 cm) long attached to make-shift floats. From experience we have learned that *Telmatherina* prefer a softer yarn and *Bedotia* quite a hard one, but colour is immaterial. The number of spawning mops is not very important, but should be not less than six. The fishes are placed in these aquariums in small shoals of six to eight, with equal numbers of each sex. In the Australian Rainbow the finnage is more colourful in the male but the sexes are roughly the same size, although the female will of course show more roundness when in spawn. The Madagascar Rainbow male is larger, more stream-lined and generally more brightly coloured than the female, and the fin margins are also darker. In the Celebes Rainbow the male is larger, more colourful and has longer fin ray extensions.

During spawning the males drive the females through the mops, where the eggs are deposited. The aquarist should make a daily inspection of the mops, removing them one by one and examining them for the presence of eggs. If a fair number are present–six or more in the case of *T. ladigesi*, 30 or more in the case of the other two species —the mops are transferred to another aquarium for incubation. When all the eggs have hatched, the mop is returned to the breeding aquarium. All rainbow fishes have slowly developing eggs; *B. geayi* about seven days, the other two species ten days or slightly longer. The smaller species, *T. ladigesi*, has very small fry which require infusoria for the first four to five days. *B. geayi* and *M. maccullochi* fry will eat newly-hatched brine shrimp from the start. Fine proprietary dry foods will be eaten by the young of all species.

A fourth rainbow fish, and a member of the *Melanotaenia* genus–*M. nigrans*, grows nearly an inch (20–22 mm) longer, but the breeding procedure is the same as that for *M. maccullochi*.

Discus *Symphysodon discus* with fry

# Marine
# Tropical Fish
## *in the Home Aquarium*

The most beautiful fishes in the world are the aptly-named damsels, butterflies and angels of the coral reefs – damsels dressed in shimmering blue, shot-silk or sequins; butterflies drifting delicately through their underwater garden, as outstanding among fishes as butterflies among insects; angels of a brightness out of this world. The reefs also hold enamelled clowns, fantastically painted wrasses and triggers, pastel-shaded surgeons, and grotesquely beautiful scorpions or dragon-fishes with their gargoyle faces and fairy wings.

The invertebrates of the reef are just as colourful and beautiful. There are some sixty genera of corals with an amazing variety of forms, with shapes like trees and staghorns, fans and lattices, roses and lettuces, mushrooms and brains. The coral we normally see and use as ornaments or to furnish marine aquariums is, of course, merely the white skeleton (except for organ-pipe coral which has a deep red skeleton). Living coral is incredibly colourful and contributes, together with the flower-like anemones and tubeworms, sponges and nudibranchs, to the effect of a magic garden, an underwater paradise.

And a paradise it is for thousands of other creatures. The reef affords a multiplicity of habitats – the living coral heads themselves, piles of coral debris, rocks, caves, sand, meadows of algae. Here thrive the molluscs: oysters, mussels, clams, scallops, snails, octopuses and squids; the spiny echinoderms: sea-urchins and star-fishes; the many-legged arthropods: crabs, lobsters and shrimps.

And so, for the small fishes, the reef affords both protection and abundant food. Predators are few, pickings are rich, and life is good for these pampered beauties.

No marine aquarium is complete without anemones and such other invertebrates as are compatible with the chosen fishes. The invertebrate aquarium, where invertebrates have priority and only compatible fishes are kept, is rapidly growing in popularity.

All the rich life of the reef depends upon the humble coral polyp. The coral polyp is part animal, part plant, since part of its body tissue is composed of algae. This algae, like all plants, needs sunlight, so coral does not grow at a depth of much more than about 130 feet, and

Cuban Hogfish *Bodianus pulchellus*

the lushest growth is down to about sixty feet on the seaward precipice of the reef, where there is also plenty of oxygen and plankton.

The coral polyp is like a miniature anemone. It feeds by filtering plankton from the water. It also extracts from the water calcium carbonate with which it builds, upon the skeletons of its ancestors, its own external skeleton. An individual coral head can grow up to ten inches in a year, and a reef can grow at a rate of six feet a year. At the same time, of course, the reef is being broken down under the stress of storms, or the attentions of the parrot-fish with its coral-crunching teeth and cement-mixer stomach, or the crown-of-thorns starfish fast demolishing the Great Barrier Reef. Now there is the additional threat of the hatchet-happy tourist. Pollution is also killing many reefs. The problem is so bad that it is quite possible that the living reefs, where the helmet-crab has lived unchanged for 400 million years, will no longer be there for our grandchildren to see.

A single reef can support up to 400 species of fishes. Each has its ecological niche, both in terms of territory and of food supply. One species will hide in a coral head, another among the debris, another in a cave or crevice, another in a shell, another among weeds or among the tentacles of an anemone, and yet another will burrow in the sand. One species will feed mainly on coral, another on small crustaceans, another on molluscs, another on echinoderms, another on algae, another on smaller fishes . . . thus the need, in a community aquarium, to offer a widely varied diet.

Some fishes habitually move about in shoals, sometimes comprising thousands of individuals. Some patrol a strictly limited territory singly or in pairs. Schooling, the tendency of some fishes to get as close to each other as possible at moments of danger, seems to work by confusing the predator, who cannot focus on or concentrate on any specific victim. Sometimes the school becomes a mob, effectively driving off a large invader by sheer weight of numbers.

The typical muscular streamlined shape of the fast-swimming fishes of the open sea, of which the shark, if we could see it without fear, is the most beautiful, is not found in coral fishes. They are specialized not for sustained speed, but for acceleration over short distances and manoeuvrability. A large school of damsels can, in a twinkling, completely disappear into a small coral head. The disc-shaped butterfly quickly slides into a narrow crevice where no predator can follow.

Though the shapes of the reef fishes can be seen to be functional, it is more difficult to see their patterns and colours as anything but the extravagance of nature delighting in variety and vividness and beauty, splashing

her paints exuberantly here, subtly shading and delicately cross-hatching there. A few species are obviously camouflaged, or have patterns which, like the stripes and patches of jungle animals, break up the outline. But in the majority of species there can be no question of camouflage. On the contrary, they are advertising their presence to the world, but especially to other members of the same species. Thus the utter distinctiveness of each species eliminates the danger both of overcrowding that particular niche, and of sterile cross-mating. The more different species of the same family there are in the vicinity, the more startling the variations of pattern and colour, which will have evolved to help them recognize their own species at a distance in the blue undersea dusk. When we expose these colours to ideal lighting in the aquarium, the result is breathtaking.

## Marine Tropical Fishes in the Home Aquarium

Marine tropicals are very much more difficult to keep in the home aquarium than freshwater tropicals, not because they are less hardy (they are, in fact, hardier) but because it is so much more difficult to create in the home aquarium

Left: *Amphiprion perideraion*
Below: *Dendrochirus zebra*

anything resembling the conditions in the reef than it is to duplicate the natural conditions of freshwater fishes. Until a few years ago the chance of keeping a butterfly or an angel alive for a year was negligible. There have been major improvements in shipping, disease control, feeding, and the artificial seawater preparations, but the crucial breakthrough has been in filtration. The undergravel bacteriological filtration system now generally in use has solved the problem of the gradual build up of nitrites highly toxic to these fishes. The system is essentially the same as that used in the gravel beds at sewage works. When an aquarium has been in use for a few weeks each piece of gravel becomes coated with bacteria. Simple airlifts pull the water down through the gravel into a chamber beneath it, then up pipes and back into the tank from just above the surface (thus aerating the water at the same time). As molecules of nitrite pass through the gravel the aerobic bacteria add oxygen, thus converting toxic nitrite into harmless nitrate. The system has the further advantage of being cheap and easy to construct with little to go wrong if the pump is kept working. An efficient pump will circulate the entire contents of the aquarium in fifteen minutes. Some aquarists advocate external power filters with activated carbon, ozonizers, protein-skimmers, etc. in addition, but they are not strictly necessary.

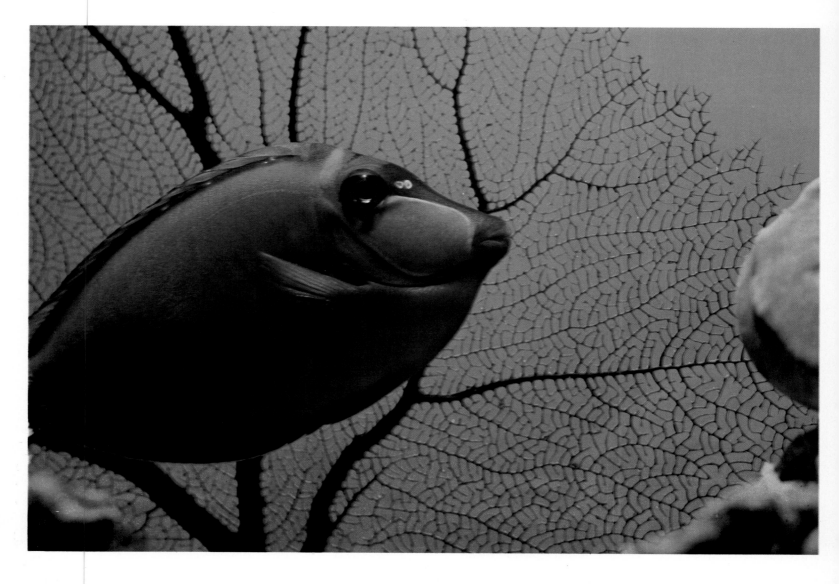

Above: Unicorn Tang *Naso lituratus*
Right: Cortez Angel *Holocanthus passer*

One of the principal difficulties in keeping a community of freshwater fishes is, as we have seen, the very different requirements of different species in terms of temperature, pH, hardness etc. Though it may be more difficult to duplicate the water conditions of a coral reef, at least there is the advantage with marines that once you have got it right, you know that it is right for all species, since there is little difference between one coral reef and another the world over. On the other hand there are so many delicate or impossible marine fishes and so many with special requirements that the aquarist who simply buys what catches his eye at the shop must anticipate high losses, even if the conditions in his tank are right. But, by restricting himself to those species agreed to be hardy (and this is no very crippling restriction) his losses need be no greater than he would expect with freshwater fishes. If the environment stays right and a fish settles in, eats well, and survives those crucial first weeks, there is no reason why it should not live happily for years.

The marine aquarist needs money, time and knowledge. There is no space here to go into all the complexities and no reader should attempt to set up a marine tank solely on the information I am able to give, but here are a few of the essentials.

The tank should be as large as possible, preferably fifty to a hundred gallons, certainly not less than twenty gallons. An all-glass or fibre-glass tank is best. If the tank has a metal frame it must be nylon-coated before glazing. Any metal in contact with the water will rapidly poison the fish. Salt water dissolves putty, so the inside of the tank must be sealed with silicone-rubber.

Plants will grow in the aquarium only if special steps are taken to provide high light intensity (in the form of spotlights) and vitamin additives, but the tank can be decorated with coral skeletons and shells. These must be cleaned, boiled and bleached very carefully to remove all traces of organic matter (and rinsed many times to remove all traces of bleach). I always try to make my own tanks look as much like a section of a coral reef as I can. This means arranging the coral to look as if it were growing from the rock, not just piling one piece on another, or arranging the pieces like ornaments on a shelf. And no plastic divers or sunken galleons!

Those who live far from the habitats of these fish should use a reputable brand of prepared salts to make artificial sea water. The specific gravity at 75°F should be 1.020 to 1.022. Trace elements should be added occasionally. It is wise to change a quarter of the water every few weeks, also to remove the sea-humus which accumulates in the gravel. Every marine aquarist needs a hydrometer, a nitrite test kit and a pH test kit. The pH should be 8.0 to 8.3. To maintain this high pH layers of crushed limestone, crushed cockle shell and coral sand should be used instead of gravel, and rockwork should be limestone or tufa. A few drops of buffer solution weekly may also be necessary.

The temperature of the water must be thermostatically controlled at about 76°F. (25°C.). The tank should be well lit with, ideally, both fluorescent and tungsten lighting, and the lights should be on the length of a tropical day. This encourages the growth of beneficial green algae.

No fishes should be put in the aquarium until all the systems and readings have been perfect for a week or two, then only two or three hardy damsels should be introduced and fed sparingly until the bacteria culture has had time to develop, and that may take several weeks. The hardiest, most nitrite resistant fish are the Humbug and Domino Damsels. Also very hardy are the other damsels, the Cleaner and Lyretail Wrasses, scorpions and triggers. Clowns are relatively sensitive and not suitable for absolute beginners.

The tank must not be overcrowded. One inch of fish to every two gallons should be an absolute limit. The beginner would be wise to limit himself to one every four gallons for a few months.

Most of the fishes offered for sale are babies. Some of them, especially scorpions, batfishes and triggers, will grow very fast and will need more and more room. This

Below: General shot of tank with Scorpion and Domino Damsel
Right: Blue-faced Angel *Euxiphipops xanthometapon*

should be allowed for in stocking the tank, unless an arrangement can be made with a dealer for trading in the big fellows. There is a demand for them from the public aquariums and from fanciers with enormous tanks.

When buying fishes, first choose your dealer. Does he seem to know what he is talking about? Is the water in his tanks clear and are the fishes active and healthy and eating? Examine a fish carefully for wounds, fungus, marks or blotches of any kind which might indicate disease. If it is marked in any way, if it is lying on the bottom or gulping at the surface or breathing very fast or listless or persistently rubbing itself or pale, if its fins are permanently closed or fully extended, don't buy it. If the dealer says it is eating, ask him to show you. If, on the other hand, a fish is immaculate in body and fins, swimming about bright-eyed and alert, in good colour, breathing normally, eating, and frequently closing or extending its fins, don't quibble if you are asked a little more for it than you had intended to pay. A cheap but sick fish may not only die, but may introduce disease into your tank and kill them all.

There are a few exceptions to this rule. Some wrasses normally lie on the bottom; batfishes stay near the surface; scorpions stay still for long periods, often hanging upside-down; and many perfectly fit fishes may hide out of normal shyness, especially if it is only a few days since

104

they were in their familiar reef.

The dealer is, to some extent, at the mercy of the collectors. In the Philippines, for example, where many of the finest fishes come from, all the collecting is done by daylight (owing to local superstitions among the fishermen) and the commonest method is to knock out the fishes by squirting sodium cyanide in their faces. Needless to say, these fishes are still groggy when they arrive in the shops and there are high losses. In the Caribbean, the standard method is the use of baited traps, but this results in a large number of injuries. By far the best method is that generally used in Sri Lanka, where the collecting is done at night with underwater torches. The fishes are asleep and can be picked up by hand.

If you have a long way to go, your fishes should be in large plastic bags with plenty of oxygen, each inside another plastic bag, inside a polystyrene-lined box packed with paper and sealed. They are shipped from the tropics like this, and will usually survive for up to forty-eight hours. When you get them home, do not suddenly expose them to light or to any other sudden change. Float the plastic bag in your tank for half-an-hour, occasionally adding half a cupful of water from the tank. Thus both temperature and water-chemistry are gradually equalized.

Most of the fishes commonly sold will live happily with other species, but many will not tolerate other members of their own. Once established, a fish will come to regard part of the tank, or even the whole tank, as its own preserve, and will resent (often violently) the introduction of new fishes. It is therefore a good plan to put a new fish behind a removable glass partition at one end of the tank, or in a perforated clear plastic box for a few days until the established fishes have come to accept its presence. Angels and surgeons are particularly territorial and it is wise to settle for one of each in a tank. This does not apply to schooling genera such as *Dascyllus, Chromis, Amphiprion* and *Apogon*, though adults of these genera will become aggressive when they pair. Every tank should have a Cleaner Wrasse (*Labroides dimidiatus*) which will remove parasites from the other fishes and clean their wounds.

Marine tropical fishes are susceptible to several kinds of parasitic and fungus diseases. There are reliable chemical treatments available, or an ozonizer is an effective prophylactic and sterilizer. It is imperative that no treatment should be used which destroys the bacteria indispensable to the filtration system. Most of the chemical treatments are fatal to invertebrates.

Since many marine fishes in the reefs eat mainly food which cannot be provided in the home aquarium – the larger plankton, coral polyps, small crustaceans, marine algae – they have to be educated to eat what can be provided and success or failure in this is obviously a matter of life and death. Some species, especially some of the most beautiful butterflies are impossible or so difficult that they should not be imported, but most of the fishes offered to aquarists can be tempted. The secret is variety. Feed the fishes as much as they will consume as you watch; feed often, and try everything. Even when your fishes are all eating well you will still have to maintain this variety, as they will all have different likes and dislikes. Here are some of the basic foods: deep-frozen and gamma-irradiated fish and shellfish, mysus and brine shrimp, and marine greenfood; freeze-dried brine shrimp, *Tubifex*, roes, plankton; live *Daphnia*, bloodworm and earthworm (chopped and washed); scraped or finely chopped raw meat; chopped spinach or lettuce; various proprietary flaked and granulated foods.

Damsels and clowns will spawn freely and the eggs will hatch, and there are reports of people in various parts of the world raising the young to adulthood. But there is no method generally available to amateur aquarists to feed the fry, which will die in a few days without live plankton. Baby seahorses and scorpions have reputedly been raised on newly-hatched brine shrimps.

The exact identification of species of marine tropicals may cause problems. A great deal of reclassification is now in progress. The old classification was very bad, consigning some fishes to the wrong family altogether, and classifying others as different species, which are now known to be only colour-phases of the same species. There are also wide variations between individuals in some species (Sea Bee Clowns for example) which have led to a multiplicity of unnecessary distinctions in classification.

The classification used in this book is based on *Pacific Marine Fishes* by Burgess and Axelrod, or, for species not covered by that work, on *Exotic Marine Fishes* by Axelrod and Emmens. Some very recent reclassifications have not yet passed into general use, so that fishes will often be offered for sale under obsolete scientific names. I have therefore also indicated some of the commonest of these.

# Marine Invertebrates

There could be few more breathtaking sights than an aquarium containing a balanced selection of marine invertebrates and small compatible fishes. Though only a few invertebrate species out of the vast range can be maintained in the home aquarium for an acceptable length of time, these provide the aquarist with a wealth of exotic colours and some bizarre shapes. Some invertebrates are surprisingly easy to keep and rarely require more attention than marine fishes.

Before choosing the size of the aquarium, you should decide which type of 'community' is to be installed. Basically, there are three types.

First, there is a marine community aquarium in which the fishes are the primary inhabitants and the invertebrates only complementary. These usually consist of an anemone to harbour a clownfish, an urchin to help keep algae under control or a large hermit crab for scavenging. Invertebrates for this type of aquarium have to be very hardy and therefore need little or no attention. Some care though must be taken in selecting the fishes, but this rule applies to all community aquariums where invertebrates and fishes are kept together.

The second possibility is an invertebrate community aquarium in which the invertebrates are the primary inhabitants and the fishes are secondary. The fishes are usually few and small in size, but add to the display. Such an aquarium, if properly set up and carefully maintained, can provide

Invertebrates of many types happily coexist and occupy every niche in the marine invertebrate aquarium

a continuous spectacle of colour and movement.

The third type is an all-invertebrate aquarium containing only compatible invertebrates, such as live crustaceans, corals and anemones.

Whichever type of community is decided on, the basic requirements for success are much the same. Choose a non-toxic and non-corrosive aquarium, preferably all glass, and as large as possible within reason. It is much easier to maintain a large aquarium because any local environmental changes are much less likely to cause problems. Whether you are keeping marine fishes or invertebrates, it is essential to keep the environment as stable as possible. Marine animals are not adapted to withstand sudden changes in temperature, water quality or pH level; if the aquarium is subjected to changes of this nature, stress will inevitably occur and this may be fatal. It is possible to keep a very small all-invertebrate aquarium, but the choice of inhabitants will be severely limited and water management must be very thorough for this type of installation. An aquarium of 50 to 100 gallons (220 to 450 litres) is ideal, particularly for an invertebrate community or a marine community aquarium. Undergravel filtration is generally considered to be the best system for an invertebrate aquarium. The filters are easy to use, relatively inexpensive and have no moving parts to go wrong.

If at all possible, choose a well established aquarium which has not been treated chemically nor disturbed for a long time, and preferably has some good algal growth. Take care when using medications in an invertebrate aquarium; most of them can be extremely toxic to invertebrates, so always consult your dealer. Ensure that there is at least 2 to 3 inches (5 to 8 cm) of oolitic coral sand covering the under-gravel filter and a constant supply of air through the air uplifts of which there should be one for approximately every 2 square feet (0.2 square metres) of base area. The outlets should be just above the surface and in a horizontal position to create maximum turbulence and aeration of the water.

Support systems for a marine invertebrate aquarium are similar to those needed for marine fishes. Density, temperature and pH requirements are no different. Lighting, though, is of more importance, particularly where corals and algae are to be maintained.

If it is not possible to start with a mature tank, then a start from the beginning must be made. Fortunately, it is now possible to buy maturing agents or bacteria which accelerate the natural process of maturing the aquarium. Without these maturing agents this process could take several weeks. Instead, a new aquarium can be

matured within days, and then a selection of invertebrates can be introduced safely. The process of maturation involves the build up of bacteria which can convert poisonous waste products produced by fishes and other animals into non-toxic substances. Without these bacteria, any waste food or dead organic matter would very quickly decompose to form ammonia and other poisonous substances which would pollute the aquarium and kill the inhabitants. There are many test kits on the market for testing the level of maturity in a marine aquarium.

Good filtration and aeration are essential, not so much for water clarity and movement but to support the population of beneficial bacteria which are essential for the successful maintenance of the invertebrates and other inhabitants. Invertebrates also require a high quality synthetic salt water mixture, so only the best available should be considered. If the density, pH, temperature and overall quality of the water are correct, success will inevitably follow given a sensible choice of subjects.

Purple Blanket Anemone *Discosoma* with its Anemone Crab *Neopetrolisthes*. Behind are Feather Dusters *Sabella pavona*, and in front are two Sea Apples *Paracucumaria tricolor*, one with a Painted Cleaner Shrimp *Hippolystmata grabbami*. To the left is Bubble Coral *Plyragyra* and to the right Polyp Coral *Goniopora lobata*. The green plant is *Caulerpa prolifera*

# The Invertebrates

One of the best known marine invertebrates is the octopus, but like many other interesting or beautiful creatures it is difficult to keep in the home aquarium. Only those invertebrates which can be maintained successfully in captivity for a reasonable length of time should be considered. They can be broadly divided into six groups: living rock, live corals, anemones, crustaceans, echinoderms and molluscs.

## LIVING ROCK

This term applies to natural rock taken from a reef. It normally contains an enormous variety of animal and plant life. The rocks should be of interesting shapes and contours and should be heavily encrusted with various forms of marine life such as bristle worms, urchins, brittle stars and various algae.

Living rock commands a high price because of high air-freight charges and the frequent need for the importer to condition the rock before sale, but it is nevertheless the best material to choose when starting an invertebrate aquarium. A small amount of good quality or first grade living rock will condition or mature a new tank and will serve as a background to the display. It will also provide an essential part of the natural environment for most invertebrates. Lower grade rock can be added when required, otherwise the cost would be very high indeed. When buying living rock, always ensure that it has been conditioned for a few days in your dealer's tanks. Newly imported rock will look very beautiful; but beware, because it often contains sponges and other forms of life which are not easy to maintain in captivity and which die very quickly, causing a high degree of pollution in the aquarium. A white bacterial growth is normally the start of such a sequence (indicated by a rising nitrite reading) which may be fatal to all the inhabitants. Never, therefore, put new unconditioned rock into an established marine aquarium.

It will be safe to introduce a small selection of invertebrates about four weeks after the last piece of living rock was introduced into the aquarium; a feather duster worm, a crustacean and a small anemone would make a good starting selection. During this

period the aquarium will have become mature either through the rock itself or with the aid of a maturing agent. If fishes are to be added, a further four weeks should elapse. The golden rule at this stage is patience, largely because of the risk of transmitting disease from the existing rock and invertebrates to any incoming fishes. Similarly, any fish which is to be added to the aquarium should be fully quarantined for a similar period, otherwise fish diseases may be introduced, and cure is difficult because most medications suitable for fishes are toxic to invertebrates.

To maintain living rock in peak condition, good lighting and good water quality are essential. The use of spotlights in invertebrate aquariums is recommended; they bring out the best colours and promote growth of the various algae. A combination of spotlights and a white fluorescent tube simulating natural sunlight is the best all-round lighting for the invertebrate aquarium. The duration of illumination will vary according to whether the aquarium receives any natural sunlight, but in general about ten to twelve hours a day will give the best results. As well as good lighting, the

Living rock supports a colony of Feather Dusters *Sabella pavona*, a Brain Coral *Trachyphillia* and a Blue Starfish *Linckia laevigata*

Bubble Coral *Plyragyra* with Polyp Coral
*Goniopora lobata* behind and living sponge to
the left

should have a density (specific gravity) reading of between 1.020 and 1.022 and a pH level of 8.1 to 8.4. Partial water changes (about 20 per cent) are essential and should be made about every six to eight weeks. Corals respond well to new water and improve noticeably in appearance. The turbulence and general water movement created by the action of the under-gravel filter will also increase the life of the corals and help with the even dispersal of suspended food particles throughout the aquarium.

All living corals benefit from the regular addition of either deep frozen or liquid marine supplements which have been specially formulated for invertebrates. If fish are present in the aquarium, their food also will benefit the corals. The juices of the *Mysis* shrimp, adult brine shrimp and red plankton are particularly beneficial. Some corals, such as *Fungia*, require direct feeding, but these are the exception; most need their food in suspension in the water.

The choice of specimens is important. When selecting your corals, always ensure that they are blossoming, look healthy and are not damaged in any way. Introduction into the aquarium should be gradual by carefully mixing the waters as for marine fishes. It is perfectly safe to take the coral out of its transit container before placing it into the aquarium and then onto a piece of rock, preferably sited under maximum illumination. Do not put corals directly on the sand or filter bed because this can lead to the polyps around the base of the coral being deprived of light and food. Any coral which starts to deteriorate can be recognized easily and should be removed immediately. Stone or hard corals usually show such deterioration by developing a brown bacterial growth whereas soft corals and polyps usually start to disintegrate.

Corals recommended for the aquarium in order of hardiness are as follows: *Plyragyra* (bubble coral), *Goniopora* (polyp coral), *Tabularia* (soft polyps on rock), *Dendronephthya* (soft mushroom corals), *Tubastrea* (sun coral), *Trachyphilla* (brain coral), *Euphyllia* (moon coral) and *Fungia* (plate coral). All these are relatively easy to maintain and under good conditions should live for between six months and three years in the aquarium.

use of specially formulated marine additives for improving algal growth and increasing the trace element and vitamin content of the water are strongly recommended.

## LIVING CORALS

The importance of good lighting has been mentioned already, but there is no better lighting than sunlight itself, and its relevance to the successful m intenance of living corals in aquariums cannot be over-emphasized. All corals, both hard and soft, have small algal cells called zooxanthellae living within their tissues. These cells need sunlight both for survival and for growth, or, in the absence of natural sunlight, a high quality 'daylight' fluorescent tube should be used. It is hardly surprising therefore that most corals áre found only in shallow seas. Under good lighting conditions, most corals will not need feeding because their zooxanthellae will make sufficient food for their host coral to live on. Other important factors are correct feeding and good aeration and filtration. The synthetic salt mixture

# ANEMONES

Anemones are by far the most popular single group of all invertebrates. They cover an enormous range of colours and sizes, are adaptable and long-lived, and make ideal subjects for the aquarium. Most anemones, once introduced into the aquarium, quickly settle down and attach themselves to a piece of rock where they will generally remain unless disturbed, but *Tealia*, *Discosoma* and some others prefer to live in the sand.

All anemones possess tentacles which vary in length and width according to the species. These beautiful flower-like structures all contain thousands of stinging cells which they use to kill their prey. The severity of the sting depends on the type and size of the anemone. Most anemones can be handled safely, but care must be taken to prevent them coming into contact with tender parts of the body such as the forearm. A rather painful and unpleasant rash will usually follow but this is not serious and will not require medical attention.

Some animals are immune to the sting of anemones and live in or near them in a state of biological harmony called symbiosis. There are classic partnerships between anemones and all species of clownfish, anemones and some damsel fish, and more rarely between anemones and crustaceans. Some of the anemones are fed by their symbiotic partners who in turn receive protection from the anemones against predators. Some species of *Discosoma* live in harmony with several different kinds of animals and as well as their clownfishes may also have crabs and shrimps living amongst their tentacles.

To keep anemones successfully in the home aquarium, it is essential, as with other invertebrates, to maintain good water quality. Anemones require a particularly high oxygen content which can be achieved by regular water changes combined with good filtration and aeration.

When handling anemones, always take great care not to damage the foot when peeling the animal away from its anchorage. A sharp nudge at the foot of the anemone, before it can contract itself, is often the best way to remove a specimen. If the foot is damaged or torn during handling, it is best to leave the anemone where it is, where it will quickly heal under normal conditions. However, if the foot is severely torn, this may kill the anemone and lead to rapid pollution of the aquarium. At the slightest sign of any decomposition or any tissue breaking away from the anemone, it must be removed at once. The unpleasant smell of a dying anemone is often a good indicator if the aquarist is in any doubt. It is quite normal for a large healthy anemone to change quickly to a small deflated specimen, but this should not cause alarm. This contraction occurs when the anemone is changing the water in its body cavity.

Feeding most anemones could not be easier. All enjoy a piece of prawn or shrimp, or similar marine food about once a week. Either place the food on the tentacles of the anemone or directly into its oral disc. Where a clownfish and an anemone are living together in symbiosis, it may not be necessary to feed the anemone, as the clownfish will probably do this. After feeding, usually the following day, it is quite possible that the anemone will have regurgitated digested food in the shape of a small ball of mucus which will float to the surface. This is highly toxic and should be removed at once. When preparing food add a proprietary vitamin supplement, either in a liquid or deep-frozen form. Evidence suggests that vitamin supplements prolong the life of anemones but, as with most animals in captivity, stress of confinement will occur and anemones will gradually decrease in size as they age.

The most suitable anemones for the invertebrate aquarium are as follows:

A Royal Gramma *Gramma loreto* swims over a Green Blanket Anemone *Discosoma*

**Radianthus malu.** This species is imported from Singapore and is available in a wide range of colours including white, pink, purple, and white with purple tips. It is very hardy and can therefore be recommended for the beginner. Not all clownfish will live in this anemone but the Tomato Clownfish (*Amphiprion frenatus*) and the Brown and White Clownfish (*A. clarkii*) seem to be the most compatible.

**Radianthus ritterii.** This species comes from the Indian Ocean around East Africa and Mauritius. Though not as colourful as *R. malu*, it does have a pink or red base and its tentacles are sometimes tipped with pale green or yellow. It is probably the best anemone for all clownfish; most species readily accept it. A shoal of Skunk Clownfishes (*A. akallopisos*) living in this anemone is an unforgettable sight.

**Discosoma.** Commonly called the carpet or blanket anemone, this genus is most common around Sri Lanka. It is usually a large anemone and often a

Tube Anemone *Cerianthus*

beautiful green or blue. It has short tentacles which contain a powerful sting and any unfortunate specimen which touches this anemone will be seized and probably devoured. It is therefore not a good anemone for the invertebrate community aquarium where slow-moving fishes and invertebrates are kept together. It is much better suited to the marine community aquarium where it makes an excellent symbiotic partner for most species of clownfish, in particular *A. clarkii*. The Domino Damsel (*Dascyllus trimaculatus*) also makes a good partner for this anemone, and a shoal of these in a large individual is a familiar sight on a reef.

**Stoichactis.** This anemone is a close relative of *Discosoma*. It has a similar, short tentacled body structure but is much more gentle with a less powerful sting and it is therefore much better suited to the invertebrate community aquarium. It will attach itself either to the rocks or to the sides of the aquarium, whereas *Discosoma* usually firmly anchors itself to the coral-sand or filter bed. It is imported mainly from Indonesia. White is the most common colour, but green and purple specimens are available occasionally. The Common Clownfish (*A. percula*) is attracted to this particular anemone though it does not accept most anemones.

**Cerianthus.** This is considered by many aquarists to be the most beautiful of all anemones, and is often referred to as the tube anemone. It is in many ways like a giant tubeworm, with a head of long thin tentacles flowing gracefully in the water, and is beautifully coloured in shades of green, purple, orange and white. Unlike all other anemones, it lives in a tube produced by secretions from its body. The tube consists of a dark brown fleshy substance and is usually partially buried in the sand. Under good conditions this anemone will multiply in the aquarium to produce a carpet of small anemones. The tentacles of *Cerianthus* are extremely toxic to most forms of marine life, including clownfish. Take care, therefore, when placing this genus in the aquarium and ensure that its tentacles are not allowed to touch other anemones, living corals or other stationary invertebrates. Most marine fish instinctively avoid the tentacles of *Cerianthus*, but sea-horses, box fish and

other slow moving fishes sometimes do not, and these should not be kept with it. Once positioned and settled, it will remain stationary in the aquarium where its tube will settle into the sand. It is imported mainly from Singapore and Indonesia and is usually shipped without its tube. This is of no detriment to the anemone as the tube will quickly develop again.

*Cerianthus* must not be confused with feather-duster worms (for example *Sabellastarte indica*) which look rather like anemones, but are in fact tube-worms. The double crowns of feathery tentacles, often striped with brown and white, are extremely attractive. Like anemones they are easily maintained and in good conditions can even propagate themselves in the aquarium.

There are many other species of anemone which can be kept successfully in aquariums. For the very small aquarium, the sand anemone (*Tealia*) is recommended. Though not colourful, it is extremely hardy and will accept readily most symbiotic partners. Similarly, the colonial anemone (*Crytodendrum*) on rock, or anemone stone as it is more commonly called, is another interesting subject. Anemone stones resemble living corals but are clusters of small colonial anemones with short mat-like tentacles. They are easy to keep and provide an excellent background to any display.

This section would not be complete without some mention of the Atlantic

Atlantic Anemone *Condylactis* with Polyp and *Tabularia* Corals, Feather Dusters, sponges, an Arrowhead Crab *Stenorhynchus seticornis* and a Bicolor Blenny *Ecsenius bicolor*

Anemone, or *Condylactis* as it is better known. This anemone has a long column, usually with a red base, and long thick tentacles which are often bright purple or white. It makes a good aquarium subject on its own, but a group of three or four make an even better display. It is not, however, recommended as a symbiont, as most potential partners are not attracted to this anemone.

## CRUSTACEANS

This group of more than 20,000 species is the largest single group of aquatic invertebrates. Although few make good aquarium subjects, there are some attractive crabs, shrimps and lobsters within the group, and most are compatible with each other. All grow by shedding their exoskeleton; new or damaged limbs being replaced during this process. It is during this moulting stage that crustaceans are most prone to attack from predators. Most species make excellent scavengers and very few have special feeding requirements.

Of the crustaceans available to the marine aquarist, the most popular by far are the hermit crabs. These crabs

live in a shell and vary in size from species the size of a small finger-nail, to large species such as the Red Hairy Hermit Crab (*Dardanus megistos*). Small hermit crabs make very good scavengers and can be safely kept, either singly or together, in any invertebrate community aquarium. Large specimens, however, can be destructive and are better suited to the marine community aquarium where they can do little or no damage. Some crabs such as *Dardanus gemmatus* carry anemones on their backs for protection against predators, and like most other hermits they need to change their shells as they continue to grow larger. This process of changing shells can be a rewarding sight; the crab carefully pulls off its host anemones from the old shell and then seems to stick them onto the new one.

Totally unlike any hermit crab is the graceful and beautiful Arrowhead Crab (*Stenorhynchus seticornis*) from the Caribbean. This species has a very small triangular-shaped body, and very long legs which seem out of all proportion to the size of its body. It makes a good aquarium subject but,

Left: Red Hairy Hermit Crab *Dardanus megistos*
Above: Arrowhead Crab *Stenorhynchus seticornis*
Below: Blue Lobster *Panulirus versicolor* with Feather Dusters *Sabella pavona* and Dancing Shrimp *Rhynchochinetes uritae*

Above: Anemone Crab *Neopetrolisthes* on
Purple Blanket Anemone *Discosoma*
Right: Painted Cleaner Shrimp
*Hippolystmata grabbami*, Polyp Coral *Goniopora
lobata* and Feather Duster *Sabella pavona* on
living rock

because of its rather delicate nature, it should be kept in a peaceful invertebrate community aquarium containing only other non-aggressive crustaceans and small fishes. It must also be kept apart from other specimens of its species unless a mated pair can be obtained – this applies to most other crustaceans. The Arrowhead Crab is perfectly hardy once settled in the aquarium, but is very sensitive to a change in water quality and when introducing it into the aquarium care must be taken to ensure that the changes of density and temperature occur as slowly as possible. The best way of doing this is to use the acclimatization technique described on page 48.

Another interesting species is the Anemone or Porcelain Crab (*Neopetrolisthes*) which, as its name implies, lives in symbiosis with most species of tropical anemones. It has a wide distribution and it is frequently imported from the Indian Ocean. These crabs should be kept singly unless each specimen can be given its own anemone. This is a small, dainty crab which feeds by filtering the water through its highly specialized feeding arms. It is not a scavenger in the accepted sense because it does not feed on the bottom.

Apart from the crabs knowingly introduced by the aquarist, it is possible that from time to time other crabs will appear in the aquarium;

these probably will have been introduced with the living rock and, although not particularly colourful, will nevertheless perform the valuable function of scavenging on the bottom.

Crabs vary enormously in their anatomy and many have very special adaptations to suit their individual life-style. Such a crab is the Fiddler Crab, whose one enormous pincer is almost twice the size of its body. Another is the tiny Lybia Crab which has small pincers specially adapted for carrying anemones which it waves at would-be predators.

The choice of shrimps for the invertebrate aquarium is quite wide. Whether you choose the tiny Anemone Shrimp, the large Mantis Shrimp or another species, each has its particular attraction and, like a crab, makes an excellent scavenger. The Harlequin Shrimp (*Hymenocera elegans*) is exceptional in that it will feed only on starfishes. It is a small shrimp with specialized pincers and attractive brown and pink markings on a white body. It will not accept any other food and so the aquarist wishing to keep this species will have to buy a small starfish from his dealer about once a month. The Harlequin is a fascinating little shrimp, however, and a worthwhile addition to any invertebrate community aquarium where starfishes are not to be kept.

The most popular of all the shrimps, and certainly the best choice for the beginner, is the almost cosmopolitan Banded Coral Shrimp (*Stenopus hispidus*). Attractively marked in red and white, it is extremely hardy and makes an excellent scavenger. Only one specimen should be kept in an aquarium unless a mated pair can be obtained; sexing is relatively easy, the female having a blue underside to her body. Similar to *S. hispidus*, though not as frequently imported, is the yellow Caribbean species *S. scutellatus*.

The Painted Cleaner Shrimp (*Hyppolistmata grabbami*) is another favourite. This species, as its name suggests, performs a cleaning operation on most fishes with which it comes into contact. This behaviour is similar to that of the Cleaner Wrasse (*Labroides dimidiatus*) which also removes small parasites and other microscopic organisms from the bodies and gills

Banded Coral Shrimp *Stenopus hispidus*

of other fishes. Cleaner Shrimps are beautifully marked with a large red and white stripe which runs the entire length of their almost opaque body. They are seasonal and are therefore only occasionally available to the aquarist. They can be kept together in the same aquarium in any quantity and are compatible with all other crustaceans.

The inexpensive Dancing Shrimp (*Rhynchochinetes uritae*) is a smaller shrimp with complex pink or red markings. It has a tendency to hide, however, and it is advisable to purchase three or four. Most Dancing Shrimps are imported from Sri Lanka which is the main source of many other beautiful crustaceans.

The Mantis Shrimp (*Odontodactylus scyllarus*) is a large magnificently-coloured shrimp which has razor-sharp claws and must be handled carefully. Ideally, it should be kept singly in an all-invertebrate aquarium containing only corals, but it can be successfully kept in the marine community aquarium providing the fishes are sufficiently agile. It is extremely colourful with bright green, red and orange markings, and has large fascinating rolling eyes placed at the end of stalks. It is also extremely active, continuously rearranging the aqua-rium, and burrowing and tunnelling in the sand and will provide its owner with many hours of amusement. When disturbed or annoyed, the Mantis Shrimp makes a distinctive clicking sound. It has a pair of very large, bright red forelimbs which it uses like hammers to smash the shells of molluscs.

The attractive female of the Anemone Shrimp (*Periclimenes*) is not only much larger than the male but has a much more brightly coloured body. The male has a smaller translucent body and is less colourful. This shrimp has a wide distribution around the world and is normally found living in symbiosis with tropical anemones, usually species of *Discosoma*. It is a graceful shrimp and greatly enhances the all-invertebrate aquarium where corals and just a few crustaceans are kept together.

Lobsters, or crayfish as most aquarists prefer to call them, are not so widely available but still have a place in the aquarium. By far the most popular is the Blue Lobster (*Panulirus versicolor*) which adapts well to captivity. It is common in the Indian Ocean where it is collected primarily for food, but small juvenile specimens usually find their way into aquarium shops. This lobster is beautifully coloured in shades of dark

Dancing Shrimp *Rhynchochinetes uritae*

119

Mantis Shrimp *Odontodactylus scyllarus*

cause disease. Little is known about invertebrate diseases and it is always better to be safe than sorry.

## ECHINODERMS

This less familiar group of marine invertebrates includes the starfishes (Asteroidea), urchins (Echinoidea), and sea cucumbers (Holothuroidea).

There could not be more peaceful members of any invertebrate community than starfishes. Exotically coloured, and in all shapes and sizes, they are ideal aquarium subjects. Most are very active and all make excellent scavengers, eating almost anything they contact. They can move through the aquarium at a surprising speed using their numerous pad-like feet. They have no sight, but have organs which they use for detecting smell and vibrations. All possess the remarkable feature of regeneration by which, under good conditions, they are able to regenerate almost any part of their bodies which has been damaged or lost.

Most widely available is the African Starfish (*Protoreaster linckia*) which is usually red and white, but some beautiful green ones can also be found. This species has a rather voracious appetite which together with its rather cumbersome nature makes it a subject more suitable to the marine community aquarium where it can do little damage. It must not be kept in aquariums containing trigger fishes, parrot fishes, large hermit crabs or other aggressive species, all of which would probably eat it. The Blue Starfish (*Linckia laevigata*) from Indonesia and the Red Starfish, another *Linckia* species from Sri Lanka, are also popular. These are both peaceful species and are well suited to the marine invertebrate community aquarium where they can be maintained safely alongside other peaceful invertebrates such as clams and scallops. Although very few starfishes need special diets, some algal growth in the aquarium will help to sustain a more balanced diet than scraps of food alone. The Crown of Thorns Starfish (*Acanthaster planci*), however, is an exception in that it feeds exclusively on live corals.

Urchins (Echinoidea) are all extremely hardy and deserve a place in almost any marine invertebrate display except those in which marine plants are to be cultivated seriously. Like the starfishes, they come in all

blue and pure white. Like all lobsters, it is shy and therefore will be seen rarely in the aquarium, except perhaps at feeding time when it becomes very active and moves through the aquarium with majestic grace. It is a good scavenger and in spite of its shyness, makes a worthwhile addition to the invertebrate community aquarium. It grows rapidly in captivity and some care should be taken when selecting a specimen for a particular aquarium.

Not so common, but almost as colourful, is the Red and White Lobster (*Justitia*). Small juvenile specimens of this lobster are not easy to collect and usually only large specimens, more suitable for the marine community aquarium, are available. Two other lobsters seen occasionally are the Slipper Lobster and the Red Lobster, both imported usually from Hawaii. Both species command high prices because of high freight charges from this area.

All the crustaceans mentioned, with the exception of *Hymenocera elegans*, will eat almost any food the aquarist puts in the aquarium. Pieces of cockle, mussel or prawn are particular favourites, and these should be cut into small pieces according to the size of the specimen to be fed. As with all marine foods, only foods sterilized by gamma rays should be used. This process of sterilization eliminates the possibility of introducing pathogens which, under tropical conditions, would multiply rapidly and

shapes and sizes and many have beautiful colours. Some have long thin spines, others have short fat ones; their beauty and variety is almost endless. Feeding is no problem; they are primarily algae-eaters but will readily accept most marine fish foods. They perform an efficient job of scavenging in the aquarium and are often kept to control the growth of excess algae. Always take care when handling sea urchins, particularly the long-spined varieties, as it is almost impossible to remove their spines once they are embedded into human flesh. Urchins, like other invertebrates, are sensitive to a change in water quality and so patience must be observed when moving a specimen from one aquarium to another. There is no mistaking a dying sea urchin; the spines or needles simply drop off.

The two most frequently imported species are *Diadema setosum*, which has long black needle-like spines, and a species of *Echinometra* which has shorter and thicker spines but is often more beautifully coloured. *Diadema* is mainly imported from the West Indies whereas *Echinometra* has a nearly worldwide

distribution. The Slate Pencil Urchin (*Heterocentrotus mannilatus*) is seen occasionally in aquarium shops. This beautiful urchin has unusual orange club-like spines and is almost exclusively confined to the tropical Atlantic. It is rare and expensive.

Sea cucumbers (Holothuroidea) are almost sessile and slow moving but are invariably beautifully coloured creatures. They need no special diets, though feeding is carried out in two distinct ways. Some are true filter-feeders whilst others are bottom-feeders or general scavengers. They are widely distributed, easy to collect and are shipped regularly from all over the world. Water quality must be constantly good, particularly for the filter-feeders and, as with most other invertebrates, the aquarium should be enriched regularly with marine vitamin supplements if sea cucumbers are to be maintained for any length of time. The scavenging types, which are much easier to feed, will help keep the bottom of the aquarium clean by scouring the surface of the sand in search of food. Filter-feeding sea cucumbers such as the beautiful, brightly coloured Indo-

African Starfish *Protoreaster linckia* with African Spade-tail Pipefish *Dunckerocampus*

Malayan Sea Apple (*Paracucumaria tricolor*) will usually attach themselves in an upright position either to the side of the aquarium or to a piece of rock where their feeding organs can be seen filtering the water for food particles. Small planktonic organisms are trapped in mucus on the surface of these feeding tentacles and then transferred to the mouth.

Other echinoderms which the aquarist may consider buying are the brittle stars and basket stars (Ophiuroidea) and the sea lilies (Crinoidea). Brittle stars are usually introduced with living rock and although they are good scavengers, they are totally nocturnal and are rarely seen in the aquarium. Basket stars, on the other hand, are worth consideration. They are available in many beautiful colours, but because they are extremely sensitive to environmental changes, they are only recommended for advanced aquarists and for those willing to accept a few losses and disappointments.

Below: Sea Apple *Paracucumaria tricolor* with sea fans (gorgonians) and *Caulerpa prolifera*
Right: Smooth-shelled Clam *Tridacna elongata*

## MOLLUSCS

The phylum Mollusca includes the clams, snails, scallops, sea slugs and many other soft-bodied animals of which the octopus is the most well known. In general, they are not easy to maintain, many having highly specialized feeding requirements. For example, the sea slugs or nudibranchs will quickly die in captivity if their special food is not available. However, these and many other molluscs do provide a very real challenge to the serious marine aquarist. Many are very beautiful and, once seen, the temptation to buy them will be hard to resist.

Two of the bivalves, the Smooth-shelled Clam (*Tridacna elongata*) and the Flame Scallop (*Lima scabra*) are well known to marine aquarists. The clam has no method of positive loco-motion, but the Flame Scallop is capable of rapid movement by vigor-ously opening and closing its shell. Both are filter-feeders and require their food particles in suspension. This is easily achieved by enriching the water with any of the specially prepared invertebrate foods Clams, like living corals, require good lighting if they are to maintain their zoo-xanthellae and keep healthy. Some, usually imported from Indonesia, have exceptionally brightly coloured ma-ntles which are almost metallic in appearance.

Very much easier to maintain are the snails and cowries. Most are predominantly algae eaters and the only food usually required will be a good growth of algae in the aquarium. The Tiger Cowrie (*Cypraea tigris*) is the best known of all cowries, and being very hardy adapts well to the aquarium. The shells of this species are attractively marked and are sold to the shell collecting trade in vast numbers. A particularly large specimen, however, can be a rather clumsy aquarium occupant and an invertebrate display can be spoilt very quickly as this cowrie bulldozes its way across the rocks in search of algae.

Sea slugs, or nudibranchs, are found on almost every coral reef in the world. Their feeding habits are so specialized that they will not usually accept food other than the various types of algae which occur in their own natural habitat. One species the aquarist will be tempted to buy is the beautiful and exotic Swimming Slug (*Hexabranchus adamsi*). This gorgeously coloured red and white beauty from the Indo-Malayan region glides through the water with un-believable grace, but it has highly specialized feeding requirements and will survive only a few days in the home aquarium.

Another mollusc which super-ficially resembles nudibranchs is the Sea Hare (*Aplysia wilcoxii*). This is a hardy animal and is common in the Caribbean. It is not brightly coloured but will thrive in aquariums where there is a rich growth of green algae.

Left: Tiger Cowrie *Cypraea tigris*
Right: Sea Slug *Casella atromarginata*

# Compatibility

When planning any invertebrate display, especially one which is to include fishes, always ensure that the specimens have been fully quarantined and that they are compatible with all other members of the proposed community. Some species can be over-aggressive and some may be the natural predators of others you may think of introducing. The specialized feeding requirements of some species also may restrict the selection of other invertebrates which may be kept with them. The following lists may be useful as a general guide when planning a community:

Flame Scallop *Lima scabra* with Atlantic Anemone *Condylactis*

| Invertebrates which must not be kept together | Fishes which can be kept with an invertebrate community (small specimens are to be preferred) | Invertebrates which can be kept with a community of large fishes (except aggressive species such as triggerfishes and parrotfishes) |
|---|---|---|
| large starfishes with bivalve molluscs | Clown Parrotfishes | large anemones |
| starfishes with Harlequin Shrimps | Regal Tangs | large hermit crabs |
| Mantis Shrimps or large hermit crabs with anything they can catch | Royal Grammas | lobsters |
| *Cerianthus* anemones with anything stationary they can touch | Pearly Jawfishes | Mantis Shrimps |
| Flamingo-tongue Cowries with gorgonians or soft corals | Longnose Filefishes | snails |
| snails with scallops | clownfishes | cowries |
| snails with clams or cowries | pipefishes | large starfishes |
|  | seahorses | large urchins |
|  | boxfishes and cowfishes |  |
|  | most blennies |  |
|  | most gobies |  |
|  | dwarf and juvenile angels |  |
|  | dwarf and juvenile wrasses |  |
|  | dwarf groupers *(Anthias* and *Mirolabrichthys)* |  |
|  | some damsels *(Abudefduf* and *Chromis)* |  |
|  | some dottybacks *(Pseudochromis)* |  |

# Disease

Although very little is known about diseases of invertebrates, there is always the possibility that a fish in the invertebrate community aquarium will become diseased. If this should happen, then it is advisable to consult your dealer who may be able to inform you of the most effective cure. At present, many medications for marine fishes are copper-based, and as copper is lethal to most invertebrates, these medications must not be put in the invertebrate aquarium. Some aquarists have had limited success with the chemical malachite green for the treatment of white spot on fishes in the invertebrate aquarium, and there is also a proprietary cure on the market which the makers claim to be effective against *Oodinium*, another common fish disease agent. The best cure must always be prevention by good management, careful feeding, sensible stocking and by quarantining all new fishes.

# Marine Plants

It is something of an anomaly to discuss plants for the marine aquarium in a chapter devoted to invertebrates. Nevertheless, they are best mentioned here as it is only in the invertebrate tank that they are safe from the many herbivorous fishes which are commonly kept. Marine plants in an aquarium containing surgeon fishes, for example, would soon be eaten. Seaweeds are so attractive and so much a part of the invertebrate world that their cultivation in an invertebrate aquarium is particularly worthwhile.

Freshwater aquarists will be quick to point out that one of the major disadvantages of keeping marines is the relative lack of plants which are available. Though this is substantially true, marine aquarists can take some comfort from the fact that there are nevertheless many beautiful algae which can be cultivated. The addition of any green plant to the invertebrate display is a welcome one, as it provides a restful colour to offset the almost endless display of exotic colours so often displayed in the marine aquarium. Green plants can also benefit the system by providing a food supply to many of the other inhabitants of the tank; care should be taken to prevent over-grazing, however, and algae eaters with excessive appetites, such as sea urchins, should not be kept in an aquarium where plant cultivation is taken seriously.

The best and most popular species of alga is *Caulerpa prolifera*. This is a bright green seaweed with long narrow oval leaves. Like other algae, it does not have a true root system, but has small clasp-like hair structures which it uses for attachment. Under good conditions, it will grow rapidly and spread throughout the aquarium, growing on the sand, rocks and even on some of the invertebrates themselves such as the stationary live corals. It thrives in a well-lit aquarium. Unlike all other marine life, it does not respond well to a partial water change and is sensitive to any change in water quality. Although this will produce only a temporary check to growth, the plant will often show its displeasure by producing a batch of small stunted fronds.

There are also other forms of *Caulerpa* which the aquarist may wish to attempt to cultivate. Some have frond structures similar to those of *C. prolifera*; others in complete contrast have grape-like frond structures. These strains normally require a high degree of lighting and the addition of marine plant fertilizers if growth is to be sustained in the aquarium. Algae and other plants not directly introduced by the aquarist may also flourish in the invertebrate aquarium if good conditions are maintained.

Not all algae are green; many are bright red or purple. Small pieces of colourful marine rock known as 'algae rock', which after many years in the sea have become heavily encrusted with many different species of algae, are occasionally imported from Singapore. This can serve as useful base material for displaying live corals, keeping them above the sand or filter bed and preventing damage to any basal polyps.

---

Invertebrates offer a new and exciting field to the marine aquarist. Many of the available species have intriguing life-styles, most are colourful and few are difficult to keep. Together with marine plants, they bring a different dimension to the aquarium. Try them – you will be delighted.

Flamingo-tongue Cowries *Cyphoma* and green Ruffled Nudibranchs *Tridachia* graze on *Caulerpa ashmeadii*

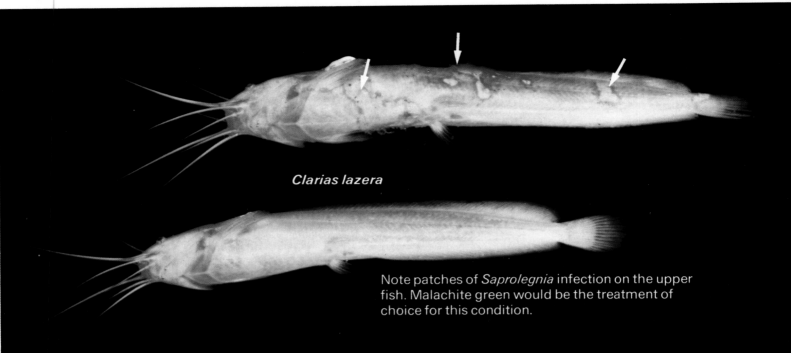

*Clarias lazera*

Note patches of *Saprolegnia* infection on the upper fish. Malachite green would be the treatment of choice for this condition.

A genetic deformation in the upper fish has resulted in malformation of the ventral musculature. Some physical injuries which heal successfully can give an appearance which resembles this condition.

Dwarf Gourami *Colisa lalia*

Cardinal Tetra
*Cheirodon axelrodi*

The large cyst on the side of the lower fish is caused by infection with *Clinostomum*. For successful treatment it may be necessary to remove the parasite surgically.

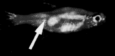

Opaline Gourami
*Trichogaster trichopterus sumatranus*

The upper fish shows a large ulcerated patch with epidermis and scale loss as a result of *Aeromonas hydrophila* infection. Antibiotics should effect a cure.

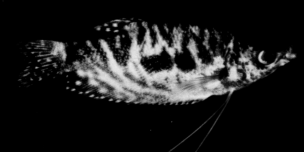

# Health

Fish disease and its diagnosis is a subject still in its infancy, but with careful observation and detailed post-mortem examination many of the commoner diseases can be identified and subsequently cured in any remaining infected fishes.

Prevention is always better than cure and the use of quarantine, disinfection, adequate diet and good fish husbandry all help to reduce the incidence of disease. The latter factor and especially the maintenance of good quality water is probably the single most important consideration in disease avoidance. Constant temperature should be maintained, usually between 65°F and 85°F (18°C and 29°C). The pH level should also be carefully regulated. This is an expression of the hydrogen ion concentration of the water–a measure of its acidity or alkalinity–neutrality being pH 7.0, with lower values denoting acidity and higher ones alkalinity; pH is usually established at 6.5 to 7.0 for freshwater fishes and 8.0 to 8.3 for marine fishes, but individual species variations do occur. Toxic waste products such as ammonia and nitrite can be reduced to an acceptable level by maintaining very low fish density and adequate plant life, or can be removed by filtration. In marine aquariums, some form of filtration is essential. Nitrite level is commonly used as an indicator of filtration efficiency; levels of up to 10 parts per million (ppm) may be tolerated by freshwater fishes but 1 ppm usually proves fatal to marine fishes.

Fishes in the wild are usually at a very low density compared with those in aquariums and water conditions are usually fairly constant–this is especially true in marine fishes. Sudden changes in water quality often have drastic effects on fish populations. Similarly, fishes in the wild often harbour parasites but these are usually in balance with their hosts and cause no great damage. The overcrowding of fishes in poor quality water often leads to population explosions amongst any parasites present, frequently with fatal results to the fishes. It is very difficult to give any hard and fast rule on fish density, but it is generally considered that the area of water surface required by an inch-long tropical freshwater fish is about twelve square inches (77 square cm); but filtration, temperature and species affect this figure. Marine fishes generally require at least twice this space.

Many problems arise soon after purchase of new fishes. Such fishes have often been through several dealers' hands (literally) and been subject to wide fluctuations in temperature and water quality. Handling a fish is itself very damaging. The epidermis, or outer layer, of fish skin is very delicate, often only a few cells thick, and it is this layer which acts as an osmotic barrier. The scales are embedded in the deeper layers of the dermis and if scales are removed, extensive, deep skin loss has taken place. At the very least, this causes a disturbance in osmotic balance and stresses the fish considerably. Secondary to

Examples of disease in freshwater tropical fishes. In each case the affected fish is shown with a normal healthy specimen for comparison

this effect, death may rapidly ensue or secondary infection of the skin wound may occur.

The gills of fishes are responsible for efficient gas exchange, both for the entry of oxygen and the removal of waste products such as carbon dioxide and ammonia. Such gas exchange is dependent on the presence of a very short distance, usually only the diameter of a single cell, between the gill blood-vessel and the surrounding water. This distance is increased by the excess mucus production which often results from irritation caused by parasites or some physical agent. In more chronic conditions a proliferation and overgrowth of the epithelia lining the gills occurs and such areas of gill are often functionless because of the increase of distance over which gas must travel. The thin epithelial cell layer may also be quickly eroded by browsing and sedentary parasites, resulting in gill sloughing and haemorrhage.

Certain diseases are very easily diagnosed, especially those caused by the larger parasites. Other diseases, such as fish tuberculosis and gill fluke infestation, though very common, are seldom diagnosed by the aquarist. A consideration of the history of any particular disease followed by a detailed post-mortem examination, as described in the following pages, should enable the aquarist to diagnose successfully a much greater percentage of fish diseases. Although a range of treatments is available, it should always be borne in mind that destruction of the stock may be the only effective remedy in some cases.

## Disease Recognition and Examination

Before any therapy is undertaken for a fish disease, it is obviously essential first to recognize that a problem is present and then to establish the nature and severity of the condition. Recognition of disease depends essentially upon frequent observation of the fishes; if this does not occur then the most frequent sign of disease is death, at which time the condition may have affected the surviving fishes to such an extent that treatment becomes impossible.

Many of the signs of disease are apparent only to the experienced fish-keeper and in order to diagnose disease in a colleague's aquarium, a series of questions needs to be asked. Such a 'history-taking' is the basis of disease diagnosis in any animal species and it is worth considering the important points at this stage, even if ultimately one only asks oneself the questions. A consideration of the history of previous diseases in the aquarium is obviously important as there may be a lingering disease which, when previously treated, was only partially cured. Previous treatment should also be noted as fishes may well die as a result of over-treatment with a variety of compounds. Any new fish or plant introductions should be considered as these may introduce a variety of diseases, although with new fishes, disease may occur only in the new stock. This could arise from drastic changes in water conditions, aggression from existing fishes, or simply because the new fishes are contracting a pathogen to which they have developed no resistance. Feeding should be examined, as a well-balanced diet is essential not only to prevent nutritional deficiencies or excesses, but also to bring fishes into condition so that they are better able to withstand the ravages of any other disease. If live food is used, the possibility of the introduction of parasites or bacterial disease should also be considered.

Monitoring of water quality parameters such as temperature, pH, nitrite level and specific gravity (in marine aquariums) should always be carried out. A sudden temperature fall, for instance, may cause extensive losses or the development of a secondary condition such as white spot disease. Aeration and filtration should also be checked—overloading of filtration units may lead to massive bacterial death within the filters and a rapid build up of toxic products, from the dead bacteria or from the fishes themselves—a rise in nitrite level is usually a good indication that this is occurring. The water supply itself should be

checked to determine whether there is copper contamination, or chlorine pollution resulting from the use of chlorinated water when topping up. The numbers and species of fishes affected should be determined. If only one fish is affected, then water quality or infectious disease problems are not so likely and the possibility of non-infectious disease, such as tumour formation, or even ageing should be considered. It must be remembered in this context that many tropical fishes have a life-span of approximately three years. If only one species of fish is affected, than specific infectious disease or specific requirements in water quality may be a distinct possibility. Plistophoriasis (Neon Tetra disease), although affecting several other species of fishes, does principally affect the Neon Tetra and in a tropical freshwater community tank other fishes may not show any signs of disease. The Cardinal Tetra is also found in the wild in soft-water areas of low pH and if recently imported may suffer from massive changes in hardness and pH.

*Visible signs of disease or stress*

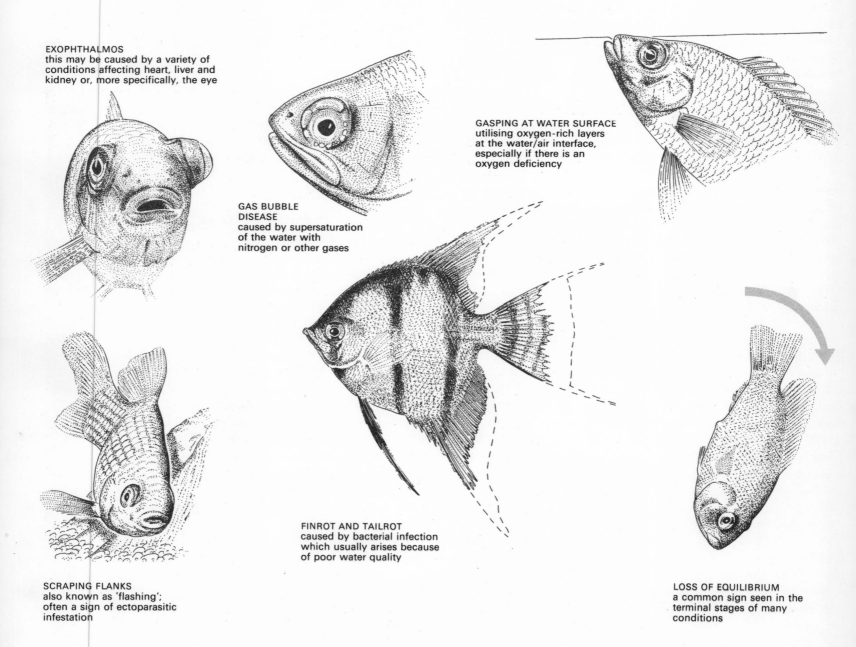

EXOPHTHALMOS
this may be caused by a variety of conditions affecting heart, liver and kidney or, more specifically, the eye

GAS BUBBLE DISEASE
caused by supersaturation of the water with nitrogen or other gases

GASPING AT WATER SURFACE
utilising oxygen-rich layers at the water/air interface, especially if there is an oxygen deficiency

FINROT AND TAILROT
caused by bacterial infection which usually arises because of poor water quality

SCRAPING FLANKS
also known as 'flashing'; often a sign of ectoparasitic infestation

LOSS OF EQUILIBRIUM
a common sign seen in the terminal stages of many conditions

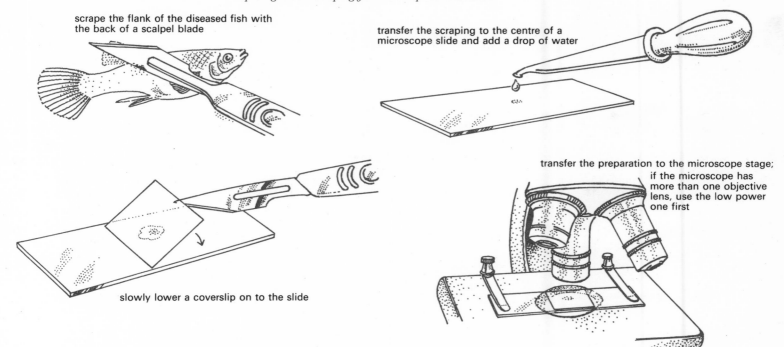

scrape the flank of the diseased fish with the back of a scalpel blade

transfer the scraping to the centre of a microscope slide and add a drop of water

slowly lower a coverslip on to the slide

transfer the preparation to the microscope stage; if the microscope has more than one objective lens, use the low power one first

Once such general points have been considered, behavioural changes in the affected fishes should be noted. Many of these are non-specific, and may include lack of appetite, swimming abnormalities, lack of coloration, or loss of equilibrium. Unfortunately, almost all fish diseases may present such signs and there are few specific signs. Scraping along stones and rocks or flicking of the fins are generally signs of irritation often brought about by parasitic infestation. Oxygen deficiency whether caused by poor water quality, overtreatment, parasitic infection, or any other cause is usually indicated by an increased respiratory rate which, for most species, is normally 60 to 90 gill beats per minute but can rise to 300 per minute in a heavily infected fish. Affected fishes are often slow-moving and move about at the surface of the aquarium as if gasping for air. This is especially noticeable in aquariums in which no aeration and filtration are used and there is consequently little water movement. In such cases oxygen-rich layers are present in surface water and the fishes gather in such areas.

Many common 'beginner's problems' are seldom found in aquariums belonging to experienced aquarists. Newcomers to the hobby often fill an aquarium with tap water and stock it with fishes and plants on the same day so that chlorine poisoning is common. Overstocking often occurs and overfeeding is probably the commonest cause of death through water pollution. Parasitic diseases are common as quarantine procedures are seldom followed and water quality is often poor, allowing a secondary build up of parasites in fishes already weakened by gill and skin damage.

Careful consideration of the above factors will often give a reasonable idea as to whether the problem is a result of poor husbandry and water quality or the result of an infectious disease. If the cause of disease is not apparent at this stage then sacrifice of fishes for postmortem examination must be carried out. If skin parasitism is suspected then it may be possible to anaesthetize larger fishes in order to remove a skin scraping for microscopic examination. A variety of anaesthetics may be used, the most readily available probably being MS222 (tricaine

methane sulphonate—Sandoz pharmaceuticals) at a dose-rate of 2.2 to 13.2 mg/litre (10 to 60 mg/gallon). However, considerable damage is often incurred, and it is usually preferable to kill the fish.

The external surfaces of the fish (preferably alive) should first be examined *in water*. If only dead fishes are available, the examination in water still shows up many lesions not immediately obvious in air. The first response of the skin to any irritant, whether physical or parasitic is usually an increased production of mucus, and this is seen as a grey-blue film over the body surface. Ragged fins may be a sign of aggression from other fishes or a result of parasitic disease or bacterial fin-rot. Ulcers may result from physical trauma, bacterial infection or from a variety of internal diseases. Cysts or swellings in the skin may be caused by parasitic, bacterial, fungal or viral lesions. Ichthyophthiriasis, probably the commonest freshwater disease caused by a parasite, results in the formation of white spots on the skin approximately 0.5 to 1 mm in diameter. These spots arise from proliferation of the epidermis over the parasite which feeds and grows in this area of the skin. The marine counterpart of this parasite, *Cryptokaryon*, produces spots which are slightly smaller. Areas of fungal infection can be seen as greyish-white tufts resembling cotton wool, and many of the larger parasites, such as *Lernaea*, *Argulus*, and leeches are easily seen with the aid of a hand lens.

The smaller protozoan parasites are visible only with a microscope using magnifications between x100 and x400. The majority of inexpensive instruments are quite sufficient for the purpose of examining skin smears. Such smears are taken following anaesthetization or killing of the fish by decapitation after removing it from the water. The back of a scalpel blade or some similar instrument is then drawn across the skin surface, removing a layer of mucus and surface skin cells. This is then smeared onto a microscope slide, a drop of water is added and the smear covered with a cover-glass. The skin surface should not be allowed to dry during post-mortem examination. Examination with the microscope may then reveal one of the skin parsites discussed in the next section.

Examination of the eyes may reveal the absence of an eye, usually either hereditary or through some disease process or trauma causing expulsion of the contents of the orbit. Endophthalmos, or decrease in the volume of the eye occurs infrequently, but exophthalmos or 'pop-eye' is quite common. This condition is only another sign of disease and is not in itself a specific disease; it may be caused by liver, kidney or heart damage, or by specific bacterial, fungal or parasitic disease of the eye. Dissection of the eye to remove the lens and subsequent squashing of the lens for microscopic examination may reveal the presence of trematodes (flatworms), especially in recently imported fishes. Spinal deformities should be noted at this stage.

The gills should then be examined for general colouration, discoloured particles or swellings, haemorrhage, fungal infection and the larger parasites. A scraping should be taken and examined microscopically as for the skin; a small piece of gill tissue should be dissected out, squashed between a microscope slide and a cover-slip in a drop or two of water and examined for the presence of parasites. Telangiectasis, a condition in which gill cells lining blood vessels break down, allows the development of large 'blisters' of circulatory blood cells. These are very obvious under the microscope and may result from chlorine, ammonia or copper poisoning, or from parasitic infections. Heavy parasitic infections of skin and gill are often a consequence of poor water quality and this should always be ckecked.

Attention should then be given to the internal organs. Any swelling of the abdomen, or conversely emaciation, should be noted and the abdominal contents then exposed by making a mid-ventral incision from the vent to the insertion of the pectoral fins. Removal of part of the body wall may be necessary to further expose the abdominal contents. Examination may then reveal fluid or adhesions within the cavity, haemorrhages, swellings or spots within organs, parasites or inflammation of the intestine or other organs. Smears of intestinal contents may reveal the presence of protozoans such as *Octomitus*, a common parasite in cichlid fishes, roundworms or (nematodes) and tapeworms (cestodes) may be found. Emaciation is a common sign of fish tuberculosis, worm infections, and *Octomitus* infection. Dropsy or abdominal enlargement, with the presence of abdominal fluid, may be a result of a variety of conditions affecting heart, liver or kidney, or may be an indication of a specific viral or bacterial condition.

Swellings present throughout internal organs and musculature are often suggestive of either fish tuberculosis or *Ichthyophonus* infection and are usually 'granulomata', the result of a chronic inflammatory reaction. Other bacterial or fungal causes may be present and parasitic cysts may be found. If the condition is not parasitic, it is often extremely difficult to diagnose the cause of an internal disease. In such cases, material may be sent to a specialist laboratory. For this purpose, small pieces of each organ should be dissected out and placed in 10 per cent formalin (=40 per cent formaldehyde, available from any chemist) and carefully packed and sent off, together with a detailed history of the problem. An affected live fish should be killed for this purpose as a partially decomposed fish is not suitable for histological examination

# Agents of Fish Disease

The living agents of disease in fishes vary widely in size and shape and represent many different groups of the animal and plant kingdoms. Fungi, viruses and bacteria cause diseases about which very little is known and the Protozoa (single-celled animals) probably cause more severe problems than any other group. The Platyhelminthes or flatworms are flat and leaf-like and include the skin and gill flukes which are troublesome pests in aquariums. Nematodes or roundworms are less often seen because they usually inhabit the internal organs, though not in large numbers. Annelids (segmented worms) are represented only by the leech, which though less often seen in aquariums, is very common in the natural habitat of fishes. Crustacean parasites, closely related to the free-living *Cyclops* and *Daphnia*, can cause damage, often because of their relatively large size.

Most of the parasites have relatives which are free-living in the aquatic environment and which never become parasitic. Fungi, bacteria, protozoans and nematodes abound in the bottom of an aquarium tank where waste food and debris collect. A little of this material examined under the microscope will reveal enormous numbers of these organisms which help to break down the decomposing matter by feeding upon it and are therefore essential to the recycling process. It is important, therefore, to be able to distinguish between organisms which are a danger to the fishes and those which live in association with them and help to maintain normal water quality.

Parasitic organisms are usually divided into two major groups, the ectoparasites (external parasites) and the endoparasites (internal parasites), but this division is not always clear cut and those called mesoparasites can be external as well as internal. The ectoparasites of fishes are the most serious pathogens and can occur over the whole body surface including the skin, fins and gills.

### ECTOPARASITES OF THE SKIN AND FINS
Although many species of fungi are pathogenic to fishes, these usually belong to the genera *Saprolegnia* and *Achlya*. They can be recognized as white or grey epidermal patches resembling cotton wool which often grow in wounds caused by handling or fighting and prevent the natural healing of the skin. Once entry has been made, fungi and bacteria can cause ulcers which may result in death if not treated. Bacteria are involved in the gradual erosion of the fins and tails of fishes living in poor environments, giving rise to the conditions known as fin rot and tail rot.

Viruses can cause tumour conditions of the skin such as Lymphocystis. This is especially common in marine fishes and appears as a wart-like or cauliflower-like growth on the skin and fins. It develops over a long period and rarely causes death but the growths are unsightly.

Relatively few species of Protozoa are parasitic on the skins of fishes, but those which are cause serious problems. Small numbers of protozoans on the skin are not harmful but in large numbers the effect is devastating. Death follows in a short time as a result of skin damage. Three types of protozoans are important pathogens in fishes; flagellates, ciliates and sporozoans. Flagellates consist of a single cell bearing long hair-like structures (flagellae) which are used for feeding and locomotion. Ciliates have large numbers of short flagellae called cilia, arranged in patterns over the surface of the cell. Sporozoans have a complex life-cycle and produce many very small, resistant spores which spread the infection.

The flagellates create a serious problem in both freshwater and marine aquariums. *Amylodinium* and *Oodinium* are oval or pear-shaped cells measuring up to 150 microns (1 micron = 0.001 mm) in length which attach themselves to and feed on skin cells. *Amylodinium* is common in marine tropical aquariums where it is known as coral fish disease and is often fatal. *Oodinium* has brownish-yellow granules inside the cytoplasm of the cell and is common in freshwater tropical aquariums. A heavy infection on the flanks of the fish can be seen as a red-brown sheen under bright light, giving rise to the names velvet, rust or gold dust disease.

A flagellate of great importance is *Ichthyobodo necator*, commonly known as *Costia*. This is a pest frequently encountered in freshwater where it survives within the wide temperature range of 36 to 86°F (2 to 3°C). It has a free living stage which is kidney-shaped and bears two pairs of flagellae. It attaches itself to the skin cells and may feed from them directly by penetrating the cell wall; this attached form is more pear-shaped. *Costia* is very small, about the size of a red blood cell (10 to 15 microns), and can only be seen under the microscope. It is very irritating to the fish, causing it to produce an excess of mucus; grey, slimy patches on the head and flanks may be the only signs of this disease prior to death of the fish. The cell can multiply very rapidly by simply dividing into two parts so that heavy infestations occur in a short time resulting in rapid death. Young and weak fishes of any species are particularly susceptible.

Perhaps the most important of all protozoan parasites of fishes is the ciliate *Ichthyophthirius multifiliis*; indeed it is considered by many aquarists to be the single most important parasite of all freshwater fishes. It is certainly very common and is known variously as ich, white spot or itch. The last name is very appropriate since it causes severe irritation of the skin. Most aquarists will recognize this parasite by the white spots about the size of a pin-head, which appear in the skin of infected fishes. This is the feeding form or trophont, embedded in the epidermis and feeding on the debris of damaged cells. In this situation it grows to nearly a millimetre in diameter and, if observed under a microscope, can be seen to be spherical in shape with a characteristic horseshoe-shaped nucleus. Its surface is covered with short hairs (cilia) which are continually beating and causing the cell to rotate. When it is mature, it escapes to the outside by rupturing the overlying skin. The wound which remains may become infected by bacteria and fungi, and large numbers of trophonts escaping at about the same time may cause the fish to lose control of its salt/water balance. The now free-swimming trophont drops to the bottom of the tank or pond and becomes a cyst in which the cell contents divide into smaller cells. When division is complete, the cyst bursts to release up to 2,000 of these oval, ciliated cells, now called tomites, which swarm in the water in search of a fish. The length of time taken for this cycle to be completed depends on temperature, and is shorter at higher temperatures. A very similar parasite, *Cryptokaryon irritans*, occurs in seawater and causes similar problems in marine aquaria.

*Chilodonella* is a ciliate 50 to 70 microns long which feeds on skin cells and cellular debris but does not become attached to the skin of the fish. It browses over the skin

*The life cycle of* Ichthyophthirius multifiliis, *the causative organism of white-spot or 'itch'*

the mature trophont escapes from the skin of the fish

the cyst bursts, releasing the tomites, which swim in the water until they contact a new fish host

the trophont eventually settles on the bottom where it encysts; its contents divide many times to produce the infective stage – the tomites

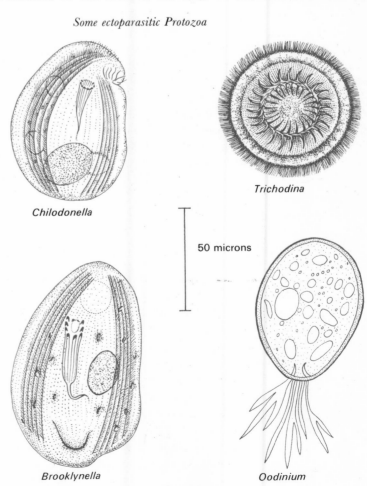

Some ectoparasitic Protozoa

Trichodina

Chilodonella

50 microns

Brooklynella

Oodinium

surface, wafting food into its mouth using the short cilia arranged in rows over the whole cell surface. The mouth is very distinctive and is the key to identifying this ciliate. The channel carrying food from the mouth is supported by a ring of long stiff hairs, sometimes described as a basket. It is very small and, unlike that of *Ichthyophthirius*, its body is flat and leaf-like. A very similar ciliate thrives in seawater and is called *Brooklynella*. Both *Chilodonella* and *Brooklynella* divide simply and tend to infect the weaker debilitated fishes.

One of the most beautiful ciliates, *Trichodina*, is a parasite of both freshwater and marine fishes. Unlike the ciliates so far described, it has very elaborate cilia which are modified for attachment to surfaces. These modified cilia or denticles form a characteristic ring 10 to 100 microns in diameter on the flattened surface opposite the mouth. This flattened surface gives the organism a hat-shaped appearance when viewed from the side. The view most commonly observed in skin or gill scrapings under the microscope is of the flattened surface. Rings of long cilia cause the cell to spin like a tiny catherine wheel as it browses over the skin surface, feeding on the cells and cell debris. It frequently attaches itself using the ring of denticles as a sucker. This is very damaging to the fish skin and causes large areas of erosion, making way for bacteria and fungi. These are generally visible as grey slimy patches often on the head or back. Two other ciliates, *Tripartiella* and *Trichodinella*, are so similar to *Trichodina* that only specialists can tell them apart. They are, therefore, referred to collectively as the *Trichodina* complex. Trichodinids, *Chilodonella* and *Brooklynella*, may be found occasionally in small numbers on healthy fishes but multiply rapidly on a debilitated fish, eventually causing death.

A group of sporozoans, the Myxosporidia, reproduce by means of small oval spores which can be found in various tissues and organs. A number of species infect the skin and can be seen as small white cysts. *Myxobolus squamosus*, for example, reproduces in epithelial cells and is visible as patchy white spots. There is no treatment for this condition and the life-cycles of the parasites are little known. However, they rarely cause mortalities.

Only one group of flatworms are ectoparasitic on fishes and these are the skin and gill flukes which belong to the class Monogenea. These are so-called because they have a simple life-history, usually involving one host. They are small slender worms with a characteristic attachment organ (the holdfast or haptor) at the posterior end of the body. The group of flukes most commonly seen on aquarium fishes has a haptor armed with one or two pairs of large anchors and 12 to 16 smaller hooks and suckers round the edge. Although this apparatus is used for attachment, the worm is able to move about the body surface of the fish in a leech-like manner, alternately gripping and releasing with the haptor and the anterior attachment organ which produces a sticky secretion. Severe damage is inflicted by the hooks and secretions during these migrations and secondary invaders can exacerbate the condition. Monogeneans feed on skin cells, mucus and blood. In heavy infections there is skin erosion, excess mucus production and small haemorrhagic spots. There are two families of Monogenea which are very common on a wide range of tropical marine and

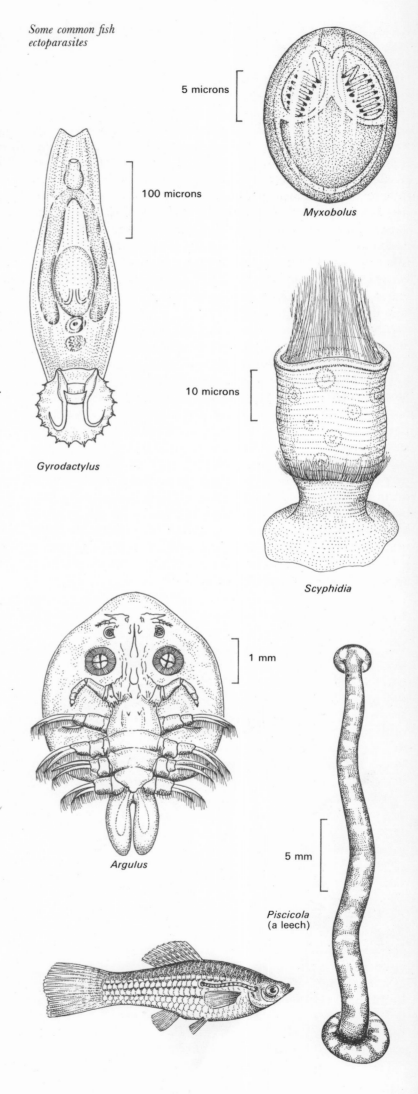

*Some common fish ectoparasites*

5 microns

100 microns

*Myxobolus*

*Gyrodactylus*

10 microns

*Scyphidia*

1 mm

*Argulus*

5 mm

*Piscicola* (a leech)

freshwater fishes. The gyrodactylids are readily distinguished because they are viviparous and an embryo can be seen in the large uterus in the central region of the body. Sometimes an embryo can be seen within the body of the larger embryo, each embryo armed with a set of embryonic hooks. This curious biological phenomenon is called scatulation. The other major family is the Dactylogyridae whose members are very similar in many respects to the Gyrodactylidae but are, instead, oviparous. The eggs hatch out into small larvae which search out a new host fish. Monogenea are dangerous in aquariums because they can reproduce rapidly, particularly the gyrodactylids, and numbers soon build up to epizootic proportions if they are not eradicated. They are not easily seen with the naked eye but, with a hand lens, they appear as small attached threads waving about vigorously.

The only parasitic segmented worms (Annelida) are the leeches which range in size from a few millimetres to the large medicinal leeches famous for their human blood sucking capacity. All leeches feed on blood by secreting substances which prevent the blood from clotting. Large numbers feeding on a fish can cause severe anaemia and wounds which will become secondarily infected. These worms are not common in aquariums but fishes may be attacked by leeches in ponds used as holding facilities prior to importation. They may also be introduced into the aquarium on plants to which they attach themselves between blood meals. Periodically a leech will leave the vegetation, secure itself to a fish using either the posterior or anterior sucker, feed and then drop off. Leeches are also known to be responsible for transmitting blood parasites and other infections from one fish to another.

The largest of the parasites of fishes are the Crustacea and these can usually be seen with the naked eye. The commonest skin-infesting crustacean is *Argulus*, the fish louse. This is up to 1 cm long, dorso-ventrally flattened and can cling to the fish using its attachment organs, which end in curved hooks, and a pair of suckers. When not attached, it moves about the surface of the fish and can move freely from fish to fish using its four pairs of swimming legs. *Argulus* feeds on the skin and underlying tissues using a suctorial proboscis bearing a sharp stylet with which it repeatedly pierces the flesh. This feeding action causes considerable damage to the fish, as do the hooks and suckers which are used for attachment. *Argulus* is particularly damaging to small fishes because the stylet can penetrate deeper into the flesh. The lice are easily removed from the fish and are rarely found in aquariums. However, they are common in holding ponds and may be introduced into tanks with live food. Plants may also act as vectors since *Argulus* lays batches of eggs which it attaches to plants or submerged objects.

## ECTOPARASITES OF THE GILLS

All of the parasitic species which infest the skin of the fish can also be found on the gills. However, there are often close relatives, some of which prefer skin and others prefer gills. This is particularly true of the monogenean flukes; there are even cases described where different species prefer different sites even on the same gill, so that each species has its own particular niche. Some parasites are specific to gills such as the fungus *Branchiomyces* which causes gill rot by penetrating and blocking the blood vessels of the gills, often resulting in rapid death of the fish.

Cysts containing spores of sporozoans are occasionally seen in gills of aquarium fishes but these are rarely in such large numbers as to impair the function of the gill. They are noticeable as swollen, yellow/white spheres or nodules which, when burst open, release hundreds of small, round or oval spores. The most important are those of the genus *Myxobolus*. Little is known about the life-history but, in some species, vegetative stages have been found in other tissues of the body. A related sporozoan, *Nosema*, lives within the skin or gill cells and causes great enlargement of the infected cells. Different species occur in both freshwater and marine aquariums but rarely cause problems unless the infection is very heavy.

All the other protozoan flagellates and ciliates previously described are found on gills. A number of ciliates are ectocommensals on fishes but can cause problems in aquariums in certain circumstances. They are not parasites because they do not feed from fish tissues, but take in bacteria and tiny particles of matter which are always present in water. The food material is wafted into the mouth by a spiral arrangement of cilia at their anterior end. They are sessile and are attached to the substrate by a flattened disc at the posterior of the body. There are a number of species varying in shape and size, the commonest being *Scyphidia*. Some are stalked but the bodies are so similar that they are called the *Scyphidia* complex. In an unnatural environment such as an aquarium, they can build up into large numbers and use the fish skin and gills as a substrate. This can happen if organic matter is allowed to accumulate and bacteria are able to multiply freely. Large numbers build up on the gills and interfere with the gas transport across the gill surface. Such fishes are severely distressed and may die from lack of oxygen. They are also commonly found around the edges of skin ulcers where they feed on the masses of bacteria infecting the ulcer and may delay wound healing. A similar stress is put on fishes by a suctorial protozoan, *Trichophyra*, which clings to the fish gills and occasionally puts out stalked suckers with which it removes food material from the water.

## MESOPARASITES

The Anchor Worm, *Lernaea*, is a very common parasite of warm water fishes, on which it spends the early part of its life as an ectoparasite but, on becoming an adult, bores its way into the skin and underlying tissues where it becomes firmly anchored for the rest of its life. *Lernaea* is a crustacean, but only the young larvae or copepodids look like crustacea, having the appearance of *Cyclops* the well-known freshwater copepod. The larvae undergo several moults before attaining maturity. After fertilizing the female, the male dies and the female attaches itself permanently to the host, penetrating into the flesh, sometimes as far as the liver and other internal organs. The embedded head then grows branched structures which act as an anchor. *Lernaea* loses all its crustacean features as it develops and all that is recognizable is a worm-like body protruding from the fish with a pair of egg sacs trailing free in the water. The movements and the feeding of the parasites cause a large unsightly ulcer to form which is often invaded by secondary pathogens. The fish also loses condition quickly as a result of the

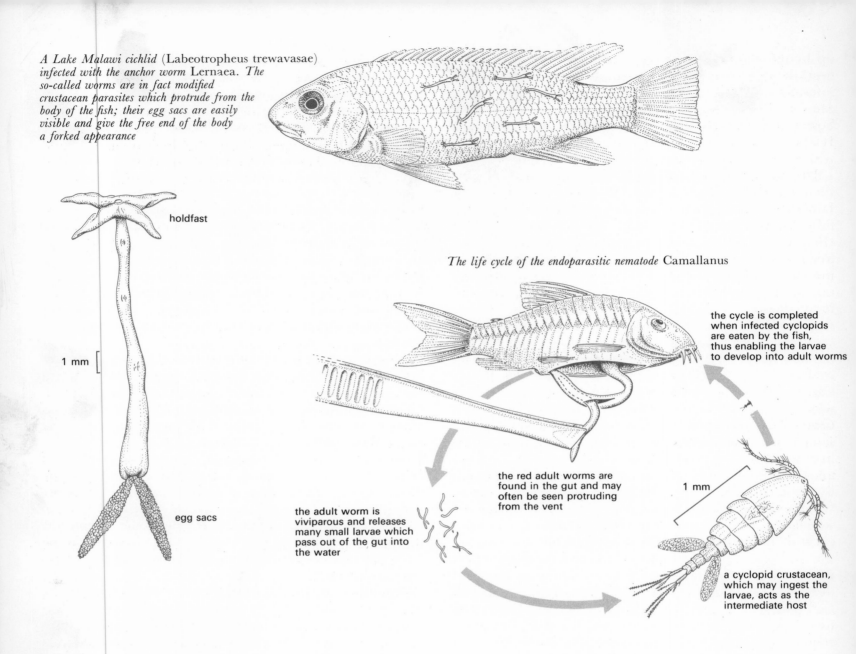

A Lake Malawi cichlid (Labeotropheus trewavasae) infected with the anchor worm Lernaea. The so-called worms are in fact modified crustacean parasites which protrude from the body of the fish; their egg sacs are easily visible and give the free end of the body a forked appearance

holdfast

1 mm

egg sacs

The life cycle of the endoparasitic nematode Camallanus

the cycle is completed when infected cyclopids are eaten by the fish, thus enabling the larvae to develop into adult worms

the red adult worms are found in the gut and may often be seen protruding from the vent

the adult worm is viviparous and releases many small larvae which pass out of the gut into the water

1 mm

a cyclopid crustacean, which may ingest the larvae, acts as the intermediate host

feeding activities of the parasite and only a few of these *Lernaea* on a fish can be fatal. The eggs hatch and hundreds of tiny, free-swimming forms (nauplii) are released which search out new hosts and large numbers can build up in this way in a closed system. Marine forms do exist but they are not common.

A completely unrelated parasite lives in a similar situation but its behaviour and life-history are quite different. *Transversotrema patialensis* is a digenean fluke. Digeneans have a complex life-cycle involving more than one host. In *Transversotrema*, the other host is a planorbid snail commonly found in aquariums. The adult worm lives in the skin of the fish, most commonly a species of *Brachydanio* in Britain, and produces eggs which pass into the water. In the water they hatch out into microscopic worms (miracidia) which are covered in cilia and swim about until they find a snail. Each miracidium bores its way through the skin of the snail and undergoes a reproductive stage within the body of the snail. As a result, thousands of infective stages are produced which burst out of the snail into the water. These new infective stages (cercariae) look quite different from the miracidia, being more worm-like and possessing a forked tail. The tail is used to locate a new fish host to which it becomes attached. At the anterior end of its body, the cercaria is equipped with glands which produce secretions enabling it to penetrate the fish skin

below a scale, leaving a wound through which eggs can escape when the worm becomes mature. The body of the worm causes the scale to be inclined at an unusual angle, thus giving a clue to its presence.

## ENDOPARASITES OF THE INTESTINE
Fishes may suffer from bacterial diseases which may be spread by the blood stream to all internal organs where they may cause considerable damage. In freshwater the causative organism is usually the bacterium *Aeromonas*, of which there are many species. In salt water the bacterium *Vibrio* is the agent of a number of diseases. These are impossible to diagnose without the use of special techniques in a laboratory. They are, however, usually the result of poor fish husbandry and water quality.

There are very few protozoan parasites which inhabit the intestine. Perhaps the commonest is *Octomitus* or *Hexamita*, a flagellate which occurs occasionally in large numbers in the small intestine, especially in weak fishes which are not feeding. The most important protozoan parasites of the intestine of freshwater and marine fishes however, are the Coccidia. These are sporozoans which live in the intestine wall and eventually produce cysts which contain the infective stages. These cysts burst through the intestine wall and are passed out of the fish with waste products into the water where they are picked up by other fishes. Once inside the intestine of the new host, the cysts hatch and the new parasites penetrate the intestine wall and the cycle is repeated. Heavy infections cause the fish to become emaciated and lose its appetite. Some coccidians cause enteritis and eventually death. It is possible, however, for a fish to be a carrier of the disease without showing any clinical signs of it.

Helminth parasites in the intestine frequently occur in small numbers and do not seem to affect a fish adversely. However, under certain conditions, in an enclosed system, numbers may increase to a dangerous level. In an artificial environment, fishes frequently encounter plants, other free-living animals and parasites which they would never meet in a natural situation. These strange parasites are not adapted to their new type of host and may then cause more damage than in their natural host. Small fishes sometimes become infected with large parasites which cause blockage of the intestine, even though only a small number are present. *Spirocamallanus*, a roundworm of freshwater fishes, has been found to cause such a problem. *Capillaria* and *Camallanus* are roundworms in the intestine which are occasionally associated with enteritis and *Contracaecum* has been found to cause loss of condition in some cases. Roundworms often have a larval stage which lives in free-living crustacea such as *Daphnia* and *Cyclops* and there is, therefore, a risk of introducing them with live food.

Tapeworms are flatworms with a complex life-history which includes one or more hosts. They are not often encountered in the aquarium but infection may occur in the wild prior to capture. However, the larvae spend part of their lives in free-living crustaceans and may be introduced into the aquarium with live food. One tapeworm, *Caryophyllaeus*, uses *Tubifex* worms (which are commonly used as live food) as a first intermediate host for the larval stages. Fortunately, most tapeworms rarely cause problems.

## ENDOPARASITES OF OTHER INTERNAL ORGANS

Fungal diseases of internal organs are not very common, with the exception of *Ichthyophonus hoferi*, a type of fungus which is not easily distinguished from some sporozoans. Wild marine fishes are often infected and the infection can be recognized by the appearance of small cysts in any of the body tissues. These cysts vary in size and contain vegetative and spore stages. Both stages stimulate a vigorous cellular response by the fish, as a result of which the cysts are formed in an attempt by the fish to isolate the offending foreign bodies. Treatment of this condition is seldom effective. A similar organism called *Dermecystidium* produces long oval cysts in the muscles and skin. These cysts are filled with minute spores in large numbers but not a great deal is known about the other stages in the life-history.

The most common bacterial disease of the internal organs of fishes is tuberculosis caused by *Mycobacterium* species. This is a difficult disease to diagnose unless histological techniques are used. The infection spreads rapidly through a batch of fishes but develops slowly within the fish. The earliest signs of the disease are loss of weight, emaciation and lack of appetite. Changes in the skin are sometimes seen and occasionally skeletal deformities. Internal signs of the disease are very similar to those of *Ichthyophonus* infection. Eventually the fish may die and it is essential to remove any dead fish as this is a source of infection to other fishes when the carcase is eaten.

Certain helminths, such as roundworms and tapeworms, use the fish as an intermediate host and, therefore, do not become mature when they enter the intestine in food. Instead, they penetrate the intestine wall, surround themselves with a cyst and wait until the fish is eaten by a bird or another fish before they become mature. Others do not produce a cyst straight away but migrate to other organs such as the liver, ovary or testis before encysting; an example is *Eustrongyloides*. Once encysted they do little harm, but migrating worms can cause irreparable damage to these internal organs; for example, large numbers in an ovary can cause sterility. Fortunately, these are not common in aquariums though infestation is common in the wild.

Sporozoans are found commonly in the internal organs and muscles of fishes but rarely cause harm. Some form milky white cysts in the muscle, liver or the intestine wall. Others inhabit the gall bladder, changing its fluid from clear to opaque as a result of the spores within. One particular sporozoan, *Plistophora hyphessobryconis*, is a serious pathogen and produces cysts in the muscles of characids and cyprinids. It was first described from the Neon Tetra (*Hyphessobrycon innesi*) and has therefore become known as Neon Tetra disease. The first indication of disease is a fading of the colour bar along the midline on the flank of the fish. The loss of colour progresses as the cysts spread; the fish becomes emaciated and often loses its equilibrium.

Roundworms are not often found in the flesh, with the exception of the blood red worm (*Philometra*) and its close relatives. These worms spend the immature stages of their lives in copepods. When the copepod is eaten by a suitable fish, the larval *Philometra* is released and bores its way through the intestine wall and into the muscles of the body. As it feeds and grows in the muscle tissue it causes haemorrhages. Mating occurs and the females migrate towards the scale pockets. Here they become ripe with hundreds of young larval worms which are released into the water through the fish skin, causing an unsightly ulcer. The young larvae are taken in by copepods and the life-cycle continues.

Resting stages of digenean flukes are encountered in the flesh more frequently than any other worms. These flukes have a complex life-history in which the fish plays the part of an intermediate host and the parasite cannot develop further until the fish is eaten by a bird (the final host). In the intestine of the bird, the worm is freed from the fish by the bird's digestive enzymes and attaches itself to the wall of the intestine. As it feeds and grows, it becomes mature and, because each individual worm is hermaphrodite (with both male and female reproductive organs), all worms produce eggs. Eggs pass out of the bird with waste as bird droppings. Since these are fish-eating birds, the eggs of the fluke are dropped either in or near water where they hatch and infect snails (the first intermediate host). In the snail a reproductive phase takes place and the cercariae emerge to seek out the second intermediate host (the fish). In the fish they inhabit the muscle and skin and occasionally other organs. The worm curls up and usually produces a cyst around itself; it is now a metacercaria. Some growth and development takes place but then it becomes a resting stage until the fish is eaten by the final host. This, of course, may never happen but the metacercaria is able to live for years. Clearly, this complicated life-cycle could not be completed in an aquarium but newly imported fishes may be often quite heavily infected with metacercariae. These may not be evident until many months later when the metacercariae have grown so large as to cause lumps on the side of the fish. In most cases, however, the infected fishes are weeded out at an early stage.

Metacercariae of the superfamily Strigeoidea are ubiquitous in freshwater fishes. One particular group, neascus larvae, stimulate the fish into producing black pigment which collects around the cyst, giving the fish a spotty appearance. The condition is known as black spot and is very unsightly. Other small metacercariae do not become pigmented and are barely visible to the naked eye, even when fully grown. Little harm is done to the fish by these metacercariae and, since they do not infect other fish, there is no reason to destroy them. In the wild only a few of these metacercariae find any one fish so that infection is very light. However, in artificial situations such as holding ponds where the number of snails may be allowed to build up and where fishes are crowded, the chances of getting heavy infections are greatly increased. Large numbers of cercariae penetrating the bodies of small fishes may cause sudden death owing to the migration of many larvae through the blood and tissues. After encystment the danger has passed.

Digenean flukes of the family Clinostomatidae are very large and cause gross distortions of the muscle on some small freshwater fishes. *Euclinostomum* grows slowly as a metacercaria and feeds on blood. If the cyst is near the surface the worm's branched intestine can be seen full of blood pigment. *Clinostomum* is a close relative which also causes large lumps on the fish body. These worms are sometimes known as yellow grub or white grub.

## ENDOPARASITES OF BLOOD

There is not a great deal known about parasites of the blood of fishes but there is no doubt that they exist. Sporozoans and trypanoplasms have been found in the blood of both marine and freshwater fishes. These are related to the organisms responsible for malaria and sleeping sickness in man, though, of course, they are different species and cannot transfer disease to man. Blood smears of fishes infected with *Cryptobia*, a trypanosome, show small, elongated flagellates which wriggle actively. With some exceptions, they do not harm the fish even in relatively large numbers. Leeches transmit the infection in the same way that the Tsetse Fly transmits the sleeping sickness infection to man.

Fishes can also suffer from the blood flukes *Sanguinicola*. The first intermediate host is a snail, as it is with other digenean flukes. The cercaria enters the fish but, instead of encysting, it penetrates the blood vessels and in the blood the adult females produce eggs. The eggs travel in the blood to the narrow capillaries of the gills where they burst through the gill tissue causing severe damage to the gill. In the water, the eggs hatch and seek out a snail to continue the life-cycle.

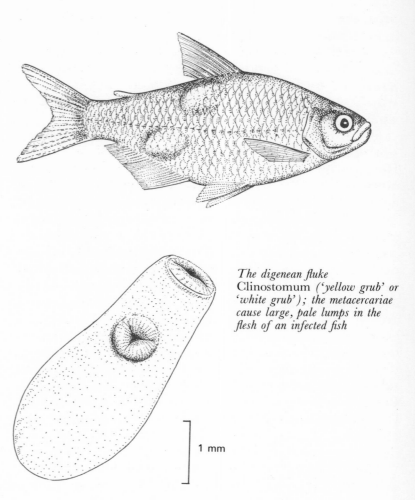

The digenean fluke Clinostomum ('yellow grub' or 'white grub'); the metacercariae cause large, pale lumps in the flesh of an infected fish

1 mm

## ENDOPARASITES OF THE EYE

Diseases of the eye are not common in aquarium fishes but certain parasites are specific to the eye. There are a number of sporozoans which infect the tissues of the eye and there are digenean flukes which prefer the lens and the eye fluids. These helminths are members of the superfamily Strigeoidea (related to the neascus larva) and are collectively known as diplosomula. The cercariae, on entering the fish, migrate to the eye where they develop into metacercariae. How they find their way to the eye is not known and they may enter the fish from all over the body surface and gills. Many seem to travel along blood vessels and escape in the vicinity of the eye orbit. In the lens or fluid, they do not encyst but feed and grow, remaining there until the fish is eaten by a bird, such as a heron. Large numbers of metacercariae cause blindness in fishes but generally wild fishes have only a few and do not appear to suffer any adverse effects. Aquarium fishes do not contract the disease in the tank but may become infected prior to capture.

# Non-infectious Causes

The previous section considered diseases caused by living agents, but there is a variety of common problems arising from other causes, and indeed a combination of both living and non-living agents can lead to major problems for the aquarist. Perhaps the most prevalent cause of death in tropical aquariums today is the inadequate maintenance of the fish's environment or water quality. Oxygen lack may occur through overcrowding or overfeeding of fishes. In the latter case, bacterial degradation of uneaten food (even if the manufacturer states that the food 'does not cloud water') may use up available oxygen and in either situation a build-up of harmful wastes such as ammonia or nitrite may occur. Filtration systems, unless they are allowed to become overloaded, help prevent such toxins from accumulating. Deaths through nitrite poisoning are particularly common in marine aquariums.

In freshwater aquariums, the plants will utilize such potentially harmful nitrogenous compounds for growth. Test kits are commercially available for monitoring the nitrite level and can give advance warning of a rise in level before deaths occur. Another commonly measured parameter in both freshwater and marine aquariums is pH. This generally varies from 6.5 to 7.0 (acid to neutral) for freshwater fishes and 8.0 to 8.3 (alkaline) for marine fishes. This value does vary, however, between species, some freshwater species living in the wild in quite acidic water with a pH level as low as 5. In the majority of fishes, variations in pH cause damage to skin and gill tissues. Hardness of water is another frequently measured parameter, the response to which is again subject to species variation. This is especially important when considering metal toxicities as most metals are more toxic in soft water.

Although oxygen lack has been considered, problems of supersaturation may also occur. If air is pumped too vigorously into an aquarium, supersaturation with nitrogen may occur. This leads to an increase in the partial pressure of nitrogen in the blood, and this may come out of solution and form bubbles of gas within the blood vessels if a sudden drop in outside gas pressure occurs (for example when the pump is switched off). The bubbles of gas may be visible in vessels near the surface of the skin, especially in the fins, or may cause exophthalmus (pop-eye). Aeration, if not excessive, will help to reduce any supersaturation problems by moving the water layers to the air/water interface, promoting more efficient gas exchange.

A variety of poisonings may occur in tropical aquariums. Amongst the commonest causes are the so-called heavy metals such as copper, lead and zinc. Copper salts are frequently used in treating fish disease, but their use is not recommended except in certain forms of disease in marine fishes. Variability of toxicity with hardness of water makes dosage difficult to compute and the therapeutic dose is often very near the lethal dose. Aquarium water is often drawn from water supplies containing a lot of copper piping (many hot water storage tanks are made of copper) and high levels of copper salts may be present. The water supply should be carefully checked for the presence of

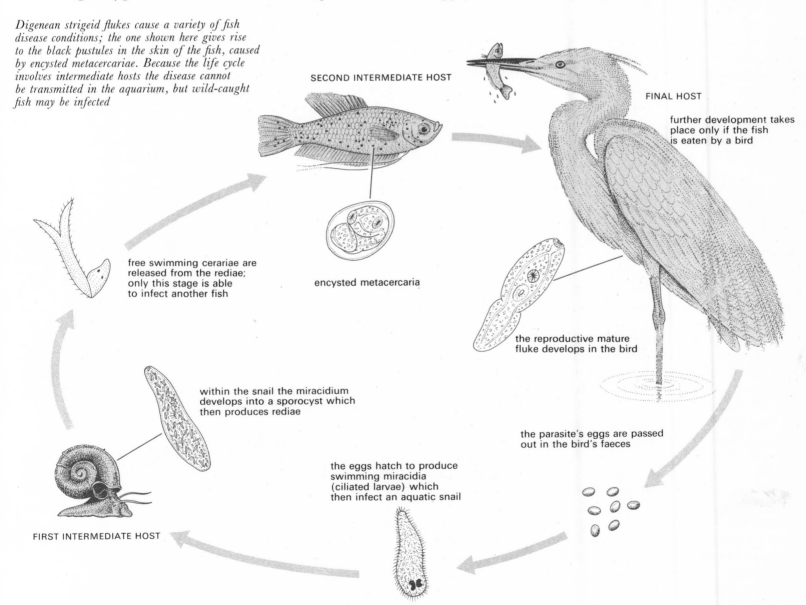

*Digenean strigeid flukes cause a variety of fish disease conditions; the one shown here gives rise to the black pustules in the skin of the fish, caused by encysted metacercariae. Because the life cycle involves intermediate hosts the disease cannot be transmitted in the aquarium, but wild-caught fish may be infected*

SECOND INTERMEDIATE HOST

FINAL HOST

further development takes place only if the fish is eaten by a bird

free swimming cerariae are released from the rediae; only this stage is able to infect another fish

encysted metacercaria

the reproductive mature fluke develops in the bird

within the snail the miracidium develops into a sporocyst which then produces rediae

the parasite's eggs are passed out in the bird's faeces

the eggs hatch to produce swimming miracidia (ciliated larvae) which then infect an aquatic snail

FIRST INTERMEDIATE HOST

such piping and a copper-free source used wherever possible. Copper salts have a direct effect on gill tissues, causing either immediate sloughing of large areas of gill epithelium, or, at lower levels of copper, a chronic overgrowth and fusion of gill epithelia.

Water taken from lead piping seldom causes any pathological effect as this piping has usually been present for a considerable length of time and has become coated with insoluble salts. Lead toxicity may, however, occur if large quantities of lead are used as plant weights. Zinc salts cause similar pathology to copper salts, toxicity being most frequently caused by using a form of malachite green containing large quantities of zinc—when purchasing this compound, the zinc-free form of malachite green should be requested.

Another common gill poisoning results from a high level of chlorine. Many water supplies are heavily chlorinated, and before adding such water to an aquarium, it should be either vigorously aerated for 24 hours or sodium thiosulphate should be added at a rate of 1 gm for 2.2 gallons (10 litres) of water in order to inactivate the free chlorine. Chlorine also damages gill and skin tissues. Care should be taken when using aerosols of various sorts, paint, or even when smoking (nicotine is poisonous to fishes) as concentrations of these compounds may reach the lethal level, especially if introduced to the aquarium water by aeration. Detergents are also toxic and great care should be taken to remove all traces of such compounds from hands or utensils prior to working in the aquarium. Certain species of fishes, such as the marine Trunk Fish, may release toxins when disturbed.

Dietary problems occur quite frequently in tropical aquariums. This is not surprising as species requirements vary considerably and no one food can be expected to be suitable for all species. Problems are best avoided by feeding a range of food including quantities of live food. The most common problems are deficiencies, especially vitamin deficiencies leading to spinal deformation or muscular defects. Differential diagnosis of such problems is often difficult. Another common problem is fatty liver degeneration and necrosis, which may occur through using diets containing high levels of rancid fat following excessive storage time. The livers often appear white in colour and the fishes become very susceptible to secondary infections.

Mechanical injury is quite common—extreme care should be taken in handling fish as the osmotic barrier of the skin, the epidermis, is easily removed and fish might die from osmotic imbalance or from some other secondary infection. Care should be taken in the selection of fish species in community tanks as aggression and fish injury may well cause secondary bacterial infection and death.

Shock, either through excessive handling or too sudden changes in water quality, should be avoided, especially in marine aquariums where deaths from such causes are particularly common.

Tumours are frequently found in fishes. Although some are caused by viruses (for example *Lymphocystis*), the cause of many is unknown and destruction of affected fish is the safest course of action. Similarly, a variety of disorders of the heart, liver, kidney and other organs occasionally occur but diagnosis is only possible using sophisticated laboratory techniques.

# Treatment

The therapy of fish disease is still at a primitive stage when compared with the treatment of other animal species. The medications used are generally very simple compounds such as dyestuffs and, because of the large numbers of species concerned, many treatments have been tested only on a small percentage of the species maintained in aquariums. The current expansion of fish farming has, however, led to a search for new compounds, initially for use with salmonids but in most cases also for trial with tropical fish.

However, before discussing the treatment of tropical fish diseases, a consideration of the methods of preventing disease should help to reduce the incidence of such problems. As mentioned previously, the maintenance of water-quality is of the utmost importance. If correct conditions of oxygenation, pH, hardness, temperature, fish density and other factors are maintained, then ill-health and death are not likely to arise from, for example, ammonia or nitrite toxicity. Fishes maintained in good conditions, will be in good health and able to respond to any infection and prevent its spread much more readily. Regular monitoring of water conditions should be undertaken, especially of parameters such as temperature, pH, hardness, specific gravity (in marine aquariums) and nitrite level. Physical trauma should be prevented—sharp-edged rocks should not be used and handling of fishes should be reduced to a minimum. Nutrition should be as varied and balanced as possible utilizing both dried and live foods. It is possible to introduce disease with live food, particularly if such food has originated in water containing fishes. *Tubifex* worms are particularly suspect of introducing parasites and bacterial infection, but disinfectant compounds are commercially available which are used to treat such foods prior to feeding. Earthworms or white worms are an excellent food source as they are not of aquatic origin. Care should be taken in feeding live foods, as they quickly pollute the aquarium if not eaten.

Plants, from any source, may contain a variety of fish parasites, and should be well washed and then immersed in 10 ppm potassium permanganate solution for several hours prior to use. Snails may carry parasites on their outside surface and act as intermediate hosts for a variety of digenean trematodes—introduction of snails from the wild should be discouraged.

Problems often arise after the introduction of new fishes into an established aquarium. Parasitic infection is particularly common, though bacterial and viral infections may be disseminated in this way. One of the best methods of prevention of the majority of these diseases is by quarantine. Essentially, the longer the quarantine period the better, but about three weeks should be adequate to check on fish health. During this period the fishes should be watched closely for any signs of disease, and tested as necessary. It is possible to carry out prophylactic treatment against the common parasitic diseases at this time. A variety of compounds may be used, amongst which are methylene blue (2 ppm as a permanent bath), acriflavine (1 ppm as a permanent bath) or formalin (1 ml 4 per cent formaldehyde/gallon, 1 hour dip). Even following quarantine, it is good practice to maintain strict isolation between aquariums. Separate nets and other equipment should be available for each aquarium, or if this proves expensive, then disinfection of equipment between aquariums should be undertaken. Several compounds are available for this purpose, but those having iodine as the active principle are probably most efficient.

Having taken all reasonable precautions, disease does still occasionally arise in the aquarium. Once a diagnosis has been made, some form of treatment will be required and several factors must be considered before choosing the most suitable medicament. For many parasitic diseases, a range of compounds is available and choice is usually dependent on a combination of efficacy at killing the parasites together with lack of toxicity to the fish. Many compounds used in treating skin and gill parasitic disease are themselves directly toxic to skin and gill and there is often danger of causing further damage resulting in death.

Water volumes must be accurately calculated so that overdosage does not occur, and there should be even distribution of the medicament. Species variation in sensitivity to toxicity may occur and fishes should be observed carefully during treatment and removed immediately they show signs of distress. When possible, one or two fishes of each species should be treated first to test for toxicity reaction. Aeration during bath treatment not only ensures even dispersal of the treatment compound but also improves oxygenation and this often proves beneficial. It should be remembered also that pH and hardness affect the toxicity of many compounds, e.g. copper salts are toxic at lower concentrations in soft water. As many of the compounds used in treatment are dyestuffs, they are quickly absorbed into organic material, especially algae. This not only reduces the effective concentration of the compound used but also makes it extremely difficult to compute additional quantities which may be needed. Consequently, organic detritus should be siphoned out of the tank before treatment, and as much algae as possible removed.

Charcoal filters have a similar absorptive effect and should be switched off during treatment. When bacterial filtration is used, care must be taken to ensure that treatment compounds do not kill the bacteria and render the filter inactive. This is especially important when using antibiotics or copper compounds in marine aquariums, and it is often best to remove the fishes to a separate container for treatment. If it is necessary to disinfect the aquarium and filter and then re-establish the aquarium, it should be remembered that a bacterial filter will take at least several weeks to become efficient and in the meantime the fishes must be maintained in good quality salt water.

Some of the compounds used may damage or kill certain plants, e.g. methylene blue, quinine and malachite green. Invertebrates in marine aquariums also usually suffer toxic effects from treatment compounds at a much lower concentration than the therapeutic dose for fishes and this should always be borne in mind when treating marine aquariums.

A knowledge of the life-cycles of many parasites is useful when planning treatments. When more than one host is involved in a parasite's life-cycle, removal of such intermediate hosts may prevent spread of a disease or even eradicate it. For this reason, many diseases, such as certain digenean fluke infections are seen only in fishes recently introduced from the wild. Many of the ecto-parasitic protozoan diseases are easily controlled by one treatment—such parasites have no resistant phase in their life-cycle and live on the surface of the skin and gills where the treatment used readily contacts them. *Ichthyophthirius* infection, on the other hand, is difficult to treat

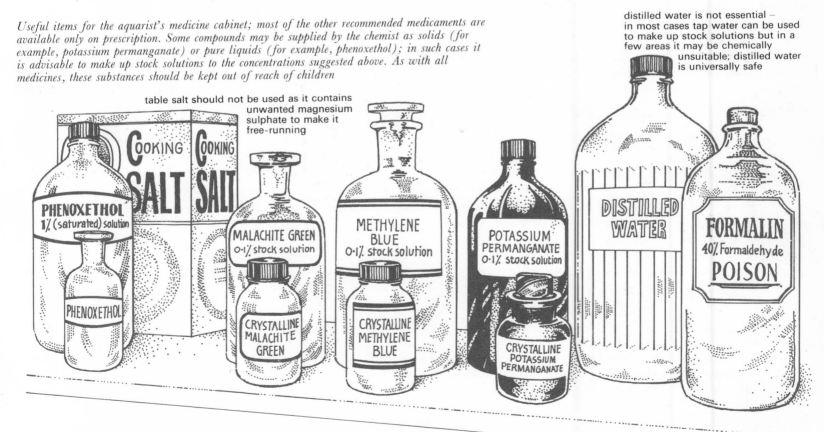

*Useful items for the aquarist's medicine cabinet; most of the other recommended medicaments are available only on prescription. Some compounds may be supplied by the chemist as solids (for example, potassium permanganate) or pure liquids (for example, phenoxethol); in such cases it is advisable to make up stock solutions to the concentrations suggested above. As with all medicines, these substances should be kept out of reach of children*

distilled water is not essential – in most cases tap water can be used to make up stock solutions but in a few areas it may be chemically unsuitable; distilled water is universally safe

table salt should not be used as it contains unwanted magnesium sulphate to make it free-running

PHENOXETHOL 1% (saturated) solution

PHENOXETHOL

COOKING SALT COOKING SALT

MALACHITE GREEN 0·1% stock solution

CRYSTALLINE MALACHITE GREEN

METHYLENE BLUE 0·1% stock solution

CRYSTALLINE METHYLENE BLUE

POTASSIUM PERMANGANATE 0·1% stock solution

CRYSTALLINE POTASSIUM PERMANGANATE

DISTILLED WATER

FORMALIN 40% Formaldehyde POISON

because the parasite is not on the surface of the epidermis but buried beneath it and there is a resistant resting phase away from the fish. In this case continual or repeated treatment is necessary as only the free-swimming forms of the parasite can be killed. The time taken for completion of many parasitic life-cycles such as that of *Ichthyophthirius* is dependent on temperature and this fact is sometimes used in treatment. Raising of the temperature will decrease the duration of treatment because each phase in the life-cycle is shortened. At higher temperatures, however, less oxygen is available in a given volume of water and the fishes' metabolic demand is increased. Consequently, fishes are often stressed and the advantages of such a method may be outweighed by the disadvantages. Such temperature manipulations are therefore not usually recommended.

The method of treatment and route for administration are also variable. The commonest treatment method is the permanent bath, when an aquarium is treated once and left. This method is suitable only if the compounds used do not persist and cause chronic damage. Also, such treatment may damage plants or invertebrates, and removal of fish and subsequent dip treatment at a higher concentration for a shorter time may have to be carried out. Obviously such treatment will not affect resistant stages remaining in the aquarium, for example in white spot, and a certain amount of stress caused through handling will take place.

Treatment of the food may be suitable when using compounds such as antibiotics but achieving an even dispersion is difficult and variations in appetite occur (sick fishes often do not feed) so that administering correct dose-rate becomes very difficult. Treatment may also be surgical (for example the removal of lymphocystis lesions or expulsion of trematode cysts) or topical (as in direct application of antiseptic compound to skin wounds). In the latter cases, great care must be taken to avoid damage during handling and an anaesthetic such as MS222 may be employed. Ozone at 25 mg per gallon (5 mg per litre) or ultraviolet light may be used as disinfectants in marine aquariums.

Consideration will now be given to the commonest types of disease and their treatment. An accurate dose-rate computation is important; note that 1 ppm = 1 mg per litre = 4.5 mg per gallon = 28.3 mg per cubic foot. Allowances should always be made for rocks and gravel when measuring the tank volume.

Ectoparasitic protozoans such as *Costia*, *Chilodonella* or *Ichthyophthirius* are particularly common and a variety of treatments exists. A bath in a 1 per cent salt solution for up to an hour is often effective and aquariums may be treated by raising the salt concentration to 0.55 per cent over three days and then leaving this concentration as a permanent bath. The latter treatment, however, often adversely affects plants and certain fish species. Formalin is another inexpensive but very effective treatment. A permanent bath of two drops of 40 per cent formaldehyde per gallon of water is often effective, though it may be used in short bath form for 1 hour using 1 ml. of 40 per cent formaldehyde per gallon of water. The latter treatment is toxic to gill tissues in many species. Methylene blue (medical quality) in permanent bath form at 3 ppm is especially used for *Ichthyophthirius* infection but this is readily adsorbed onto organic material and it may be necessary to add further methylene blue over an extended period. It will stain silicone sealant compounds and may damage plants. Malachite green is also very effective at 0.1 ppm in permanent bath form or 2 ppm in a dip for 30

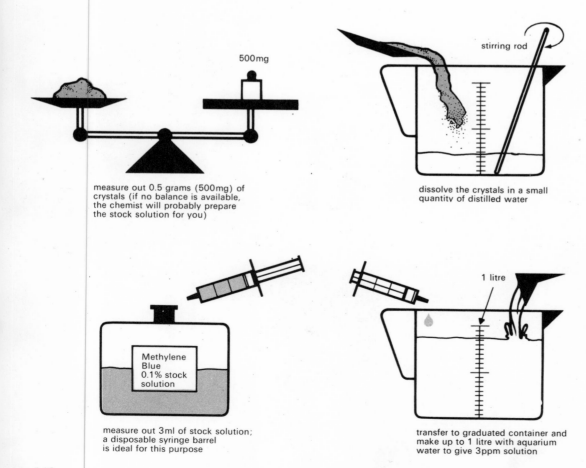

measure out 0.5 grams (500mg) of crystals (if no balance is available, the chemist will probably prepare the stock solution for you)

dissolve the crystals in a small quantity of distilled water

make up to 500ml with distilled water to give 0.1% stock solution and transfer to stock bottle

measure out 3ml of stock solution; a disposable syringe barrel is ideal for this purpose

transfer to graduated container and make up to 1 litre with aquarium water to give 3ppm solution

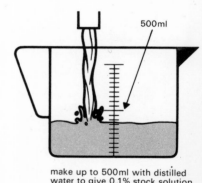

*Making up and using stock solutions; for example, 500ml of a 0.1% methylene blue solution which can be used as a permanent bath at a final concentration of 3ppm*

minutes. The zinc-free form should be used and organic detritus removed. Neutral acriflavine may be used at 0.02 ppm over a period of three days. The water should then be changed and if necessary a repeat treatment carried out three days later. This compound also can kill plants and may produce sterility in some species. Quinine hydrochloride is often used at 30 ppm but is unstable in solution and may kill plants and possibly cause sterility. Potassium permanganate has been used as a 30 minute bath at 10 ppm and chloramine T has proved effective over 24 hours at 10 ppm. Protracted treatment is necessary when using any of these compounds to cure white spot.

Skin and gill fluke infestations, though seldom diagnosed without the aid of a microscope, are also very common. Formalin or chloramine T are the treatments of choice for these parasites.

Fungal infections may respond to salt, acriflavine or permanganate treatment, but malachite green is the most effective. Phenoxethol (2-phenoxyethanol) is also frequently used. This compound forms a saturated aqueous solution at 1 per cent and should be used at 45 ml of this solution per gallon of water (10 ml per litre). The compound also has anaesthetic properties.

Crustacean parasites and leeches are much more difficult to kill but usually respond to organophosphorus compounds such as Dipterex and Masoten (Bayer Agrochemicals Ltd). Such compounds are dangerous and toxic to humans and care should be taken to avoid contact with the skin. They are used in permanent bath form at 0.25 to 0.5 ppm. A two minute dip in a 3 to 5 per cent salt solution often removes leeches (usually accidentally introduced with plants or live food).

Secondary bacterial infections are often treated with antibiotics, usually in bath form over a period of five days, as in the treatment table. The pure compound should be used whenever possible as many of the feed additives available for veterinary use contain a large percentage of bulking powder which is often insoluble and used merely to ensure even dispersion in food. If antibiotics are used, they should be used at the correct dosage for the specified length of time to avoid the dangers of build-up of drug resistance. Because of the danger of the transfer of resistance from one bacterium, often to a species which could be a human pathogen, antibiotics should be used only if absolutely necessary. Correct water quality and avoidance of overcrowding will prevent many of the bacterial problems from occurring. If fin-rot occurs, a variety of compounds such as acriflavine and phenoxethol may often be used with success. In bacterial diseases such as fish tuberculosis, lesions have usually advanced so far prior to disease diagnosis that treatment will not be effective and destruction of the affected stock and sterilization of the aquarium and equipment may be the only course of action. The compounds already mentioned are particularly useful in freshwater aquariums. In marine aquariums, antibiotics will destroy the bacterial filter. Copper sulphate is commonly used to combat *Oodinium* infection, one of the commonest marine parasites, but it will kill bacterial filters and is also toxic to invertebrates. It is used at 0.1 to 0.4 ppm concentration over an indefinite period. Baths in freshwater replace salt water for treatment of many of the ectoparasitic protozoans. Neguvon may be used for larger crustacean parasites but is also toxic to crustacea in aquariums. Acriflavine is insoluble in salt water but malachite green and formalin are quite useful compounds for the treatment of external protozoans and for skin and gill flukes. They should be administered at the recommended freshwater concentrations.

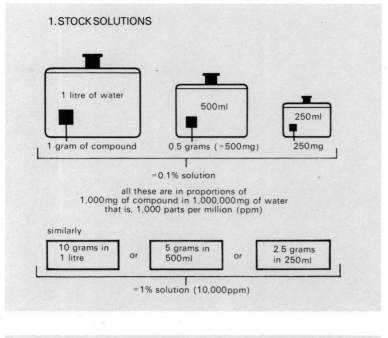

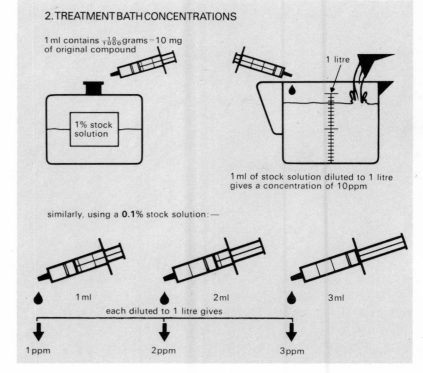

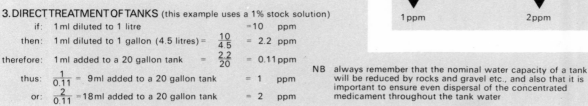

*How to work out dilutions and concentrations*

# COMMON MEDICAMENTS USED IN FISH DISEASE THERAPY

| COMPOUND | DOSE-RATE | TREATMENT | DISEASE |
|---|---|---|---|
| Salt | 3–5% | 2 minute dip | Leeches |
| Salt | 1% | 1 hour bath | External Protozoa |
| Salt | 0·55% | Concentration gradually increased from zero over 3 days | External Protozoa |
| Formalin | 1 ml/gallon (2·2 ml/10 litres) | 1 hour bath | External Protozoa and flukes |
| Formalin | 2 drops/gallon (4 drops/10 litres) | Permanent bath | External Protozoa and flukes |
| Methylene blue | 3 ppm | Permanent bath | External Protozoa |
| Malachite green | 2 ppm | 30 minute bath | External Protozoa and fungi |
| | 0·1 ppm | Permanent bath | External Protozoa and fungi |
| Organophosphorus compounds | 0·25–0·5 ppm | Permanent bath | External Parasites generally |
| Acriflavine | 0.02 ppm | 3 day bath | External Protozoa, fin-rot and fungi |
| Chloramine T | 10 ppm | 24 hour bath | External Protozoa and flukes |
| Copper sulphate | 0·1–0·4 ppm | Permanent bath | External Protozoa especially *Oodinium* |
| Phenoxethol | 45 ml of 1% sol. per gallon (10 ml/litre) | Permanent bath | External fungus and fin-rot |
| Quinine hydrochloride | 30 ppm | 3 day bath | External Protozoa |
| Potassium permanganate | 0·1% sol. | Local treatment | *Lernaea* |
| | 10 ppm | 30 minute bath | External Protozoa and fungi |
| *Antibiotics:* | | | |
| Chlortetracycline | 13 ppm | 5 day bath | Bacterial infections |
| Nitrofurazone | 20 ppm | 5 day bath | Bacterial infections |
| Oxytetracycline | 20 ppm | 5 day bath | Bacterial infections |
| Sulphanilamide | 200 ppm | 5 day bath | Bacterial infections |

Many of the internal diseases of both freshwater and marine tropical fishes are not only difficult to diagnose but also difficult to treat. With many conditions, for example fish tuberculosis and *Ichthyophonus* infection, the fish may have to be destroyed. There are, however, a few compounds which have been tested only on one or two species, but which nevertheless may prove useful. Amongst these is phenoxethol which may be effective against internal helminths when incorporated into the food. Metronidazole at 31.8 mg per gallon (7 mg per litre) in permanent bath form has proved effective against *Octomitus* infection, as has nitrofurazone incorporated into the food at 3.1 mg per ounce (110 mg per kg) of fish per day over a five-day period. Nitrofurazone has also been used to treat coccidial infections. Quinacrine (May and Baker Ltd) has been used on one or two species to control sporozoan infections at 3 mg per litre for three days, but destruction is usually indicated with such infections. Phenothiazine may control cestode infections at 113 mg per ounce of fish (4 mg per gram) given in the food for three days.

Many remedies are available at fish-dealers' premises and these usually contain a mixture of the above compounds. Purchase of the chemicals from a pharmacy should, however, enable considerable savings to be made, but be sure that your dose-rates are accurately measured. Although relatively few well-tested compounds are available for the treatment of fish disease, the maintenance of water quality and quarantine procedures together with prompt diagnosis and treatment will usually allow the establishment and maintenance of a healthy aquarium.

Above: A stained section (magnified 500 times) through the skin of a fish infected with the protozoan *Costia*. If untreated, this condition may result in massive colonization of the skin surface by the parasites and the damage to the skin can cause death from osmotic imbalance

Below: A stained section (magnified 500 times) through the secondary lamellae of a gill showing the condition known as telangiectasis which can be caused by treatment with excessive quantities of medicaments such as copper sulphate, formalin or methylene blue. Blood vessel walls break down and large 'blisters' of blood are formed which may interfere with gas exchange; the blood eventually clots and fibrin is deposited

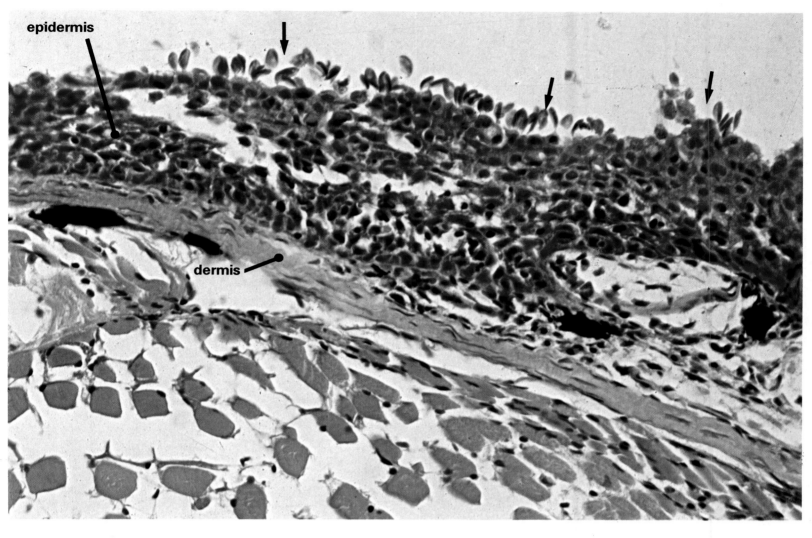

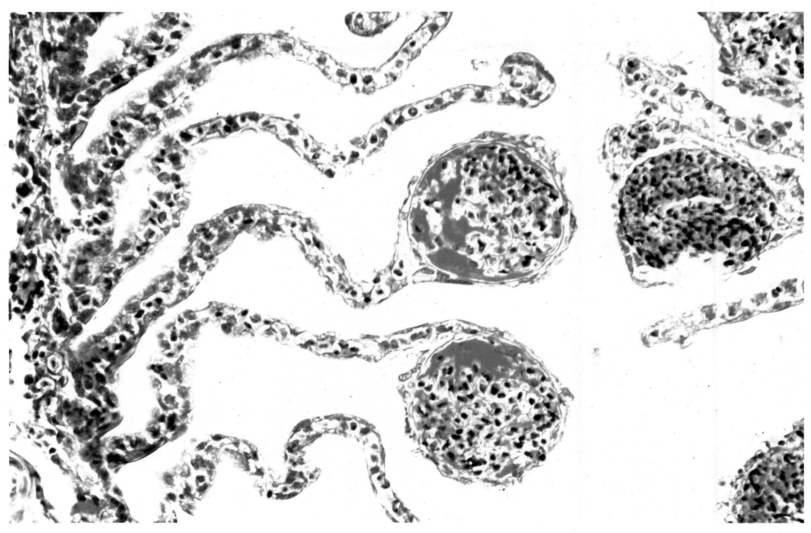

# *Families of Marine Tropicals*

## FAMILY POMACENTRIDAE
### Damsels

Damsels are hardy and cheap and of great character. Some species are hardly to be beaten for beauty by fishes at any price. The beginner would be well-advised to start with damsels, particularly of the genus *Dascyllus*: the Humbug Damsel (*D. aruanus*), the Domino or Three-spot Damsel (*D. trimaculatus*) or the Cloudy Damsel (*D. carneus*). The Atlantic Domino Damsel (*D. albisella*) differs from the Indo-Pacific Domino in having larger and more elongated white spots. In both species the spots reduce with age until they disappear altogether. The Pacific Cloudy Damsel (*D. reticulatus*) is a duller fish than its counterpart *D. carneus*, which is found in the Indian Ocean and the Red Sea. Black, white and grey are the predominant colours in *Dascyllus*, and they prove that bright colours are not necessary for attractiveness. They are resistant to disease, low pH and the high nitrite level which is inevitable in the first weeks after a new tank has been set up. They will, like all the damsels, eat almost anything.

Although they will not grow to much more than two inches in captivity, damsels are very territorial and

aggressive and quite capable of buffeting to death a much larger fish which has no means of escape in a small tank. *Dascyllus*, especially the Domino Damsel, puts his head down and charges like a little bull. He will also charge the hand that feeds him, and his aggression call, a loud grunting, can be heard at the other end of the room. Damsels will attack other members of their own species with particular savagery. They should be bought singly or in groups of ten or more. With a large number the schooling instinct seems to override the territorial instinct. In the reef a school of damsels will mob even an octopus or a barracuda.

Damsels should be provided with large coral heads. They will dart through the narrow convolutions of the coral with incredible agility, sometimes even swimming backwards, and are so attached to their coral refuge that they will remain in it even when it is lifted out of the water. Many a piece of coral has been taken to the sink to wash with a Cleaner Wrasse and half a dozen damsels completely concealed within it.

The Domino Damsel has the ability, unique among damsels, to enter the tentacles of even the most poisonous

Left: Yellow Tang *Zebrasoma flavescens*
Above: Yellow-tailed Blue Damsel *Abudefduf parasema*

anemones (including those from the Mediterranean where there are no damsels) with impunity. Presumably the purpose of this and the manner in which it is achieved are much the same as in the case of clowns, which are also known as anemone fishes for this reason.

Several damsels can change colour radically as a result of fright or changes of light. An Electric Blue Damsel (*Abudefduf uniocellata*, formerly *Pomacentrus caeruleus*) which lives up to its name in the dealer's tank, may be almost black in its plastic bag. Don't tell the poor man he has brought the wrong fish! The Green Damsel (*Chromis caeruleus*) is similar in that it is constantly changing from green to blue as the light catches it.

Some damsels such as the Yellowtail Blue (*Abudefduf parasema* formerly *Pomacentrus melanochir*) and the Thai Damsel, excavate caverns for themselves by carrying the larger pieces of debris away in their mouths and wafting the smaller ones away by rapidly vibrating their tails. Another lovely damsel, but rarely imported is the Fijian Blue Damsel.

Damsels will often spawn in the aquarium. The male, who becomes even more aggressive than usual, lures the female, or several females, to his chosen spot where the eggs are deposited. Then he drives off the female, guards the eggs, and oxygenates them by fanning them with his tail until they hatch. The babies are then on their own.

## Clowns or Anemonefishes

Clowns are not as suitable as damsels for the beginner because they are less tolerant of nitrite and generally less hardy. But, if conditions are right, they are excellent aquarium fishes, particularly the Common Clowns (*Amphiprion ocellaris* or *percula*) which are cheap and easily available, omnivorous, sociable, entertaining, and very gaily coloured with their distinctive bands of bright orange and enamel white. *A. percula* has a thicker black border to its white bands than *A. ocellaris*. Nearly all the clowns have these white bands on a background of red, orange, pink, maroon or brown. Other species, such as the Tomato or Fire Clown (*A. frenatus*, previously

Above: Sea Bee *Amphiprion clarkii*
Below: Humbug Damsel *Dascyllus aruanus*

*ephippium*), the Sea Bee (*A. clarkii*, previously *sebae* and *xanthurus*) or the Maroon Clown (*A. biaculeatus*) are less sociable and should not be mixed. (The Maroon Clown differs from all other *Amphiprion* species in having gill-plate spikes like those of angels. For this reason it was until recently allocated to a different genus, *Premnas*.) The Pink Clown (*A. perideraion*) is a schooling fish and should not be kept without anemones. Clowns are found throughout the tropical Indo-Pacific, but not in the Atlantic.

The changed scientific names of so many species (not only of clowns) are the result of recent reclassification in the light of evidence that fishes formerly thought to be of different species because of their quite distinct markings are in fact colour phases of the same species. The Tomato Clown, for example, is bright orange-red as a juvenile, except for his white head-stripe but as he grows the middle of his body becomes darker, eventually almost black. The background colour of the juvenile Sea Bee is bright orange-yellow, but in the adult it is uniformly brown.

Clowns differ from damsels not only in coloration but in their whole life-style, which centres on their symbiosis or partnership with anemones. The flower-like anemone gently waves its tentacles in the current. But each tentacle is loaded with stinging cells (nematocysts), little hypodermics triggered at a touch to inject a paralysing poison into the victim. Only the clown is immune. Not only does he survive contact with the anemone, he even seeks it, nestling in the very mouth of the anemone, and rubbing himself constantly and with evident enjoyment among the lethal tentacles.

This relationship was first observed over a century ago, but it has only recently been explained. If the anemone's stinging mechanism were triggered by any kind of touch, it would constantly be stinging itself and its neighbouring anemones. To prevent this, anemones secrete a mucus which inhibits the stinging mechanism. The clown has cracked this secret. He has found that by tentatively rubbing himself against the non-stinging parts of the anemone or by enduring for a while the light stings as he gingerly flicks against a tentacle, he can gradually coat himself with this protective mucus and become as safe as if he were part of the anemone. When the mucus is removed experimentally, *Amphiprion* is stung like any other fish until he has had time to repeat the process of acclimation.

The anemone becomes home for the clown, which chases off the anemone's enemies (several butterflies, for example, will nibble at the tentacles) with a ferocity amazing in so small a fish. Even human divers will be attacked by breeding clowns, and if the going gets too rough the clown can always retreat to the protection of the anemone.

Compared with the damsel, the clown is sluggish in his movements, not venturing far from his anemone and not needing the manoeuvrability the damsels have evolved to swim in and out of coral heads. His bright and distinctive coloration is also probably related to his symbiosis with the anemone. If a predator comes too near and is stung, he comes to associate the clown's colours with getting stung and may thereafter give him a wide berth even when the clown is away from his anemone refuge.

In the aquarium a clown will feed his host anemone by dropping into it any pieces of food too big for him to swallow. It is not known whether this also happens in the reef, but seems likely. If a clown has no anemone to feed in the aquarium, he will often choose an anemone-substitute in the form of a conch or other hollow shell, and assiduously 'feed' it with large morsels. Unless some other fish or invertebrate regularly cleans out this larder, there could soon be pollution from the rotting mass.

The anemone also offers protection for the eggs of *Amphiprion* which are usually laid in its shadow on a smooth patch of rock which the clown has carefully cleaned. All the Pomacentridae anchor their eggs firmly. *Amphiprion* may lay several hundred cylindrical eggs, each about an eighth of an inch long. The male watches over them for about ten days constantly fanning them with his fins. Many, nevertheless, are eaten by crabs, and many are infertile. The remainder hatch and become part of the plankton which is the main food supply of the parents. The process is repeated several times at intervals of ten days.

To spawn clowns in captivity a healthy adult pair should be given a tank to themselves with a few large anemones and adjacent smooth rocks.

Top: Maroon Clown *Amphiprion biaculeatus* with Yellow-tailed Blue Damsels *Abudefduf parasema*
Above: Common Clowns *Amphiprion ocellaris*

They seem to prefer a lower pH than other marines – perhaps even slightly acid. The eggs will hatch in about six days, but the young will quickly die without live plankton.

## FAMILY LABRIDAE
### Wrasses

The family of wrasses covers a great range of species, from the diminutive genus *Labroides*, seldom exceeding three inches, to the giants of the genus *Cheilinus* several feet long. Most of the smaller imported species live on small invertebrates, which they crush with their strong protruding teeth; but they rarely trouble other fishes in the aquarium.

Many species are extremely colourful. The Clown Wrasse (*Coris gaimard*) is trebly so, since he passes through three quite different but equally gaudy colour phases. The juvenile is vivid orange with five, large, black-edged, white spots or saddles along his back. These soon disappear, the tail becomes yellow, the body-colour darkens, particularly the rear half which becomes spangled with bright blue dots. The fish undergoes another complete transformation before it becomes an adult.

The wrasses have a strangely laboured method of swimming, with the pectorals used like oars, jerking their length along. But this applies only to cruising. When a wrasse wants to move, he can move. Drop a mussel in the opposite end of the tank and he will streak across to snatch it from under the noses of the nearer fishes. Some wrasses, the Lyretail (*Thalassoma lunare*) for example, like to lie on the bottom, often resting their chin on a shell. Others, such as the Clown Wrasse or Green Wrasse (*Halichoeres melanurus*) spend the night under the gravel and will do a spectacular nose-dive into it if frightened.

In the reef the wrasses have a unique mating procedure. A large group will mill around excitedly near the bottom. Several will suddenly break away, dash to the surface, then abruptly turn back, releasing at that moment a cloud of eggs and sperm. The turbulence created ensures that most of the eggs are fertilized. The eggs immediately float to the surface.

Wrasses are very susceptible to shock and consequently do not travel well. A wrasse in a state of shock should be left in darkness until the natural light of dawn slowly infiltrates the tank. Once settled in they present no problems.

One of the most fascinating sights to be seen in the aquarium is that of a tiny silver and pale-blue fish with a black central stripe swimming between the deadly spines, in and out of the gills, or even in and out of the mouth of a large scorpionfish, which would swallow in one gulp any other fish of that size. Or sometimes you will see a queue of larger fishes waiting their turn and when it comes, presenting themselves to the attentions of this intrepid little fellow. For he is the Cleaner Wrasse (*Labroides dimidiatus*), the barber and general practitioner of the reef, who removes the parasites from the skin, mouths and gills of all the other fishes and cleans their wounds. With the help of the cleaner shrimps, which also have their recognized surgeries or cleaning-stations, he keeps the other fishes healthy and comfortable, and in return they give him safe conduct wherever he goes.

The cleaning operation must be of tremendous importance to override such primary instincts as the predatory instinct of the clients and the fear of the cleaners. Moreover, a general truce seems to hold for the whole cleaning station area, where fishes will patiently queue next to fishes they would be in mortal fear of anywhere else. Even sharks will come in from the open sea for cleaning and abide by the general truce. When a population of Cleaner Wrasses was removed experimentally from a crowded reef, the reef was abandoned within two weeks. When the wrasses were replaced, the others rapidly returned.

Apparently, the Cleaner is recognized as such by his uniform, for the Neon Goby, which performs the same function wears the same uniform. And so, with fiendish cunning, does the Saw-tooth Blenny (*Aspidontus taeniatus*) who is not a cleaner but a confidence trickster, for he exploits the immunity his uniform brings him to get in close only to take a chunk out of his unsuspecting host before beating a hasty retreat.

In the reef the Cleaner Wrasse may get his entire food supply from his cleaning operations, but in the aquarium he will eat almost anything. No tank should be without its Cleaner Wrasse. Perhaps it would be kinder to have two, or who cleans the Cleaner? I have kept two together for a short

time, but never observed them cleaning each other. Cleaner Wrasses are very susceptible to nitrite and to immature synthetic sea-water and should not be introduced to a new aquarium for at least two months.

The strangest of the wrasses in appearance is the Bird-mouth Wrasse (*Gomphosus varius*, formerly *coeruleus*), whose mouth is elongated into the shape of a duck-bill. The male is a deep blue-green, the female predominantly brown. *Gomphosus* is an active, hardy and entertaining aquarium fish.

## FAMILY CHAETODONTIDAE
### Butterflies

There are over two hundred species of butterflies. The greatest concentration is around the islands of Indonesia where there are over sixty species. But they are found in every coral reef. Butterflies are very territorial, and a single pair may lay claim (as far as their own species is concerned) to a stretch of reef a quarter of a mile long. Thus, if the particular ecological niche filled by butterflies is to be fully exploited, it can only be by a proliferation of species, much to the delight of the natural historian, aquarist and photographer.

Most species have a wide distribution throughout the Indo-Pacific, but some are more localized. *Chaetodon collaris* and *C. xanthocephalus* are found only in the Indian Ocean, *C. larvatus*, *C. semilarvatus*, *C. fasciatus* and *C. mesoleucus* only in the Red Sea, *C. capistratus*, *C. ocellatus* and *C. striatus*

151

only in the Atlantic. Fishes from the Red Sea are happier at a rather higher temperature (80–85°F.) and salinity (at least 1.025) than those from anywhere else.

All the butterflies are basically disc-shaped and so laterally compressed that a four-inch fish can swim with ease through a half-inch gap. In the sea the smallest species grow to about four inches, the largest to about twelve, but in the aquarium growth is inhibited, and a specimen acquired at two or three inches will seldom grow to more than four.

Butterflies are not as spectacular as angels, but more subtle and delicate in their patterns and coloration. Several species have an attractive reticulated pattern, each scale outlined in a darker colour. This is most clearly seen in the Pakistani Butterfly (*C. collaris*), *C. rafflesi* and *C. xanthurus*. Two other species show an interesting chevron pattern – *C. triangulum* and *C. mertensi*.

One of the most striking butterflies is the Saddleback (*C. ephippium*), found only in the Pacific. The juvenile is about four inches long. As he matures he will lose his eyestripe and gain a long filament at the back of his dorsal fin. *C. auriga* has a similar filament.

The Bannerfish (*Heniochus acuminatus*) differs from all other butterflies in having an extremely elongated fourth dorsal spine, often longer than the body, carrying a white fin like a banner. *H. acuminatus* is probably the hardiest of all the butterflies. They survive the pollution of Colombo harbour, and I have know them none the worse after twenty-four hours in cold water. Another characteristic of the genus *Heniochus* is the development in mature specimens of horns on the forehead in several species but not in *H. acuminatus*. The Bannerfish also differs from other butterflies (except *C. semilarvatus*) in its schooling habit. All others pair for life.

The Moorish Idol (*Zanclus canascens*) is not strictly a butterfly, but has a family all to itself, the Zanclidae. It is similar to the Bannerfish, though completely unrelated and much more exotic. Some call the Bannerfish 'the poor man's Moorish Idol'. The Moorish Idol is one of those fishes which, like the seahorse or scorpion, seems to belong more to the world of fantasy than that of nature. Small groups of Moorish Idols move about the reef, peacefully browsing on invertebrates and algae. They eat ravenously in captivity, but nevertheless commonly die in a very short time.

Apart from their markings, butterflies differ from angels in being slimmer, in lacking the cheek-spine, and in the fact that the young pass through a larval stage, called the *tholichthys*, during which the head is covered with bony plates which gradually disappear as they approach the juvenile stage.

Above top: Butterfly *Chaetodon mesoleucus*
Above: Butterfly *Chaetodon rafflesi*
Right: Butterfly *Chaetodon mertensi*
Opposite page top: Pakistani Butterfly *Chaetodon collaris*
Opposite page bottom: Addis Butterfly *Chaetodon semilarvatus* with Cleaner Wrasse *Labroides dimidiatus*

Again unlike angels, there is little significant difference in markings between juveniles and adults. Thus, the juveniles would be attacked and driven off if they approached the territory of the adults, and must find different feeding grounds often in the tidal pools.

It is common for butterflies to have an ocellus, or false eye, somewhere on the fins or body towards the rear. Usually the real eye is disguised by a stripe running through it, or, in the case of the Long-nose (*Forcipiger flavissimus* or *longirostris*) by a black mask which makes him look like a rather sinister highwayman. The combination of realistic false eye and well-disguised real eye is particularly evident in the Copperband (*Chelmon*

Far left: Copperband Butterfly *Chelmon rostratus*
Left: Rainbow Butterfly *Chaetodon trifasciatus* with Bannerfishes *Heniochus acuminatus*
Below: Saddleback Butterfly *Chaetodon ephippium*
Bottom: Long-nosed Butterfly *Forcipiger longirostris*

*rostratus*). Apparently the aggressor normally aims at the eye. If he aims at the wrong one, he gets a mouthful of water, for his intended victim has gone the other way. Copperbands even fool one another. When fighting they can be seen to be concentrating their attack on the false eye, thus doing much less damage than if they were to attack the real one. The very small mouths of these two species make it essential to give them such foods as mussel and earthworm finely chopped.

Butterflies have relatively small mouths, with several rows of close slender teeth, like a brush. Hence the name chaetodonts which means 'bristle-teeth'. They eat the larger plankton, small crustaceans and coral polyps. Those with long snouts such as the Long-nose and Copperband are obviously specialized for picking or sucking out small crustaceans from crevices in the rocks and corals. Those without snouts such as *C. trifasciatus*, *C. meyeri*, *C. ornatissimus*, *C. plebius*, *C. larvatus*, *C. octofasciatus*, and *C. trifascialis* probably feed almost exclusively on coral polyps, and are therefore extremely difficult to feed in the aquarium. Unfortunately, these are some of the loveliest species, and aquarists find them irresistible. But the temptation should be resisted to discourage their importation. A good rule of thumb for the aquarist buying butterflies is – the shorter the snout the harder to feed. An exception is *C. triangulum*, which has a snout, but will not eat.

The easiest butterflies are the Long-nose and Copperband, the Bannerfish, *C. auriga*, *C. lunula*, *C. vagabundus*, *C. pictus*, *C. ephippium*, *C. rafflesi*, *C. semilarvatus*, *C. falcula*, *C. mertensi*. The very distinctive and attractive Pakistani Butterfly (*C. collaris*) may be reluctant to start feeding, but once started will eat anything and is as tough as they come.

To say that these are the easiest butterflies is not to say that they are easy. Few butterflies will stand a low pH or the slightest trace of nitrite. A great variety of food, including fresh and live food must be offered initially. Then whatever the fish has been eating live can be offered in its deep-frozen or freeze-dried form, especially mysus or brine shrimp. Gradually most species will learn that whatever is put into the water at feeding time is tasty, and within a few weeks should be eating flakes.

A newly-acquired butterfly which is not eating may often be tempted by small earthworms chopped into half-inch lengths, by mussel offered in the half shell, or by pieces of mussel rubbed onto the coral where the fish has been vainly pecking. A temporary lowering of the specific gravity to 1.8 or 1.9 often has the effect of stimulating appetite.

Apart from Bannerfishes and *C. semilarvatus*, which are schooling fishes, butterflies should be kept apart from their own species. An established butterfly will probably resent the introduction of a new butterfly of any species to his tank. The first six or seven dorsal spines on a butterfly are

pouring medicaments into the tank; when the light has been on for a few minutes he will be swimming normally again.

## FAMILY POMACANTHIDAE
### Angels

The angels are the most resplendent of all the reef fishes, the aristocrats of the reef as their common names imply – Regal, Majestic, Queen, Emperor. They are expensive because they need to be shipped singly with a good deal of water, so that, as with other large fishes, only 20% of the cost to the dealer is the price of the fish; the other 80% is what it costs him for transportation. Fortunately, though shy, they are less delicate than many butterflies in the home aquarium.

long, sharp and erectile. Fortunately, they are used mainly for defence. They attack with the snout and by general buffeting, seldom killing each other. But the loser (which is always the new fish, even when he is the larger) may be so bruised and frightened that he skulks in a corner and soon starves to death. You may be lucky and have no trouble, but there is nothing lost by having a perforated plastic box ready just in case.

A note of warning, finally, to owners of Long-nosed Butterflies. This fish has thrown many an aquarist into a needless panic by its habit of sleeping upside-down. There is no need to start

They are disc-shaped, like the butterflies, but not so slender, and, except for the dwarf angels, are considerably larger. Some species grow to two feet in the sea. They are usually found in deeper water than butterflies – at least fifty feet, which probably explains the need for brighter colours to be seen in the dimness.

Angels are easily distinguished from butterflies by the bony spike which projects backwards half an inch or so from the gill-plate. This spike is useless as a weapon. It seems to be used rather as a means of locking the fish in a crevice so that it cannot be pulled out backwards.

Little is known of the mating of angels. They have kept this secret as well as their heavenly namesakes. The eggs are free-floating. The larvae are carried out to sea where the currents give them a wide distribution. At about one inch they transform into the juvenile fish and find the nearest reef. Like butterflies, adult angels pair for life and defend their territory to the death against others of the same species. Evolution has two answers to the problem of survival for juveniles in this situation. They can live in territory unlikely to be claimed by adults, as butterflies do, or evolve markings so different from the adults that they are not recognized by them as belonging to their own species. This is what happens with the majority of angels.

There is, however, no advantage to be gained from being different from the juveniles of other species, so nature has made several species which bear no resemblance as adults, but which are almost identical as juveniles. (For the convenience of aquarists she has been considerate enough to provide just sufficient differences to help in identification.) As for Cleaner Wrasses, there seems to be a recognized uniform for juvenile angels, which presumably entitles them to immunity from attack by adults. This uniform is black with circular or semicircular white markings, which become pale blue then electric blue as they near the periphery. The species whose juveniles wear this uniform are all those of the *Euxiphipops* genus and all of the genus *Pomacanthus*

Left: Blue-faced Angel *Euxiphipops xanthometapon*
Below: Juvenile Blue-ring Angel *Pomacanthus annularis*

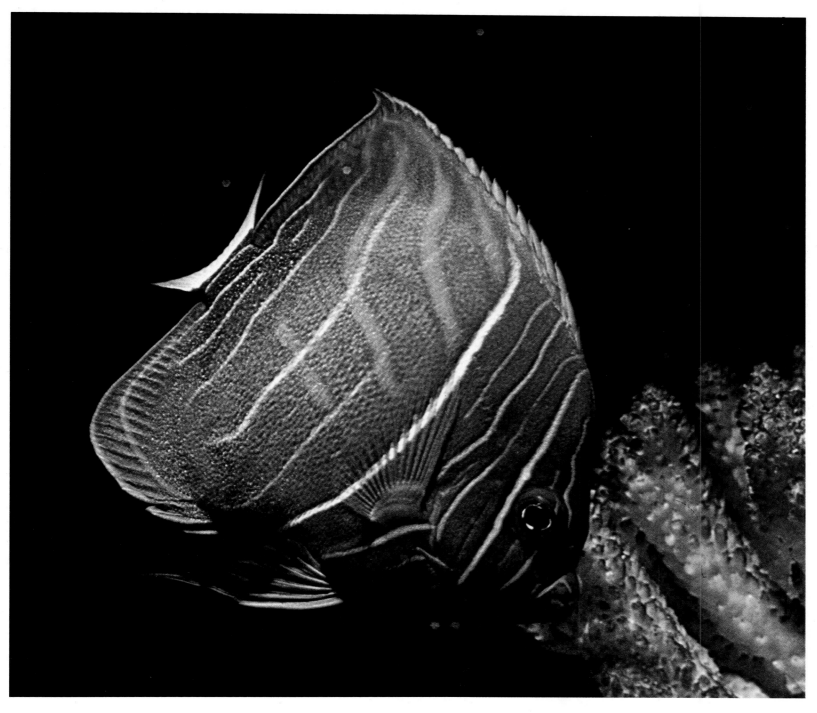

except the two Atlantic species, *P. arcuatus* and *P. paru*.

The photographs show a juvenile Blue-face Angel (*Euxiphipops xanthometapon*) from the Philippines, and the adult it will become at about four inches. The Blue-ring Angel (*Pomacanthus annularis* from Sri Lanka is in the middle of its change. When adult the vertical white marks will disappear, the diagonal lines will extend and become bright green on a light brown body.

Atlantic butterflies cannot compare with those of other tropical oceans, but angels redress the balance. Off Florida, the Caribbean Islands and Mexico are found the Rock Beauty (*Holacanthus tricolor*), vivid yellow with a large patch of jet black in the rear half, the French Angel (*Pomacanthus paru*), the juvenile, with broad yellow bands on black, the adult without the bands, but with every scale edged with yellow, the Blue Angel (*Holacanthus isabelita*), and, brightest of angels, the Queen Angel (*Holacanthus ciliaris*). The juvenile Queen Angel has several blue stripes on the body and a dark band through the eye.

Above: Queen Angel *Holacanthus ciliaris*
Right: Emperor Angel *Pomacanthus imperator*
Far right: Juvenile Blue-faced Angel *Euxiphipops xanthometapon*, left; Pakistani Butterfly, below; Lyretail Wrasse, right

Opinions naturally differ as to which is the most beautiful of all marine tropical fishes. My own leaning is towards the surgeons. Those who prefer a more dazzling beauty will probably choose the Emperor (*Pomacanthus imperator*) or Regal Angel (*Pygoplites diacanthus*). But of the angels my own favourite is, I think, the Majestic (*Euxiphipops navarchus*).

Angels must not be kept with others of the same species, and must be given plenty of room in a tank with places to hide. They may need some coaxing at first, but will soon be eating everything and losing some of their shyness. I have found juveniles less shy, more eager to eat, and well able to look after themselves among larger fishes. As a bonus they afford the unique pleasure and interest of watching the transformation as they grow into a new beauty.

## FAMILY ACANTHURIDAE
### Surgeons

Surgeons are so called because of the retractable scalpel or flick-knife at the base of the tail. This blade is razor-sharp and up to a quarter of an inch long. By swimming alongside another fish and lashing with its tail, the surgeon can cause grievous wounds. It will do this to another fish of the same species in the aquarium, and sometimes, when established, to newly introduced fishes of other families such as butterflies and angels.

Surgeons spend much of their time browsing on algae, which forms a larger proportion of their diet than of

Left above: French Angel *Pomacanthus paru*
Left below: Rock Beauty *Holacanthus tricolor*
Below: Majestic Angel *Euxiphipops navarchus*

any other reef fish. In the aquarium, if algae is not present in quantity, chopped spinach, parsley or lettuce will be readily taken. Surgeons are not choosy and will eat most other foods as well.

Surgeons spawn in a similar way to wrasses, a small group breaking away from a school and releasing eggs and sperm simultaneously. The eggs hatch into semi-transparent larvae. This stage is called the 'acronurus'. The larvae drift in the open sea for several weeks before returning to the reefs and changing rapidly into juveniles, usually of the same colours and markings as the adults.

Some surgeons, particularly the Regal Tang (*Paracanthurus hepatus*) and the Clown Surgeon (*Acanthurus lineatus*) are very susceptible to shock and travel badly, but most, once settled, are hardy. The Regal Tang, which has been called 'the bluest thing on earth', likes to lie inside or under the coral, dashing out for food and immediately back again. It will lie quite motionless, often on its side, for long periods. This does not indicate illness, and the fish should not be interfered with. The other surgeons are in constant movement and should have plenty of room. The Regal Tang is the smallest of the family, growing to only seven or eight inches. It is also the only species of which several may be kept together. (There are significant differences between the Pacific and Indian Ocean Regal Tangs. Those from Sri Lanka are larger, less shy, more active, and have bellies the colour of egg-yolks. Pacific Regals are the same royal blue all over.)

One of the largest of surgeons, and the most spectacular, is the Japanese, Unicorn or Lipstick Tang, (*Naso lituratus*) which grows up to eighteen inches. Japanese Tang is a bad name, since the Powder-brown Surgeon is now called *Acanthurus japonicus*. Unicorn is also a bad name. Species of the *Naso* genus are called unicorn fishes because they develop a horny projection from the forehead. But *Naso lituratus* is the one exception to this rule. *Naso lituratus* may be a unicorn without a horn, but he does have a remarkably equine head, and might have been called seahorse had that name not been preempted. The horse-like appearance is accentuated by a sculpted jawline inside the line of the gill-case, which in the adult is picked out in yellow. The adult has a further distinguishing feature in the form of long filaments extending from both tips of the tail. Perhaps I should have called *Naso lituratus* 'she'. With her lipstick, her turquoise eyeshadow, and her filamentous adornments, she is almost too selfconsciously glamorous. This species differs from the other tangs in having two non-retractable blades at the base of the tail.

Another horse-faced surgeon is the Powder-brown, with his white flashes along cheek and nose. I once obtained a Powder-brown at about one and a half inches, not long emerged from the larval stage and completely trans-

Right: Emperor Tang *Zebrasoma xanthurum*
Far right: Unicorn Tang *Naso lituratus*

parent but for a silver gutsack. I don't know how the dealer knew that he was a Powder-brown, but sure enough, over the next few months, the faint colours came, gathered strength and asserted themselves, until after about a year and grown to three inches, he looked like the photograph at the top of this page.

Equally beautiful is the popular Powder-blue Surgeon (*Acanthurus leucosternon*), plentiful in the reefs off Sri Lanka. Unfortunately, this fish does not seem to retain in captivity quite the original richness of pastel blue.

Identical with the Powder-blue and Powder-brown in shape and behaviour, but very distinctive in colour and markings is the Achilles Tang (*Acanthurus achilles*) a fish from the mid-Pacific atolls. The name derives from the Greek hero Achilles who, as a baby, was dipped by his mother in the river Styx to make him invulnerable. But she held him by the heel, which the magic water did not touch. (Hence the term 'Achilles heel' meaning the single weak spot in a man's defences.) The Trojan prince Paris knew of this, and during the seige of Troy shot Achilles in the heel with a poisoned arrow and killed him. The Achilles Tang seems wounded in the heel with that bright-red blood-drop at the base of his tail. There are other bright red markings. Body and fins are finely edged with pale blue. In the dorsal and ventral fins red suffuses the body colour, which is like no other colour I have seen in nature, half-way between maroon and brown. I look at my own four-inch Achilles as I write, his colours enhanced by Growlux lighting, and realize how badly I have failed him with my camera. He is the most handsome fish I have ever seen.

The genus *Zebrasoma* is characterized by a greater depth of body and fins, giving the fish a shape, especially when his fins are extended, quite different from other surgeons. The young are often deeper than they are long. This is most evident in the Sailfin Tang (*Z. veliferum*), but can be seen also in the Yellow Tang (*Z. flavescens*), which is most common near Hawaii, and a brighter yellow there than elsewhere in its range. The Emperor or Purple Surgeon (*Z. xanthurum*) is found only in the Indian Ocean and the Red Sea.

## FAMILY BALISTIDAE
### Triggers

Triggers are easily recognized by their strange rhomboid or diamond shape, as though half of them were head and the eye were in the middle of the back. This is seen at its most extreme in the genus *Rhinecanthus*. Actually in the middle of the back, just behind the eye, is the trigger from which this family gets its name. This is a long, first, dorsal spine which will lie in a groove flush with the back, or stand up at right angles. It can be locked in the upright position by the second spine so that it cannot be lowered without releasing the second spine first. It performs the same function as the gill-plate·spikes in angels, enabling the trigger to wedge itself in a crevice from which it cannot then be pulled out.

Some triggers, including all the species pictured here, have a rasp at the base of the tail which is used for attack as the surgeon uses his tail-blade.

Triggers have strong teeth, and the distance between mouth and eye helps them to attack urchins and spiny star-fishes without damaging themselves. The spines of the sea urchin are sharp, poisonous, mobile, and over a foot long, but they present little problem to the trigger. He carefully takes hold of the tip of one of the longest spines and pulls the urchin over. Then he dashes round to rip into the unpro-tected underside before the urchin has

Below: Yellow Tang *Zebrasoma flavescens*
Top left: Powder-brown Surgeon *Acanthurus japonicus*
Centre left: Achilles Tang *Acanthurus achilles*
Bottom left: Powder-blue Surgeon *Acanthurus leucosternon*

time to right itself. Alternatively, he may choose to blow the urchin over with a jet of water. If these methods do not work he has yet another in reserve. Picking up the urchin by the tip of a spine, the trigger tows him towards the surface, lets go, dives beneath it as it drifts down and attacks from below before it reaches the bottom. These same methods can be employed with equal success against the Crown of Thorns Starfish. The introduction of large numbers of triggers and puffers (the only other fish to prey on them) has been considered as a means of controlling these starfishes in the Great Barrier Reef, parts of which they have overrun and are laying waste.

Triggers spawn in large pits in the sand, about a yard across. Here they watch over and fan the eggs, savagely attacking any trespasser, including divers.

Triggers are fairly popular because of their hardiness and odd beauty, and also because they are 'personalities', becoming very tame and learning tricks. But there are several disadvantages in keeping triggers in the home aquarium. They eat a great deal of almost anything, leaving little for their tank mates. They grow fast and go on growing. Some species reach two feet in the wild. They can be very aggressive, though there are differences here not only between species but even between individuals. The Green Trigger (*Odonus niger*) seems to be the most consistently peaceful. I once saw a black trigger (*Melichthys* spp.), foiled by the dealer in its attempt to demolish a heater, turn in its frustration and take a neat half-moon out of the throat of the nearest fish. This happened to be a Pinnatus Batfish which slowly keeled over and sank – very dead.

You will never reach agreement with a trigger about the layout of your tank. He will carry pieces of coral much larger than himself industriously to the site of his choice, and excavate large trenches in the gravel.

Possibly the most famous, and certainly the most conspicuous of all marine tropicals is the Clown Trigger (*Balistoides niger*, formerly *conspicillum*). The first specimen to reach Europe alive was brought from Sri Lanka in 1953 and sold in Frankfurt for £260 ($650). Now they can be bought for a tenth of that. Most triggers are imported as juveniles, but the juvenile

Clown Triggers do not return to the reefs until they are several inches long. I have never seen a specimen smaller than this one (left), which was four inches. One would really need to keep such a fish alone in a very large tank with no moveable decor. I prefer to leave it to the public aquariums.

The Orange-striped Trigger (*Balistapus undulatus*) is often available quite small, but does not stay that way for very long. Unfortunately it does not develop its superb adult coloration until it is very large. The green body colour we see in this three-inch juvenile becomes purple, the orange stripes become brighter and those on the face are replaced by orange spots.

Perhaps the best trigger for a community tank is a juvenile *Rhinecanthus aculeatus*, which is relatively peaceable. The juvenile has the same markings as the adult. It is difficult to imagine how these markings could have been acquired other than by the brush strokes of a modern painter – hence the name Picasso Triggerfish.

The closely related filefishes are smaller and vegetarian, and are therefore more suitable for community tanks.

## FAMILY CANTHIGASTERIDAE
### Sharp-nosed Puffers

There is only one genus of sharp-nosed puffer, and one of these species is the strangely-shaped Saddled Puffer (*Canthigaster valentini*).

These small fishes have the ability to inflate themselves with water or air until they are spherical. This understandably deters predators from swallowing them. Filipino children frequently use them as footballs on the beach. The long snouts end in strong teeth capable of crushing shells and coral (and biting fingers). They have neither scales nor pelvic fins.

Apart from a tendency to nip the fins of other fishes, they are good aquarium fishes, disease-resistant and eat whatever is offered.

## FAMILY OSTRACIONTIDAE
### Boxfishes

The boxfishes are distinguished by the hard box-like carapace which serves both for skeleton and armour. Some, like the little *Ostracion cubicus*, are almost exactly cubic; some, the cowfishes (genus *Lactoria*) have long horns; and others have several spiky projections like the Thornback or

Top left: Orange-striped Trigger *Balistapus undulatus*
Centre left: Clown Trigger *Balistoides niger*
Bottom: Picasso Trigger *Rhinecanthus aculeatus*
Above: Puffer *Canthigaster valentini*

Hovercraft Boxfish (*Tetrasomus gibbosus*). There are holes in the box for the eyes, mouth, gills, anus and fins. The fins are small and transparent so that the box has no visible means of support as it sails slowly and rather comically along.

Boxfishes are intelligent and develop many quaint habits in the aquarium, such as spitting a considerable distance to attract attention. Their mouths are so small that they are obliged to suck in their food like spaghetti. They have no enemies since they must be as appetizing as old boot soles.

Some boxfishes exude a toxic foam when frightened. They are not immune to this themselves, and many a boxfish dead on arrival has poisoned itself in the bag. Before you leave the shop, check that there are no surface bubbles in the bag. If there are, get the dealer to change the water. The fish is unable to repeat the emission immediately.

Boxfishes are easy to feed, hardy, peaceful and tame.

## FAMILY SYNGNATHIDAE
### Seahorses

Even stranger than the boxfishes, but sharing with them the carapace or external skeleton, are the seahorses known at least since Roman times, and probably the only marine tropical fish which can be identified by everybody. Its quaint shape has fixed it in the popular imagination. It shares the characteristics of several very different animals, and has some uniquely its own. The head is so horse-like (and is carried so like a horse's, since the seahorse swims upright with its head at right angles) that it is disconcerting to find the chest leading not to legs but to a long prehensile tail like that of no other fish, but very like that of some reptiles and tree-dwelling mammals. The whole body is armour-plated and ridged, with many protruberances. It is so rigid that the fish has no need of an internal skeleton. This again is a feature more common in other animal classes, in insects, for example, and the independent eyes are like those of lizards.

The seahorse has only one fin, the dorsal. It moves slowly, with unshakeable dignity, as though in another dimension of time. It looks more like a brooch than a living creature, and this, sadly, is what many become.

But the most amazing characteristic, unique not only among fishes, but in the whole animal kingdom, is the fact that it is the male which becomes pregnant and gives birth. In that case, one might ask, why not call it the female? But it is the female which produces the eggs, the male the sperm. At mating the seahorses wind round each other and the female injects her eggs through a tube into the male's brood pouch. There they incubate for several weeks until, a few at a time over several days, hundreds of perfect miniature seahorses emerge. Many attach themselves to the father as he lies exhausted by this protracted labour. I am at a loss to know why the seahorse has not been chosen as the emblem of the Women's Liberation Movement.

There are several species of seahorses not differing very much from each other. The most frequently offered for sale in Europe is the Oceanic Seahorse (*Hippocampus kuda*). Specimens may be black, brown, yellow, white, or, occasionally, red. These are colour phases, not permanent differences, and they may change colour in a short time.

Seahorses live where warm currents bring a steady stream of plankton to them. Anchored by their tails to the bottom growth they reach out and suck in small creatures through their pipette-like snouts. They will eat nothing but live food (or what they take to be alive) of exactly the right size, and are consequently difficult to feed in captivity, (small live prawns are excellent if available). Newly hatched brine shrimp are too small except for the Dwarf Seahorse (*H. zosterae*), and few aquarists can raise brine shrimp to adult size. Sometimes they will take daphnia and glassworm. Baby Guppies or other livebearers are often suggested, but these tend to swim on the surface and in taking them the seahorses swallow air, which they are unable to expel, and which eventually kills them. Frozen brine or mysis shrimps offer a new hope. A block of frozen shrimps floated on the surface gradually releases shrimps which sink, are caught in the filter current and taken by the seahorses.

Top left: Boxfish *Ostracion cubicus*
Bottom: Hovercraft Boxfish *Tetrasomus gibbosus*
Right: Seahorse *Hippocampus kuda*

Since they cannot compete with other fishes for food, seahorses must have a tank to themselves, perhaps with invertebrates, or a few, gentle, slow-moving fishes, such as clowns.

## FAMILY POMADASYIDAE
### Grunts

Grunts are so called because of the noise they make by grinding their teeth together. They are usually to be seen in large numbers around the reefs by day, scattering at night to forage for invertebrates.

Grunts of the genus *Gaterin* are known as 'sweetlips' because their lips are rather thick. The young sweetlips has an odd way of swimming, the large pectorals doing all the work, as if a small boy were trying to man-oeuvre a large rowing boat with oars too big for him.

The juvenile Polka-dot Grunt or Clown Sweetlips (*Gaterin chaetodonoides*) has large white dots on a brown background. As it grows, small brown dots appear in the centre of the white ones which extend and run together until in the adult the colour scheme

becomes completely reversed.

Polka-dot Grunts make very attractive aquarium inmates, though large specimens can be bullies. They will grow to three feet in the wild, but modify their growth in the aquarium, despite eating a great deal.

## FAMILY HOLOCENTRIDAE
### Squirrelfishes

The large eyes which are the primary feature of squirrelfishes indicate that they are nocturnal. Prolonged exposure to bright aquarium lighting is distressing to them and they must be provided with shaded areas. Red coloration also seems to be common among nocturnal species, though at a depth of thirty or forty feet red cannot be seen, and they might just as well be grey or black.

Squirrelfishes grow to several inches. Their diet is mainly of crustaceans. They eat voraciously in captivity, especially if fed in the evening. But they cannot be trusted with small fishes such as damsels.

Within a genus, the differences between species are very small, so

Left: Polka Dot Grunt *Gaterin chaetodonoides*
Above: Squirrelfishes *Myripristis* sp.
Below: Soldierfish *Adioryx* sp.

that exact identification, especially from photographs, is very difficult. Squirrelfishes of the genus *Myripristis* (also known as soldierfishes) are likely to be found in groups or schools, those of the genus *Adioryx* singly or in pairs. Squirrelfishes are considered to be a delicacy in many parts of the world, particularly in Hawaii.

## FAMILY APOGONIDAE
### Cardinals
Cardinals are not necessarily always red, as their name suggests. They are small, shy fishes, spending much of their time in the aquarium quite

Left: Mandarin Fish *Synchiropus splendidus*
Below: Cardinal *Apogon nematopterus*
Right: Round Batfish *Platax orbicularis*

motionless, as if suspended, not far from a hiding place, darting forward at feeding time to swallow some sizeable morsels with their large mouths.

In the reef many species move about in enormous shoals and some have a symbiosis with the sea-urchin, living among its spines. Cardinals occasionally incubate their eggs in their mouths.

They are found in a wide variety of habitats, some in shallow water, others in deep, some in salt water, others in brackish or even freshwater.

## FAMILY CALLIONYMIDAE
### Dragonets
The dragonets are small fishes whose markings remind one of fine oriental silks – hence the name mandarin fishes (*Synchiropus*). They are bottom-dwelling fishes, highly territorial, with greater differences between the sexes than are usual in marine fishes. In the male the first two dorsal rays are highly extended, as in cichlids. Two males will often fight to the death. The most popular species is *S. splendidus* but an equally attractive species, *S. picturatus*, known as the Psychedelic Fish, is occasionally available. Mandarins are fussy feeders, only likely to do well in invertebrate aquariums.

## FAMILY GRAMMIDAE
### Grammas
This beauty from the Caribbean area, the Royal Gramma (*Gramma loreto*) is a full-grown specimen of about three inches. Grammas have a habit of swimming upside-down in caves or under ledges which makes them hard to catch and expensive. They are hardy and omnivorous in aquariums.

## FAMILY PLATACIDAE
### Batfishes
The young Round Batfish (*Platax orbicularis*) looks very like a bat, though a less fanciful name would be leaf-fish, for batfishes drift with the surface currents among the dead mangrove leaves and are virtually indistinguishable from them. As an adult he will have lost his beautiful russet colour and become a dirty brownish-grey.

The two other species of batfishes, *Platax teira* and *Platax pinnatus* have even more elongated fins, which make them look more like boomerangs than bats, especially as juveniles. The fins grow, initially, much faster than the body, but the body later catches up, so

that the adult *P. orbicularis* is quite round, as his name implies, while the Long-finned Batfish (*P. teira*) whose height as a juvenile is several times its length, seems, as an adult, still to be wearing its juvenile fins, now much too small. Only *P. pinnatus* retains some of the majesty of his juvenile height and colouring. He has an orange rim all round which makes him look as though silhouetted against a bright orange light concealed behind him. The first photograph I saw I had assumed to have been achieved with trick lighting; I was amazed, when I saw a live specimen, to find that nothing had been added to nature. *P. pinnatus* is the most dignified of all fishes.

All the batfishes eat literally anything in the wild. The Round Batfish retains that habit in captivity, growing an inch a month, and vies with *Pterois volitans* (one of the scorpions) for the title of hardiest marine tropical fish; but the other two species are loth to eat at all in the aquarium, especially *P. pinnatus*, which gives the impression that even to glance at food would be altogether beneath its dignity. Round Batfishes can be bought as babies but *P. pinnatus* is rarely less than six inches high.

Batfishes are very tame. They will take food from the fingers (as will many marines), and do not seem to mind being tickled. But they are quite defenceless and must on no account be kept with potentially aggressive fishes, such as triggers, puffers, or even the larger damsels.

Left: Pinnatus Batfish *Platax pinnatus*
Above: Royal Gramma *Gramma loreto*

*Pterois volitans*

## FAMILY SCORPAENIDAE
### Scorpions

The scorpion is also sometimes known as the dragon-fish, the lion-fish, the turkey-fish and fire-fish. He is adapted to bottom-living, splendidly camouflaged, his long pectoral rays floating like the fronds of a plant, his face disguised by grotesque flaps of skin, his body shape broken by stripes. He has only to sit still and his prey will usually come to him. A lunge, a snap and a gulp and the unsuspecting shrimp or small fish has become a bulge in the scorpion's belly. If he needs to go hunting, he can gently shepherd his prey into a dead end, using his wings like nets. When danger threatens he spreads his fins, puts his head down, and ripples his dorsal rays, presenting a fearsome appearance. If this should not deter the aggressor, those rays are loaded with deadly poison.

There is some danger in keeping scorpions. Not that they ever use their poison spines to attack – in fact they carefully collapse them when another non-aggressive fish swims near – but that the aquarist might thrust his fingers onto the spines when moving something on the bottom of the tank. If this happens, the victim must be rushed to hospital at once. Another disadvantage of scorpions is that they grow fast and cannot be kept for long with small fishes such as clowns and damsels (Cleaner Wrasses are quite safe with them).

There are two genera of scorpions, *Pterois* and *Dendrochirus*. The most obvious difference is that the latter have pectoral rays connected for most of their length by membranes.

Luckily, the most spectacular scorpion, with the longest wings, *Pterois volitans*, is also the commonest and easiest to keep. For the first few days it may be necessary to tempt him with live shrimps, baby guppies or earthworms, but after that he will eat most things. Other scorpions take longer to extend their diet beyond live foods and some, including the handsome *Pterois radiata*, rarely, if ever, do so.

# Feeding

There are many brands of fish food on the market and yet is there really such a thing as a specific fish food? Look at the variety and form of human foodstuffs; and we are but one species. There are at least 20,000 species of fishes. Over millions of years they have exploited every niche of their environment and each species has adapted to some special supply of nutrient so that countless billions of fishes live together in all the waters of the Earth in a complex, interdependent but balanced way. The variety and range of feeding methods are incredible. The Grass Carp (*Ctenopharyngodon idellus*) grazes like a cow and the flesh-eating Piranha (*Serrasalmo nattereri*) rivals any lion. The Anglerfish (*Lophius piscatorius*) has its own rod and line and a 'bait' that dangles near its mouth, and the Blackswallower (a deep sea fish) can swallow whole fishes bigger than itself.

Like every ecosystem, any body of water has a fish population in balance with the total food supply. So a particular lake or sea will support a certain poundage of fish. This support is based on the fundamental fact that life eats life. The eating patterns may be connected in cycles, chains, or webs, but they are all part of a food pyramid. A classic example of the pyramid is the Humpback Whale, a marine mammal which needs a tonne of herring to fill its stomach, or about 5,000 fishes. Each herring needs over 5,000 crustaceans to fill its stomach and each crustacean needs over 100,000 diatoms. So the whale depends on several million, million diatoms every few hours for survival.

The food pyramid is powered by the sun which pours untold millions of photons onto the Earth's surface every day, and out of every million, 90 photons are turned into plant food by photosynthesis–about half by the land plants and half by marine phytoplankton. The annual net production of the phytoplankton is estimated to be 500,000,000 tonnes and the majority, the nanoplankton (from *nanus*, meaning dwarf), are too small to be seen without a microscope. Feeding on them are the zooplankton (animal-like plankton) and the shrimp-like krill. This plankton is eaten by shoals of fishes, either throughout life, like the herring families, or only during the larval stages when practically all fishes feed on plankton. So plankton forms the base of the pyramid and the plankton-feeding fishes form the next layer.

The plankton needs nutrients in the form of mineral salts as well as sunlight, so it flourishes where nutrient-rich cool waters well up in storms, trade winds or thermal currents such as the Gulfstream. Here also are the shoals of plankton-feeders. The shoaling fishes also show seasonal growths and migratory patterns but all are dependent on the supply of plankton. Three-quarters of the sea is a biological desert because the mineral nutrients are below the critical level in the open sea but, as there are 300,000,000 cubic miles of sea on the Earth, the quarter occupied by marine life still represents a huge base to the pyramid of food.

Carnivorous fishes feed on these shoals of herbivores to form another layer of the pyramid. The pyramid shape results from the fact that the biomass of the layer of life that can be sustained from the layer below is ever shrinking. This is because of the conversion rates. These rates are the ratio of the weight gained over the weight of foodstuffs eaten. A trout farm for example expects each trout to eat about $3\frac{1}{2}$ lb (700 gm) of commercial food to gain 1 lb (450 gm) in weight, which is 29 per cent weight conversion efficiency. Herbivores are only 20 per cent efficient and the predatory carnivores are only 10 per cent efficient. So the supportable life-forms reduce in quantity as we move up the scale. The predatory carnivores or the second-level carnivores are at the tip of the apex. The classic example of a second-level carnivore is the shark.

## Basic Nutrition

The food pyramid is simply a means of supplying one of the basics of life: nutrition. Nutrition is the support of a life-form via food, and food is any material which when ingested will provide the three basic needs:

1. Energy–for work and heat
2. Materials–for growth, maintenance, repair and reproduction
3. Substances–to control 1 and 2.

Fishes belong to that huge and successful life-form called the vertebrates, in which food is ingested through a mouth, passed through an alimentary canal and the residues expelled from a vent. The canal absorbs the nutrients from the food by breaking down the complex molecules to simple molecules that can dialyse (absorb across membranes) into the bloodstream for transportation around the body. The form of the canal varies greatly but most species have a stomach where water-soluble materials are absorbed (sugars, mineral salts, vitamin C and the B group vitamins) and an intestine for more complex materials (carbohydrates, protein, fat and the vitamins A, D, K and E).

There are six types of nutrient: proteins, fats, carbohydrates, vitamins, minerals and water; fishes require them all.

### PROTEINS

Proteins are the building blocks of all life-forms. They are composed of huge molecules made up from different blends and proportions of amino acid molecules. In fishes there are about 20 of these amino acids combined in long chains called polypeptides and bundles of these polypeptides are cross-linked to form the proteins. They all contain the basic elements of life-forms–carbon, hydrogen and oxygen–but they also contain nitrogen. When proteins have been metabolized (passed through the digestive process) the nitrogen content is excreted in the form of urea and ammonia, which rapidly converts to nitrite. These are the chemicals that pollute the aquarium –especially the marine aquarium.

Some of the amino acids can be synthesized by the fishes from digested nitrogen-containing molecules. Some

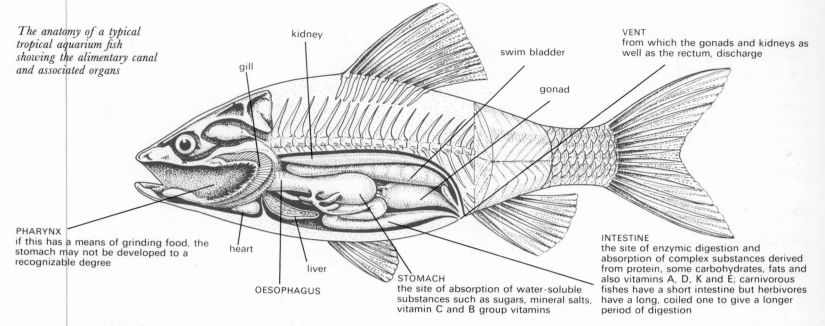

*The anatomy of a typical tropical aquarium fish showing the alimentary canal and associated organs*

kidney

gill

swim bladder

VENT
from which the gonads and kidneys as well as the rectum, discharge

gonad

PHARYNX
if this has a means of grinding food, the stomach may not be developed to a recognizable degree

heart

liver

OESOPHAGUS

STOMACH
the site of absorption of water-soluble substances such as sugars, mineral salts, vitamin C and B group vitamins

INTESTINE
the site of enzymic digestion and absorption of complex substances derived from protein, some carbohydrates, fats and also vitamins A, D, K and E; carnivorous fishes have a short intestine but herbivores have a long, coiled one to give a longer period of digestion

cannot, and these are known as the essential amino acids. Without them an animal will weaken and die, no matter how much food is taken. About eight of the 20 amino acids are essential in both fish and man. Every protein source has its own combination and proportions of the various amino acids. If the protein intake falls below the fish's requirements then the most scarce amino acid becomes the limiting one. In most protein sources, this limiting amino acid is methionine, which is unfortunate because fish require more methionine than any other vertebrate. On the other hand, it makes fishes a rich source of methionine for other vertebrates and fish meal is used widely as a food supplement for farmed animals.

One of the best protein sources because of its ideal amino acid profile is a hen's egg. This is why boiled egg yolk, pressed through muslin, is very useful for feeding to newly hatched fry.

## FATS
Fats are not just lard or oil. They are a very complex family of lipids, phospholipids, fatty acids, alcohols, oils and esters, all of which have long or very long carbon chains. These chains can be single- or double-bonded between the carbon atoms and each type is known as a saturated or unsaturated fat. Saturated fats are usually solid, and unsaturated fats are usually oils. Fishes use unsaturated fats because they are cold-blooded and their fat must be mobile even in the Arctic seas. Just like proteins, fats are a complex mixture of components some of which are essential and can be limiting.

## CARBOHYDRATES
Carbohydrates are the energy source of fishes. Like the other nutrients, their range is wide and complex. The most complex of this widely ranging group is cellulose, a nutrient source which is chemically difficult to digest and is therefore usually treated as roughage by many species. Some carp, however, can digest cellulose using bacterial help, just like the ruminant mammals. Starch is the next most complex carbohydrate and is a particularly cheap source of energy because it is widely stored by plants. Sugars, of which the domestic form – sucrose – is but one, are another form of complex carbohydrate. If excess carbohydrates are ingested, a complex body chemistry converts them to fats to be stored as an energy

source if the food supply fails. Fishes are well adapted to use this storage method because their natural food supplies are so variable. These fat stores can be extensive (as in sardines, for example) and it is good practice to make a fish draw on its store of fat by imposing periods of starvation (during your holidays or by feeding only six days per week).

## VITAMINS
Vitamins are the catalysts or activators of the complex biological processes and as with all catalysts, a little goes a long way. They fall into two major groups, the fat-soluble and the water-soluble. Despite some advertizing claims, each vitamin has a multifunctional role. No one food source has all the vitamins a fish requires but all food sources have some vitamins. There is also evidence that fishes need more vitamins per unit body weight than do mammals, probably because they are lower in the evolutionary scale and their biochemical pathways are simpler and less efficient than mammals. This explains why a diet of exclusively human food (kitchen scraps) is inadequate for aquarium fishes.

## MINERALS
These materials are also activators like the vitamins, but are usually reactants in the body chemistry and therefore cannot be considered catalysts. A good example is iron which is necessary for the manufacture of haemoglobin in the fish's blood. The list of minerals is long and complex, and interaction is important too: calcium and phosphorus, for example, must be present in a ratio of about 3:2 for a fish's teeth and bones. There is little calcium and phosphorus in beef heart and so an exclusive diet of this popular food will lead to bone deficiencies in aquarium fishes.

## WATER
Water is essential to life, particularly to fishes since it is also their habitat. The primaeval seas in which the fishes evolved were less saline than modern seas. Modern fishes have body fluids that reflect the salinity of those primaeval seas, so a sea fish is less 'salty' than the surrounding water. By the process called osmosis (the passage of water across membranes to equalize concentrations of solution on either side) the sea fish is continually losing water to the

surrounding sea and it must drink continuously, extract and excrete the salts, and digest the water to make up the loss. A freshwater fish, however, has a higher salt level than its surroundings and so absorbs water by osmosis through its outer surface. This excess water is simply excreted and the fish does not drink the water in which it swims. This explains why a marine tank is more difficult to maintain than a freshwater tank; the marine fishes drink their own pollution but the freshwater fishes do not.

# Aquarium Foods

### DRIED FOODS

Walk into any aquarists' shop and you will probably see a bewildering display of commercial fish foods. The well advertized products are made by large companies, often of international standing and represent years of research and development. Many of these foods are similar in constitution, but even so, they vary considerably in price and often this does reflect the quality. If you want a bulk food to feed to a large collection of fishes, supplemented by considerable amounts of live or wet foods, then choose a cheap variety. If you want to feed an exclusive diet of a convenience food, then choose the best quality (and probably the dearest). The problem of the commercial fish food producers is to supply the nutrients chosen for your pet fish in a stable form. A blend of foodstuffs will deteriorate unless stabilized in some way. Drying the foods is an ideal method of stabilization because, for the reasons given earlier, the fishes do not need the natural water content of the foods.

The dried food can be pelletized, granulated or flaked. Pellets are useful for pond fishes and the larger cichlids because they are 'mouth-sized' and, by incorporating a little air in the processing, they can be made to float for a long time. This allows surplus pellets to be netted from the tank surface after feeding, whereas a sinking pellet may be lost and eventually pollute the aquarium water. Granulated foods are accepted by some varieties and the fine granules are useful for baby fishes. Dried foods in flake form are the most popular. The reason is that flakes will float on the surface for top feeders, sink for middle feeders as they become wet, and finally lie discretely on the gravel for bottom feeders. Flakes can be crumbled for small fishes or fed individually to the aquarium fish as desired. The flakes made from the cheaper raw materials are powdered foods (called meals) glued together with gelatin and are sold in cardboard drums because they are quite stable and odourless. The better quality meals are used in high class flakes and these are usually packed in rigid plastic containers since the odour can attract insects and lead to infestation. Flakes made directly from whole fish, fresh meats and fresh vegetables have to be hermetically sealed into a metal can to preserve the freshness.

One of the advantages of using fresh fish and meats rather than meals in a flake food is that a better balanced diet can be formulated. The meals often have low levels of the essential amino acids because of the heat damage to the proteins in the drying process. To compensate, the total protein levels have to be very high and although this is nutritionally adequate it does lead to an imbalance in the protein/carbohydrate intake. The high protein content has to be metabolized, and so tank polluting nitrogenous residues are formed (ammonia and nitrite for example).

Another factor to be aware of is the method of measurement. The traditional method is to measure chemically the total nitrogen content and use a factor to convert the result into 'probable' protein (per cent nitrogen × 6.25 = per cent protein is the common formula). This means that gelatin used to glue fish meal together, or any other material containing nitrogen, will be recorded as protein. If this formula gives a high value, coupled with the necessary high protein level to raise the essential amino acid content, the label claim on the fish food container may show a very high value indeed (40, 50 even 60 per cent). Traditional marketing methods always make a feature of any outstanding values and this has led to an advertizing campaign where the proportion of protein is quoted as being higher than anyone else's. This in turn has led the hobbyist to believe that the higher the protein value, the better the food. This is quite wrong, of course; the ideal diet should be properly balanced and if any one nutrient, be it protein, fat or carbohydrate, is in excess, then that diet is not balanced. The important factor in protein content is not the quantity but the quality.

### FREEZE-DRIED FOODS

Freeze-drying is a method of producing the stable dried form of a foodstuff without using heat. This avoids any heat damage and keeps the cells of the food in their original physical shape, hence freeze-dried food can be reconstituted by wetting it. The water is removed by a process called sublimation which is the conversion of the solid form (ice) directly to gas (water vapour). The process speeded up by applying a vacuum to the frozen food. This is known as accelerated freeze-drying (AFD). It is an expensive process and AFD foods tend to be dear, but the food can be prepared in its original shape, and thus AFD Shrimp, *Daphnia*, *Tubifex* and others can be made available. The AFD process also kills any parasites that may be present, but not all bacteria, so only good, clean, disease-free ingredients should be treated in this way. The aquarist should again choose the best quality products to ensure that such good ingredients are used. Buying the cheap varieties is a false economy. Some nutrient loss does occur in the process, so freeze-dried foods should not be considered a complete diet.

### FROZEN FOODS

Deep-freezing avoids all the problems of drying, but a freezer is required to store the foods. Although freezing stops bacterial degradation, enzymic (chemical) degradation continues, albeit at a slow pace and deep-frozen food must therefore be considered to have a limited shelf life. A year is the maximum period for safe storage. Another problem is that unlike heat drying or AFD, deep-freezing does not kill bacterial spores and some parasitic spores which can survive to infect the fishes, especially in marine aquariums. Some manufacturers have overcome this problem by irradiating the frozen product to kill such spores, but this is an expensive process, as is freezing, transport and storage at low temperatures. Irradiated fish foods are consequently very expensive. However, for exotic species requiring a special diet, particularly the coral fishes, they are a useful addition to the range.

## SCRAP FOODS

Fish is a very good for man and so many hobbyists believe that man-foods must be good for fish. Kitchen scraps, from boiled peas to sliced cherries, are often used. Up to a point, these hobbyists are quite correct. Fishes can utilize human foods, but they are not suitable as an exclusive diet. The reason is that man is more highly evolved than fishes and his biochemical processes are more sophisticated; vitamins particularly are utilized more efficiently by man and so smaller quantities are required than are needed by fishes. Hence a permanent, exclusive diet of scrapings from your evening meal would eventually lead to the fishes' death from vitamin deficiency. But as a treat food, or as a variation from a basic flake diet, such scrap foods are appreciated by most species. Vegetarian fishes, such as many livebearers, appreciate some crushed lettuce, a boiled pea or a little spinach. The carnivorous fish, such as many cichlids, like a piece of fish or meat. Beef heart is a popular food for difficult feeders and should always be tried with newly installed, nervous fish which are refusing to eat. The high blood content gives an attractive 'flavour' in the water but also leads to rapid pollution, so do not over-feed this particular food. The beef heart may be bought quite cheaply from any butcher and, for the reasons explained earlier, should be trimmed of all fat before freezing for storage (preferably deep-freezing for long storage). The frozen beef heart can be shredded with a cheese shredder or, for large fish, bite-size pieces can be cut prior to freezing. Small frozen sections can be fed directly to the fish, but large pieces should be thawed before being fed, to prevent any chilling of the fish's gut. Liver is also appreciated by most fishes but again any fat must be removed. The liver and heart which are often packed in a plastic bag inside broiler chickens are a useful supply.

Avoid starchy foods such as bread and biscuit, and any foods that are soluble or spiced. Egg, cheese and many fruits can be fed, but first reduce the food to a size suitable for the fish's mouth by cutting, or even chewing. The fishes themselves will show their likes and dislikes. Always remove excess or rejected foods and remember that no scrap food is suitable for exclusive feeding; all forms must be considered only as a source of variety in the diet and as emergency foods.

## AQUATIC LIVE FOODS

The ideal food for a fish is the food it would eat in its natural habitat. For many species this will be a seasonal range of aquatic creatures, from the tiny infusoria and rotifers to *Daphnia*, nematodes, snails and the many types of shrimp, not forgetting any other fish that can be fitted into the mouth and even their own offspring. The diet may also include plants, from algae to land varieties and fruits that fall into the water.

For the aquarist, the problem with such a diet is that eventually and inevitably, live foods collected from the wild will introduce some disease or parasite. In nature the fishes are in balance with all the parasitic diseases, but when these parasites are added to the crowded, closed environment of the aquarium, the balance is tipped in favour of the parasite. Disease spreads rapidly and is usually fatal to the delicate fishes, some of which may have been bred for generations in the sterile conditions of the aquarium and as a result have no resistance to even the mildest of diseases.

You will always find an aquarist who has fed *Daphnia* from his local pond, or *Tubifex* worms dug from a local river, for years and years and so claims the disease problem is nonsense, but this is simply because infestation and infection is always a biological gamble. He may win for years; you may lose all your fishes after the first feeding. When there are so many alternatives available to the hobbyist, why take the risk? Many aquarium shops sell live food such as *Daphnia*, usually in a bactericidal solution, and *Tubifex* worms. If you are having problems in feeding a particular fish, or have many mouths to feed because you are breeding, then these foods can be used. The risk is slight with screened *Daphnia*, but there is a greater risk with *Tubifex*. These worms feed on detritus and are found only in polluted waters. Storing them in running water to flush away contaminants helps reduce the risk.

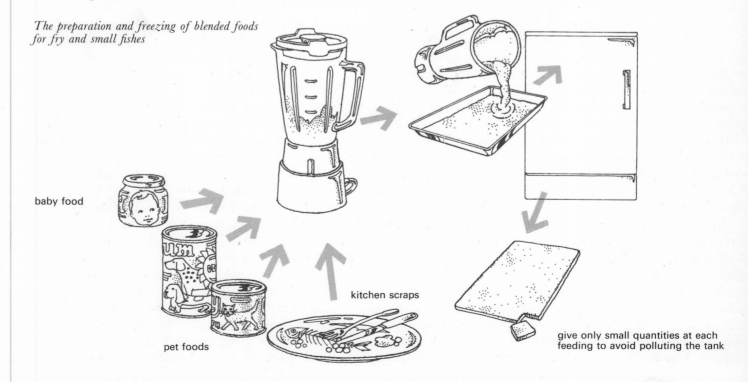

*The preparation and freezing of blended foods for fry and small fishes*

baby food

pet foods

kitchen scraps

give only small quantities at each feeding to avoid polluting the tank

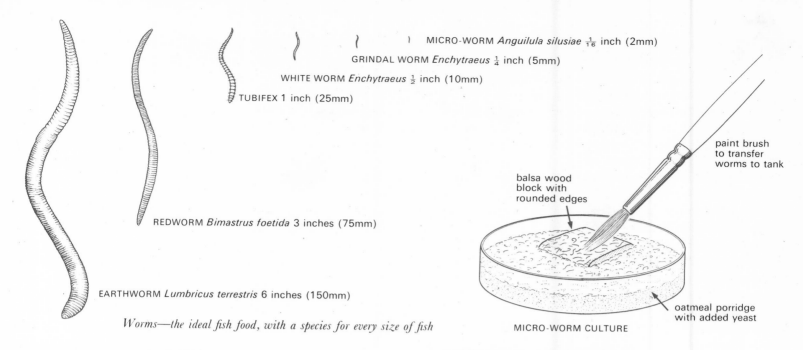

MICRO-WORM *Anguilula silusiae* $\frac{1}{16}$ inch (2mm)

GRINDAL WORM *Enchytraeus* $\frac{1}{4}$ inch (5mm)

WHITE WORM *Enchytraeus* $\frac{1}{2}$ inch (10mm)

TUBIFEX 1 inch (25mm)

REDWORM *Bimastrus foetida* 3 inches (75mm)

EARTHWORM *Lumbricus terrestris* 6 inches (150mm)

*Worms—the ideal fish food, with a species for every size of fish*

paint brush
to transfer
worms to tank

balsa wood
block with
rounded edges

oatmeal porridge
with added yeast

MICRO-WORM CULTURE

## NON-AQUATIC LIVE FOODS

There is no doubt that many fishes appreciate live foods. They help bring breeding pairs into condition and give that extra sparkle to fishes on the show bench. It is much safer to feed these live foods from a non-aquatic source and so almost eliminate the danger of parasitic, bacterial or viral diseases. Practically anything of the right size can be considered, but a few obvious precautions must be taken. Do not take worms, slugs or snails from lawns treated with weedkillers or other chemical gardening aids. Do not use flies, moths or other insects from situations where insecticides have been used.

Top of the list is the Common Earthworm (*Lumbricus terrestris*). This worm can be found on any lawn, the best time being after rain and at night. Use a torch to collect the worms, but tread softly because vibrations send the worms back to their holes. A spade will turn up many worms from below and help the garden too. They can also be encouraged to gather under a sack laid on a spare patch of earth, especially if the sacking is soaked in tea-leaves, coffee-grounds and kitchen scraps. The smaller red-worms (*Bimastrus foetida* and *Lumbricus rubellus*) are often found with the Common Earthworm. These species are ideal for fishes and can often be fed whole, whereas the larger worm usually has to be chopped. Wash the worms in running water. The Dung Worm (*Eisenia foetida*) should be avoided because of its faecal diet. It is easily identified by its yellow, rather than brown or red colour.

Next are the assorted flying insects, especially the swarms on a late summer's evening. To collect these, use a fine fish net, or stretch a nylon stocking onto a frame, and attach it to the bumper of your car. A return from any drive will yield a harvest of live foods. This technique is not recommended if you live in the heart of an industrial city because of the pollution you will also collect.

Garden plants, especially roses, will yield a variety of live foods. Collect aphids from the roses (unsprayed, of course) with a small paint-brush and collecting pot. Larger fishes will appreciate caterpillars, although some species have defence mechanisms against predators in the form of irritant bristles or toxic secretions. Your fishes will simply reject them too. Slugs and snails can be fed whole, or sliced (if you can bear to do it). They can be found in any damp and shady place, especially after rain.

## CULTURED LIVE FOODS

These are the safest living foods because you can control the conditions of storage to ensure that diseases are absent.

**Aquarium fishes** If you have a voracious carnivore as a pet fish, it is possible to keep it supplied with a constant source of live fishes by keeping a spare tank with live-bearers such as Guppies or mollies and feeding these on a high quality flake food. The ethics of such a diet you must justify to the lovers of the Guppy and the molly. A predator in the marine aquarium such as a lionfish (*Pterois*) can be fed runts and sickly freshwater fishes often available cheaply from your local dealer. The reason is that there are few freshwater fish diseases that can be transferred to marine fish. Never feed sickly marine fishes or invertebrates to a lionfish.

**White worms** There are several species of these small white worms (*Enchytraeus*) of 5 to 10 mm in length. The smaller varieties are also called grindal worms. They normally live in very moist soils, such as river banks, feeding on decaying vegetable matter. All are eaten greedily by small or medium-sized tropical fish, although the worms must not be fed routinely because they can lead to digestive problems. Some aquarists have reported constipation in tropicals fed on large numbers of the worms. Once or twice weekly feeds should avoid such problems.

To culture these worms any non-toxic container filled with a good quality loam, or soil with added peat can be used. Avoid sandy or clay soils and chemically fertilized soils. The soil must have a loamy consistency to retain moisture and yet be friable. Add enough water so that the soil can be squeezed into a ball without water dripping or the ball collapsing. White worms can be bought from some aquarium shops or via mail order from advertizers in aquarists' magazines. Place the seed culture on the soil and cover with a close fitting sheet of glass or plastic to retain moisture. Spray with water to keep the soil moist and feed with a spoonful of porridge placed on the surface. The porridge can be made from any kitchen scraps that will form a creamy mass, such as bread and milk, biscuits, potatoes and cakes, with additions of baby foods, fruit and vegetables. The more nutrients you pack into the worms, the more you pass on to your fish. The more you feed, the more worms you produce. The culture can also be reduced by restricting the amount of food. The box should be stored in a cool dark place. The fish house is unsuitable because the worms will die off at 68°F (20°C). Near freezing point reproduction ceases; the ideal temperature is 59°F (15°C). A shelf in a garage is a good place, and is likely to be free from invasions by ants or mice. When a crust forms on the soil and unpleasant smells develop, start a new culture. The worms like an alkaline pH so a slight dusting of baking soda helps.

To collect the worms, peel up the blob of porridge and they will be seen feeding beneath or around the edge. They can be collected individually with a pair of tweezers, or a piece of worm-rich soil can be placed in a jar of water; the jar is shaken and the muddy water poured off after allowing the heavier worms to settle to the bottom.

**Micro-worms** The micro-worm is a nematode (*Anguilula silusiae*) and is only 2 or 3 mm long. The young are small enough to replace brine shrimp larvae as first foods for fry. The worms are cultivated in the supplied foodstuff which is usually a very thick oatmeal porridge, but a little added yeast will raise the nutritional value. Micro-worms feed and breed at the surface, so the porridge should be stored in a shallow container covered by a glass sheet to prevent the mix drying out. A culture, bought from an aquarium shop or mail order supplier, is placed on the surface of the porridge and the container is stored in a warm dark place at between 68°F and 86°F (20°C to 30°C). The worms will breed and multiply during the first few days. The culture can be used to seed new cultures when the porridge becomes stale or dries out. A culture should last 10 or 12 weeks with occasional use.

To remove the worms, place moist pieces of balsa wood (or other porous wood) on the surface a few hours before feeding; the worms will swarm over the wood and can be washed into the aquarium. Some aquarists keep a small block of wood permanently in the centre and sweep the worms off the top of this wood. The corners of the block should be rounded off to help the worms climb aboard. Other techniques include placing some of the culture in a saucer over a warm spot (such as a cooking stove pilot light cover) to drive the worms from the porridge. They can be swept from the saucer edges into the tank.

**Brine shrimps** The newly hatched brine shrimp larvae (the scientific name is *Artemia salina*) are an excellent first food for fry. The eggs are bought from a dealer and hatched in salt water at about 86°F (30°C) in 24 to 36 hours. In recent years the percentage hatchings of the traditional American brine shrimp eggs has been falling steadily. The reasons have been blamed on pollution, biological rhythms, improper preparation and over-harvesting. Perhaps all these factors are involved. The usual formula is two slightly heaped tablespoons of rock salt per two litres of tap water. Do not use table salt because it usually contains an iodide and an anti-caking chemical. Make up the brine in a glass jar and place it in a brightly lit place because light aids hatching. A very bright light (use a pencil torch for example) will make the newly hatched larvae congregate in the beam of light, when they can be siphoned off or sucked into a pipette. This prevents the spent eggshells getting into the aquarium – the shells are

very tough and are not suitable food for the fishes. Unless the fry are marine fishes, the brine should be removed by filtering off the shrimps in a fine cloth (handkerchief) and rinsing them lightly before they are added to the fry tank. For species that like a little salt in the water (e.g. live-bearers and goldfish) the rinsing can be omitted. In marine aquariums a small plastic pot with a small hole drilled about two-thirds up from the bottom can be mounted by means of a sucker in one corner of the tank. Brine shrimp eggs added to the pot will hatch and the shrimps, seeking the light, will swim through the hole to give a steady supply of food for many filter feeders and small marine animals. Where large numbers of brine shrimp are needed, they can be hatched in a glass filter-funnel with the spout sealed over an air-stone to blow air continuously into the funnel. The oxygen-rich water gives rapid hatching if the light and salinity is correct and if the air is stopped, the shells sink into the V-shaped base of the funnel leaving a supernatant layer of water rich in shrimps for siphoning off.

It is possible to mature the brine shrimps for feeding to adult fish. The larvae should be placed in a small aquarium prepared earlier by filling with salt water and exposing it in a sunny window to turn green with algae. The shrimp may also be fed with a little live yeast. The art is to provide the shrimp with sufficient food without polluting the water.

**Infusoria** Infusoria are the smallest of live foods and are suitable for newly hatched fry. For the very small fry of fishes such as the Anabantidae, infusoria are indispensable for the first few days. Infusoria is the common name for a collection of hundreds of different species of Protozoa (single-celled animals) which can be found in any body of mature water. The maturity is necessary to provide the infusoria with their food, bacteria.

To make an infusoria culture, a container of water must be seeded with organic material to grow the bacteria and then with infusoria to feed on the bacteria. The container can be anything transparent – large jars are ideal. The organic material can be anything too, but experience has shown that lettuce leaves, hay, banana skins, potato peelings and hard-boiled egg yolks all give good cultures. The amount needed is only small; for example, two small lettuce leaves per litre of water. The leaves should be beaten with the back of a spoon to break up the plant cells and so release the cell fluids into the water. To make an infusion of hay, boiling water can be poured over a little broken hay. The solution of organic material should be left to mature, preferably in a warm, dark (or dull) place for a few days. The culture is ready for seeding when the water is turbid and probably has a stale smell. If left standing with no cover, the infusoria will develop spontaneously from airborne spores. Seeding can be made from other cultures, pond water, aged aquariums or the water from a vase of flowers. Within a few days the water will clear as the infusoria eat the bacteria. The minute protozoans can just be seen with the naked eye, especially if the jar is held up to the light. Once the culture is clear, sweet smelling and full of infusoria, it can be poured unceremoniously into the aquarium to feed the fry. Obviously timing is the important factor, so the cultures must be started ahead of any planned spawnings. Do not rely on a single culture—make several to ensure a good supply.

# Principles of Feeding

All beginners and most aquarists overfeed their fishes. Actually you cannot overfeed the fishes, only the aquarium, but since most fish can eat more food than they require and simply excrete the excess, they themselves can pollute the aquarium. In the wild, fishes pass through lean times as food supplies wax and wane. To overcome the lean times, fishes store fat as oil in various internal organs. To mobilize this store of fat, periods of starvation are advantageous to aquarium fishes, so they should be fed only six days a week and left unfed when you are away from home for a few days.

How much should one feed the fishes is the first question any beginner will ask, and it is the most difficult one to answer. Quantity depends on such variables as species, age, size, number, stock density and even temperature. With experience, every aquarist develops a feel for the quantity of food his particular collection of fishes requires. A good rule of thumb is to add small quantities of the particular food and let each fish eat for a minute or two. Feeding should then stop and any surplus be netted out (not forgetting to leave a small amount on the bottom of the tank if bottom feeders such as catfishes are present). If flake food is the main diet, a 30 or 40 gram tin of high quality flake

should last the average 22 gallon (100 litre) tank of community tropicals about a month. This is based on two feeds per day, six days a week. Fishes soon recognize their owner (or at least associate him with food) and rush to 'greet' him when he approaches the tank. The aquarist must resist the obvious response to this display if it is not feeding time.

When feeding fishes observe their reactions, especially if a varied or experimental diet is being fed. Because of bullying or differences in feeding habits some fishes may always get the lion's share. The bully can be chased away with a net handle and a timid fish can be fed individually using tongs, dip-tube or even by hand. Notice also if the food is rejected after experimental tasting. Do not confuse rejection with playing with the food; angelfish, for example, are prone to suck and blow bits of food before taking the morsel.

## FRESHWATER FISHES

There are three major groups of freshwater tropical fishes, the carnivores, the herbivores and by far the largest group, the omnivores. There is no such thing as an 'absolute' carnivore because even predatory fishes will swallow smaller herbivorous fishes and digest them, including their stomach contents. A typical example in the world of

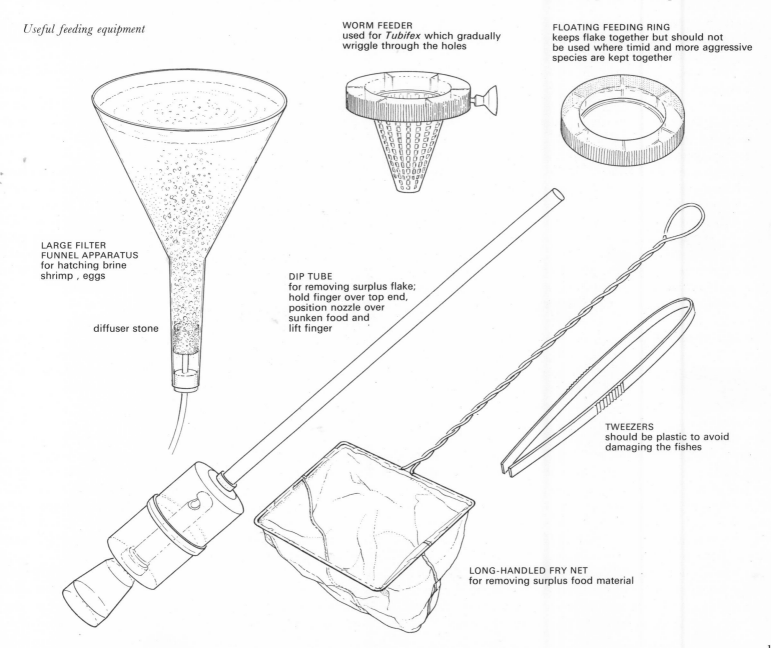

*Useful feeding equipment*

**WORM FEEDER**
used for *Tubifex* which gradually wriggle through the holes

**FLOATING FEEDING RING**
keeps flake together but should not be used where timid and more aggressive species are kept together

**LARGE FILTER FUNNEL APPARATUS**
for hatching brine shrimp , eggs

diffuser stone

**DIP TUBE**
for removing surplus flake; hold finger over top end, position nozzle over sunken food and lift finger

**TWEEZERS**
should be plastic to avoid damaging the fishes

**LONG-HANDLED FRY NET**
for removing surplus food material

mammals is the lion. This carnivore will eat the intestines, including their vegetable contents, before eating the muscle and bone of their prey. Similarly there is no such thing as an absolute herbivore because even algae eaters will always take the odd insect or larva when presented. The chemical processes of digestion can cope with any proteins, fats and most carbohydrates whatever the source. It is physiological difference that allows a fish to obtain more benefit from a generally carnivorous or vegetable or mixed diet. Hence you can feed a community of fishes with as wide a variety of foods as you can devise, with confidence that they will all benefit from such a diet.

The particular nutritional requirements of a given species can be found in the ichthyological literature. The diet can then be biased in favour of the type of foods preferred by that fish. An example is the Black Molly (*Poecilia sphenops* var.), which is a herbivorous fish. This species loves to eat algae and so some should be left on the glass, or on plastic plants, for the fish to browse upon. Commercial vegetable diet flake foods are also available for such fishes. Another example is the family Cichlidae, most species of which are carnivorous and readily take lumps of raw meat as part of their diet.

## MARINE FISHES
The digestive processes of marine fishes are no different to those of their freshwater cousins. The large difference in aquarium conditions between fresh and salt water species tends to make the hobbyist believe that the diet must be different too. This is not so. All the foods listed previously are equally suitable for marine fish. Again there are the general groupings into carnivores, herbivores and omnivores. There are more difficult feeders in the marine aquarium and the diet should be biased towards foods of marine origins to help feed these fishes. Suitable foods can be found on any fishmonger's slab–boiled crabs, prawns and shrimps and any fillets of fish. It is also possible to obtain live shellfish from most coasts, but there is always the danger of introducing diseases and parasites.

## FRY
Fry and young fishes need much more food relative to their body weight than do adult fishes. Most tropicals are adult within six months and then require only a maintenance diet. The fry need to have permanently full bellies and this must be checked by observing them with a magnifying glass. Where commercial considerations demand rapid growth, fry can be raised to a selling size by combining frequent feeds and frequent water changes. The fish density should be low and when the fry have to be divided between tanks it is best to move the smaller fish. The best rate of growth is shown by fishes which remain in their tank of birth; fishes which are moved to new surroundings show a marked check in their growth rate, so leave the best fishes in the first tank.

The frequent feeds can be round the clock, in which case the light should be left on all the time. Another technique is to use a spotlight which concentrates infusoria, and then brine shrimp larvae, in a small area. The fry can then feed intensively without wasting energy chasing such foods all over the aquarium. An average quantity of infusoria culture is two or three tablespoons every two or three hours for 50 fry in a 5 gallon (20 litre) tank.

If the infusoria fail during the crucial first few days after the egg sac has been absorbed, a useful substitute is hard-boiled egg yolk squeezed through a handkerchief into the water, with a little shaking motion to distribute the cloud of food. Care must be taken not to pollute the tank by overdoing the quantity fed. Another substitute is 'Aylott's Soup' (so called after the British aquarist who swears by it!). To prepare this, place a cleaned red earthworm in a pestle and squash it with a mortar; add a flake or two of cereal or fish food and grind into a paste; add a little water, grind again and then add more water, until the mortar is full; leave to stand for about 20 minutes and the heavier particles will settle leaving a supernatant soup of particles in suspension which are of typical infusoria size and very nutritious. This liquid can be poured into the fry tank every two hours or so in quantities enough to keep the fishes showing a full belly but never more.

## REFUSAL TO FEED
Wild fishes may have been under considerable stress after capture and shipment. It is common for such fishes to go into a state of shock and to refuse all foods until they die of starvation; persuading them to feed requires much patience. Do not startle them at feeding time by approaching the tank carelessly, banging covers or switching on bright lights. Have an assortment of foods available to tempt them and use a pair of forceps (plastic ones are preferable to avoid possible damage to the fishes) to offer the food. This is better than handling the food because your fingers can impart repellent flavours as any angler will confirm.

Try every food listed in these pages and once a preference is shown, fatten the fish on this particular food before trying to wean it onto a more conventional or varied diet. There are two groups of foods which may trigger feeding–those with strong flavours, such as canned flake food or beef heart, and moving live foods, such as *Daphnia* or *Tubifex*.

Some species, for example Discus, will not feed because of a timid nature. A good technique in this case is to add a companion fish who is well adjusted to your tank and foods. The companion fish will show the timid fish what to do, or competition may trigger a feeding response.

# Special Feeders

There are many aquarium dwellers that require a special diet or presentation of the foodstuff. If you want to keep such specimens you must be aware of their particular needs.

## PIPEFISHES (Syngnathidae)
These fishes from the fresh, brackish and salt waters of Thailand are as difficult to feed as the seahorses of the marine aquarium. A constant supply of small live foods is essential such as brine shrimp larvae, white worms and screened *Daphnia*.

## SPINY EEL (*Mastacembelus pancalus*)
The Spiny Eels are found in the Far East and are considered difficult aquarium fishes because of their tank-wrecking activities. They also are difficult to feed because although their bodies are large their head is small with a

tiny mouth. *Hydra* are taken readily but this is not a food that can be cultured in sufficient quantities (*Hydra* is a pest in the breeding tank because it will eat fry). In their natural habitat they eat blood worms. Sometimes these aquatic worms (which cannot be cultured) are available from the aquarium shop. White worms and the smallest earthworms should be suitable for these fishes.

## CLOWN KNIFE FISH (*Notopterus chitala*)
This is one of the few aquarium fishes which feeds at night, and it must be fed after the lights have been turned out.

## LARGE FISHES
Flake food is not suitable for big fishes such as Cichlidae. Chunks of meat, fish and offal can be used instead, but wrap these around a few flakes to ensure that vitamins and minerals are present. Whole worms, maggots, boiled peas, and pond pellets can all be fed. Pet food from cans and some dried cat-foods are suitable, but do not feed the so-called semi-moist pet foods. These look like plastic minced meat and are sold in plastic or cellophane bags. The preservation system of these foods is based on sugar (they are literally meaty candy) and the sugars will pollute the aquarium and cause obesity in the fish. Trout pellets are useful but not as a continuous diet. These are very high in protein (for rapid growth of trout fry) and so will very quickly pollute the aquarium.

## ALGAE EATERS
Fishes which eat algae, such as the Sucking Loach (*Gyrinocheilus aymonieri*) or Black Molly (*Poecilia sphenops*

var.) can be fed by allowing algae to grow in controlled areas. A useful technique is to have a spotlight beaming into the tank (through a glass cover). The algae will grow prolifically only in the beam of light.

An alternative supply of green food can be supplied if algae are excluded from the tank. Lettuce leaves, for example, can be scalded with boiling water to make them edible. Boiled peas can be squashed from their skin and the pulp fed to the fish. Boiled spinach is an often recommended vegetable, but this should not be fed to excess because of its high oxalic acid content. Commercial vegetable flake foods are available and these make an ideal diet for these vegetarian fishes.

## PREDATORY CARNIVORES
There are a few fishes which will eat only live foods. Some piranhas fall into this category, although with patience they can be weaned onto flake food. Many lionfish (*Pterois*) will often refuse any food unless it is alive, but again there are some species, such as the Common Lionfish (*P. volitans*) which can be weaned onto chunky scrapfoods. To supply such predators regularly with live foods, a spare tank will be needed to raise live-bearers. These fishes should be well fed with a good quality flake just prior to feeding them to the lionfish or piranhas.

Finally, remember that in the wild, fishes seek their preferred foods and the species will thrive where that food is both suitable and nourishing as well as plentiful. In the aquarium the fishes are totally dependent on you, the aquarist. So for healthy, colourful, active fishes, study their needs and supply them with food that is suitable and nourishing – but not too plentiful.

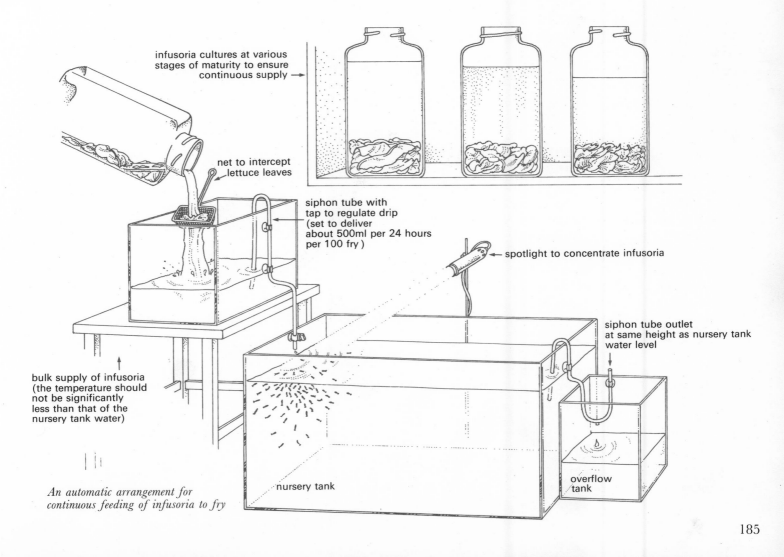

infusoria cultures at various stages of maturity to ensure continuous supply →

net to intercept lettuce leaves

siphon tube with tap to regulate drip (set to deliver about 500ml per 24 hours per 100 fry)

spotlight to concentrate infusoria

siphon tube outlet at same height as nursery tank water level

bulk supply of infusoria (the temperature should not be significantly less than that of the nursery tank water)

nursery tank

overflow tank

*An automatic arrangement for continuous feeding of infusoria to fry*

# FEEDING GUIDE

KEY TO FEEDING TYPE:
**E** easily fed on all types of food
**D** difficult to persuade to eat in captivity
**F** finicky feeder; offer a wide variety of foods and carefully watch to see what it will take
**L** will eat live foods only

**W** initially requires live foods but may be weaned gradually onto a wider variety
**G** requires some green food such as algae, lettuce and green flake
**C** cannot compete for their food with larger or faster fishes
**N** narrow- or small-mouthed fishes which can take only small items
**I** more likely to feed in a marine invertebrate aquarium

## FRESHWATER TROPICAL FISHES

| | Popular name | Scientific name | Feeding type | First foods for fry | Remarks |
|---|---|---|---|---|---|
| **THE TOP TWENTY COMMUNITY FISHES** | Angelfish | *Pterophyllum scalare* | E | infusoria | greedy but may be temperamental |
| | Swordtail | *Xiphophorus helleri* | E, G | powdered foods | algae browser and top feeder |
| | Platy | *Xiphophorus maculatus* | E | powdered foods | frequent small feeds preferred |
| | Zebra Danio | *Brachydanio rerio* | E, N | infusoria | |
| | Neon Tetra | *Paracheirodon innesi* | E | infusoria | small fish and so may become food for others |
| | Dwarf Gourami | *Colisa lalia* | E | infusoria | fry are very small so infusoria must be fine |
| | Black Molly | *Poecilia sphenops* var. | E, G | powdered foods | algae browser |
| | Red-tailed Black Shark | *Labeo bicolor* | E, G | difficult to breed | algae browser and bottom feeder |
| | Harlequin | *Rasbora heteromorpha* | E | infusoria | |
| | Cardinal Tetra | *Cheirodon axelrodi* | E | infusoria | fry are difficult to feed and raise |
| | Whitecloud Mountain Minnow | *Tanichthys albonubes* | E | infusoria | prefers to feed in shoals |
| | Siamese Fighting Fish | *Betta splendens* | E | infusoria | |
| | Guppy | *Poecilia reticulatus* | E, G, N | fine foods | benefits from small live foods occasionally |
| | Glowlight Tetra | *Hemigrammus gracilis* | E, C | infusoria | |
| | Flame Fish | *Hyphessobrycon flammeus* | E, C | infusoria | |
| | Scissortail | *Rasbora trilineata* | E | infusoria | |
| | Blind Cave Fish | *Anoptichthys jordani* | E | infusoria | blindness is no handicap to finding food |
| | Black Widow | *Gymnocorymbus ternetzi* | E | infusoria | |
| | Kuhli Loach | *Acanthophthalmus semicinctus* | E | infusoria | bottom feeder and good scavenger |
| | Sucking Loach | *Gyrinocheilus aymonieri* | E, G | difficult to breed | will browse on excess algae |
| **SPECIALITY FISHES** | Killifishes | Cyprinodontidae | E or F | microworm and newly-hatched brine shrimp | live foods need to be part of diet |
| | Discus | *Symphysodon discus* | E or F | fed by parents | can be temperamental |
| | Cichlids | Cichlidae | E | infusoria or fine foods | chunky food preferred |
| | Piranha | *Serrasalmo nattereri* | E or F | difficult to breed | not a ferocious feeder in the aquarium |
| | Barbs | *Barbus* | E | infusoria | no teeth, so food must be mouth-sized |
| | Rasboras | *Rasbora* | E | infusoria | |
| | Characins | Characidae | E | infusoria | have teeth and some will bite at anything |
| | Catfishes | *Corydoras* | E | microworm and newly-hatched brine shrimp | bottom feeders |
| | Labyrinth fishes | Anabantidae | E | fine infusoria | midwater feeders |
| | Gobies | *Brachygobius* *Gobius, Stigmatogobius* | L, C E | difficult to breed difficult to breed | |

# MARINE TROPICAL FISHES

| Popular name | Scientific name | Feeding type | Remarks |
|---|---|---|---|
| Angels | *Pomacanthus, Holocanthus* and *Centropyge* | W, G | may learn to be hand fed |
| | *Euxiphipops* and *Pygoplites* | F, G, N | |
| Anthias and Purple Queens | *Anthias* and *Mirolabrichthys* | F | |
| Batfishes | *Platax orbicularis* | E, G | may outgrow tank |
| | *Platax pinnatus* and *teira* | D, F, G | some can be hand fed |
| Blennies | *Blennius* and *Ecsenius* | W, C, I | mainly bottom feeders |
| Boxfishes and cowfishes | *Ostracion, Acanthostracion* and *Lactoria* | F, C, N | midwater feeders |
| Butterflies | *Heniochus acuminatus* | E | |
| | *Chaetodon auriga, ephippium, fasciatus, lunula mertensi, rafflesi, semilarvatus* and *vagabundus* | W then E | these are the easiest *Chaetodon* species to feed; most others are temperamental |
| | *Chaetodon collaris* | D, W then E | |
| | *Chaetodon larvatus, meyeri, ornatissimus, triangulum* and *trifasciatus* | D, L | will almost certainly starve unless a continued supply of living coral is provided |
| | *Chelmon* and *Forcipiger* | F, N | |
| Cardinals | *Apogon* | W | many are small and need cover; such species are also C |
| Catfishes | *Plotosus* | E | bottom feeders |
| Clowns | *Amphiprion akallopisos, sandaracinos* and *perideraion* | W | body colouration is enhanced by feeding a flaked colour food |
| | other *Amphiprion* species | E | the fish will also take food to its anemone |
| Damsels | *Dascyllus, Abudefduf* and *Chromis* | E | useful fish to stimulate finicky feeders |
| Eels | *Gymnothorax, Gymnomuraena* and *Muraena* | E | like chunky food |
| Filefishes | *Monacanthus, Cantherhines, Amanses* and *Pervagor* | D, F, G, N | with patience, a fish that would otherwise starve may be persuaded to handfeed |
| | *Oxymonacanthus longirostris* | D, F, N, I | |
| Gobies | *Amblygobius, Zonogobius, Lythrypnus* and *Gobiodon* | E, G | amusing feeding antics |
| Grammas | *Gramma loreto* | E | |
| Jawfishes | *Opisthognathus* | W | small live foods preferred |
| Mandarins | *Synchiropus* | F, C, I | bottom feeders |
| Moorish Idols | *Zanclus canescens* | F | W with luck |
| Parrotfishes | *Scarus* and *Bolbometapon* | E, G | coral crushers |
| Puffers | *Canthigaster* | E | may squirt a jet of water at its feeder |
| Scorpions/lionfishes/ dragonfishes | *Pterois volitans* | W | use chunky food |
| | other *Pterois* species and *Dendrochirus* | L | |
| Seahorses and pipefishes | Syngnathidae | L, C, N, I | some may be D |
| Snappers | *Lutjanus* | W then E | chunky food preferred; all benefit from some live food |
| Soldierfishes | *Myripristis kuntee* | L | |
| | *Myripristis murdjan* | W then E | nocturnal but will adapt to day feeding |
| Squirrelfishes | *Adioryx, Flammeo* and *Holocentrus* | W then E | nocturnal but will adapt to day feeding |
| Surgeons/tangs | *Acanthurus, Paracanthurus, Naso* and *Zebrasoma* | E, G | |
| Sweetlips | *Gaterin* | W | |
| Triggers | Balistidae | W then E | will bite chunky food; sometimes aggressive at feeding time. |
| Wrasses and Hogfishes | Labridae | E | the useful Cleaner Wrasse will eat parasites off other fish |

# Aquarium Photography

Aquarium photography is not difficult given the right equipment—a good single-lens reflex camera and an electronic flash gun with extension lead. Most of the photographs in this book were taken with a Pentax 35 mm camera. Nearly all single-lens reflex cameras will focus down to eighteen inches, which is near enough for the larger fishes or a school of small ones. To move in closer you will need close-up lenses or automatic extension tubes. Tubes simply increase the distance between the lens and the film, which has an enlarging effect; they are sold in sets of three. Remember to allow half-a-stop additional exposure when the small tube is used; one stop for the middle tube and $1\frac{1}{2}$ stops for the large.

Distortion is likely to occur if the camera is held at an angle to the glass. If a rubber lens-hood is fitted, this enables the camera to be pressed against the front glass, thus eliminating both reflection and distortion, and steadying the hand-held camera.

Do not attempt to illuminate from the front; this results in almost inevitable glare or reflection from the front glass, and in any case produces a very unnatural effect with fishes staring glassy-eyed and throwing black shadows. Place the flash gun on the cover-glass, at the front, over the part of the tank where you intend to take your photographs. If you want a special background or if you know the fish you want will repeatedly pass your chosen spot, you can use a tripod, but it is not really necessary as the speed of the flash reduces the risk of camera shake. If the camera is hand-held you must resist the temptation to follow fishes out of the range of the flash. If you want to photograph a whole aquarium or a large section of it you will need more than one flash gun. An adaptor can be bought very cheaply which enables you to fire two or three guns simultaneously.

If the flash gun is at the front of the cover-glass and is not tilted, the background will be black. If you want the decor behind the fish to show, either use a second flash gun or move the gun to the middle of the cover-glass and wait until the fish goes to the back of the tank. If your subject is in front of the flash it will become a silhouette. If it is directly underneath, its lower half will be in deep shadow. Ideally the gun should be positioned four to six inches in front of the subject.

The nearness of flash to subject allows the use of a very slow film such as 25 ASA, which has a very fine grain. Most flash exposure guides go down only to a metre, but in any case they do not apply when the flash has to travel through water. By keeping a record of all your exposures you will soon be able to calculate exactly the right exposures for your own tanks. As a rough guide, using 25 ASA film and a single flash gun with a guide number of 35–40, the following exposures will be needed: if the flash-to-subject distance is less than eight inches f16; eight to twelve inches f11; twelve to eighteen inches f8; eighteen to twenty-four inches f5.6. With 50 ASA film use one stop less. Flash guns with guide numbers 30–35 will need one stop more, and those with 40–45 one stop less.

Many otherwise excellent photographs are spoiled by distracting background detail and glimpses of aquarium equipment. All-black backgrounds are dramatic, but most photographs benefit from some background in the form of plants, rocks or coral which can be used to frame the subject, and, if out of focus, to create a three-dimensional effect. It is more natural to show a fish as part of a total environment, especially if it can be made to resemble the environment of that fish in the wild.

When photographing marines a background of limitless blue can be achieved by putting a sheet of blue acetate behind the back glass, covering the inside of the back of the cabinet with a pale blue material, and making a display of corals, sea-fans and plastic plants in the space between. This effect can only be photographed by placing a second flash-gun to illuminate the area behind the tank. Since this will be brighter than the flash passing through water, it may be necessary to use a neutral filter or to place a ground-glass screen or white handkerchief under the flashgun.

Before you start a photographic session clean the inside of the front glass, which is almost bound to have some algae on it even if this is not evident at a distance. Also turn off all aeration or every tiny bubble in the water will be brightly illuminated by the flash.

Finally, remember that however good your equipment and technique you will not get good results without perfect specimens. The camera cannot lie.

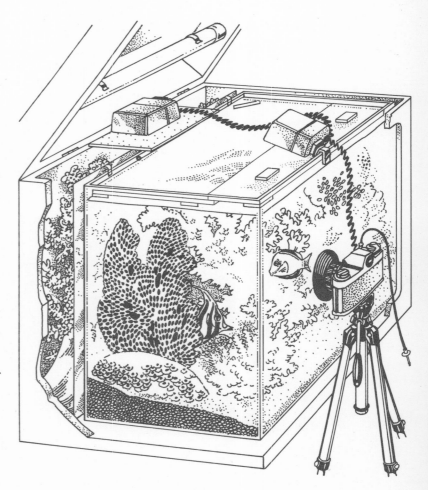

# Bibliography

## Freshwater

### GENERAL REFERENCE

**Complete Aquarist's Guide to Freshwater Tropical Fishes**
ed. Gilbert, J./Ward Lock, 1970

**Encyclopaedia of Tropical Fishes**
Axelrod, H. R. and Vorderwinkler, H./Tropical Fish Hobbyist Publications (TFH)

**Exotic Aquarium Fishes**
Innes, W. T./Innes Publications, 1959; TFH

**Exotic Tropical Fishes**
Axelrod, H. R. and others/TFH

**Freshwater Fishes of the World**
Axelrod, H. R./TFH

**Freshwater Fishes of the World**
Sterba, G./Studio Vista, 1964; TFH

### PLANTS AND TANK DECOR

**Aquarium Plants**
Brunner, G./TFH

**Aquatic Plants**
Rataj, K. and Horeman, T./TFH

**Encyclopaedia of Water Plants**
Stodola, J./TFH

**Aquarium Decorating and Planning**
Weigel, W./TFH

### BREEDING

**Breeding Aquarium Fishes**
Axelrod, H. R. and Burgess, L./TFH

**Breeding Behaviour of Aquarium Fishes**
Wickler, W./TFH

**Genetics for the Aquarist**
Schroder, J./THF

**Spawning Problem Fishes**
Jocher, W./THF

**Tropical Aquarium Fish: Their Habits and Breeding Behaviour**
Nieuwenhuisen, A. van den/van Nostrand, 1964

### HEALTH

**Diseases of Aquarium Fishes**
Goldstein, R.J./TFH

**Water Chemistry for Advanced Aquarists**
Huckstedt, G./TFH

### MONOGRAPHS

**Livebearing Aquarium Fishes**
Jacobs, K./TFH

**Guppy handbook**
Emmens, C. W./TFH

**Fancy Swordtails**
Gordon, M. and Axelrod, H. R./TFH

**Sharks and Loaches**
Walker, B./TFH

**Anabantoids: Gouramis and Related Fishes**
Goldstein, R.J./TFH

**All About Bettas**
Maurus, W./TFH

**Cichlids of the World**
Goldstein, R.J./TFH

**African Cichlids of Lakes Malawi and Tanganyika**
Axelrod, H.R. and Burgess, W.E./TFH

**Angelfish**
Walker, B./TFH

**All About Discus**
Axelrod, H. R. and others/TFH

**Catfish**
Emmens, C.W. and Axelrod, H. R./TFH

**Enjoy Your Killifish**
Turner, B.J. and Pafenyk, J.W./Pet Library

### MAGAZINES

**The Aquarist**
Buckley Press, Brentford, England

**Tropical Fish Hobbyist**
TFH, New Jersey, USA

## Marine

### GENERAL REFERENCE

**Exotic Marine Fishes**
Axelrod, H.R., Burgess, W.E. and Emmens, C.W./TFH

**Marine Aquarium Guide**
de Graff, F./Pet Library, 1973

**Salt-water Aquarium Fishes**
Axelrod, H.R. and Burgess, W.E./TFH

**Pacific Marine Fishes**
Burgess, W.E. and Axelrod, H.R./TFH

**Caribbean Reef Fishes**
Randall, J.E./TFH

### HEALTH

**Diseases of Marine Aquarium Fishes**
Dulin, M.P./TFH

### MONOGRAPHS

**Anemonefishes**
Allen, G.R./TFH

**Damselfishes of the South Seas**
Allen, G.R./TFH

**Sea Horses in Your Home**
Bellomy, M.D./TFH

### MARINE INVERTEBRATES

**Starting with Marine Invertebrates**
Walls, J.G./TFH

**Marine Invertebrates**
Friese, U.E./TFH

**Encyclopaedia of Marine Invertebrates**
TFH

**Sea Anemones**
Friese, U.E./TFH

**Nudibranchs**
Thompson, T.E./TFH

### MAGAZINES

**The Marine Aquarist**
Marlboro, USA

# Index

Figures in square brackets [ ] indicate the number of references on the page.
Page numbers in bold type indicate illustrations.

# ACKNOWLEDGEMENTS

*The Publishers would like to thank the following individuals and organizations for their kind permission to reproduce photographs:* Biofotos: 10, 20, 21, 68, 70; British Killifish Association: 78, 79; Jacana Agence de Presse: 14, 19, 52/53, 61, 65, 75, 76 above, 161, 172 below; Moorfield Aquatics: 74 below, 76 below; Randolph H. Richards: 128, 145; Roy Skipper: 12/13, 26, 27, 31, 80, 97; Spectrum: 32.
All other photographs are by Keith Sagar who would like to express his gratitude to all the aquarists who have allowed him to photograph their fishes: Q.S.S. Aquatics, Bradford, for most of the freshwater fishes; Oceanarium Cleveleys, for most of the marines; Waterlife Centre, Matlock, for most of the invertebrates; Foley's Pets, Manchester; Aquascope, Blackburn; and members of the Blackburn Water-Life Society.